ROBERT MORRIS

This is a volume in the
Arno Press collection

Dissertations

in

American Economic History

Advisory Editor
Stuart Bruchey

Research Associate
Eleanor Bruchey

See last pages of this volume
for a complete list of titles.

ROBERT MORRIS

Land Speculator
1790-1801

Barbara Ann Chernow

ARNO PRESS
A New York Times Company
New York ● 1978

Editorial Supervision: JOSEPH CELLINI

First publication in book form 1978 by Arno Press Inc.

Copyright © 1974 by Barbara Ann Chernow

DISSERTATIONS IN AMERICAN ECONOMIC HISTORY
ISBN for complete set: 0-405-11024-3
See last pages of this volume for titles.

Manufactured in the United States of America

Library of Congress Cataloging in Publication Data

Chernow, Barbara Ann.
    Robert Morris, land speculator, 1790-1801.

    (Dissertations in American economic history)
    Reprint of the author's thesis, Columbia University, 1974.
    Bibliography: p.
    1. Morris, Robert, 1734-1806. 2. Capitalists and financiers--United States--Biography. I. Title. II. Series.
E302.6.M8C47 1978   333'.0092'4 [B]   77-14762
ISBN 0-405-11029-4

ROBERT MORRIS: LAND SPECULATOR, 1790-1801

Barbara Ann Chernow

Submitted in partial fulfillment
of the requirements for The Degree
of Doctor of Philosophy in the
Faculty of Political Science
Columbia University
1974

To my mother,

Blanche B. Chernow

and

my father,

Harry F. Chernow

ACKNOWLEDGMENTS

The author would like to thank the following
scholars, librarians, and archivists for their help:
Mr. Bruce Baker, Canandaigua, New York; Mr. John
Catanzariti, Associate Editor, The Papers of Robert
Morris, The City University of New York; Mr. James
Corsaro, Assistant Librarian, The New York State
Library, Albany; Mr. Thomas Dunnings, The New-York
Historical Society; Dr. W. J. van Hoboken, Director,
Gemeentearchief Amsterdam, The Netherlands; Ms. Sara
Horner, Principal Clerk, Miscellaneous Records, Di-
vision of Corporations and State Records, Department
of State, Albany; Mr. William D. Liebig, Recorder of
Deeds Office, Bucks County, Doylestown, Pennsylvania;
Ms. Terry A. McNealy, Librarian, Bucks County His-
torical Society, Doylestown, Pennsylvania; Mr. Clyde
Maffin, Corresponding Secretary and Curator, Ontario
County Historical Society, Canandaigua, New York;
Mr. Peter Parker, The Historical Society of Penn-
sylvania; Ms. Doris Savage, Local History Division,
Rochester Public Library and Monroe County Library,
Rochester, New York; Ms. Martha Simonetti, Pennsyl-
vania Historical and Museum Commission, Harrisburg.

Special thanks go to the following three scholars for their advice and cooperation throughout the preparation of this manuscript: Professor Stuart Bruchey, Columbia University; Professor Richard B. Morris, Columbia University; Professor Harold C. Syrett, Editor, <u>The Papers of Alexander Hamilton</u>, Columbia University Press.

KEY TO MANUSCRIPT SOURCES

BCHS	Bucks County Historical Society
CCHS	Crawford County Historical Society
CHHL	Henry E. Huntington Library and Art Gallery
CLB	Cazenove Letter Books
DLC	Library of Congress
DNA	National Archives
GA	Gemeentearchief Amsterdam
GMLB	Gouverneur Morris Letter Books
GMP	Gouverneur Morris Papers
GWP	George Washington Papers
HLCP	Holland Land Company Papers
HR	Hall of Records
HSP	The Historical Society of Pennsylvania
JNLB	John Nicholson Letter Books
JNP	John Nicholson Papers
NALCP	North American Land Company Papers
NC	Columbia University Libraries
NYHS	The New-York Historical Society
NYPL	The New York State Library
NYSSO	New York, Secretary of State's Office
OCHS	Ontario County Historical Society
PC	Proceedings of the Commissioners

P-GP	Phelps-Gorham Papers
PHMC	Pennsylvania Historical and Museum Commission
RMLB	Robert Morris Letter Books
RMP	Robert Morris Papers
RPL	Rochester Public Library and Monroe County Library
WRHS	Western Reserve Historical Society

TABLE OF CONTENTS

LIST OF ILLUSTRATIONS

CHAPTER I

THE MERCHANT PRINCE

Robert Morris' rise from merchant apprentice to
merchant prince was unequalled in his generation; so
was his later descent into bankruptcy by the familiar
path of land speculation. First as a member of the
influential Philadelphia firm of Willing and Morris,
and later as the head of an extensive network of partnerships with prominent merchants, Morris was the most
eminent businessman throughout the colonial and revolutionary periods. His reputation, which led to his
appointment as Superintendent of Finance in 1781, was
based on the fortune he acquired from his commercial
activities and his ability to command almost limitless
credit at home and abroad. Always the nationalist who
believed in the inevitable growth and economic development of the United States, Morris invested exten-
sively in shipping, merchandising, securities, internal
improvements, and land during the Confederation and
early national periods.

Instead of great wealth, these investments resulted in the ruin of his financial empire. His effort
in the 1780's to corner the market on the tobacco trade

between the United States and France brought him to the edge of bankruptcy. To restore his financial security in 1790, he turned his attention almost exclusively to the expansion of his landholdings. Morris was convinced that land values would spiral upward, and his weakened financial position made this potential source of new profits an attractive investment. Although he had limited cash reserves with which to finance these purchases, he still had significant domestic and foreign credit resources during the early 1790's. Curiously, for a merchant whose earlier financial empire had been the result of mercantile ventures, at no point during this decade did Morris take advantage of the profits to be gained from investing in the expanding re-export trade. His obsession with the land market, and his failure to consider any alternative investments, raise serious questions about Morris' financial judgment during this era. His participation in the land boom of the 1790's must therefore be examined in the light of his earlier career.

Morris had advanced quickly in the commercial world of colonial Philadelphia. In 1747 or 1748 he sailed from Liverpool, England, to join his father,

Robert Morris, Sr., in Oxford, Maryland.[1] There, the
elder Morris acted as the agent for Foster Cunliffe
and Sons, a firm of Liverpool tobacco merchants. Soon
after his arrival, his father sent Robert to Philadelphia
to study, and arranged for him to live with Robert
Greenway, a Philadelphia merchant. Greenway secured
the younger Morris a position in the firm of Charles
Willing.

Greenway had chosen well, for Morris remained of-
ficially connected with the Willing firm until 1778.
When Willing died in 1754, his English educated son,
Thomas, assumed the direction of the company's business.[2]
Willing's ships traded with Europe and the West Indies,
and Morris' new responsibilities included serving as

---

[1]The year in which Robert Morris sailed from
Liverpool is not clear. His father, in his will, dated
Apr. 17, 1749, states that his son arrived "sometime in
the year 1748..." (PHMC). Ellis P. Oberholtzer, Robert
Morris: Patriot and Financier (New York, 1903), 1,
Clarence L. Ver Steeg, Robert Morris: Revolutionary
Financier, with an Analysis of his Earlier Career
(Philadelphia, 1954), 3, and Robert Waln, Jr., "Robert
Morris," in Biography of the Signers of the Declaration
of Independence, V (1824), 189.

[2]Thomas W. Balch, ed., Willing Letters and Papers
(Philadelphia, 1922), viii; Burton A. Konkle, Thomas
Willing and the First American Financial System
(Philadelphia, 1937), 9.

supercargo on several voyages. His friendship with
Willing grew stronger and on May 1, 1757, Thomas
Willing and Robert Morris, then twenty-three, formed
a partnership.[3] Thus Morris, a relative newcomer to
commercial Philadelphia, gained from the established
business and social contacts of the Willing family.

Under the resourceful leadership of the two young
partners, the firm became one of the most prominent
in Philadelphia, and Willing and Morris became two of the
most respected merchants in the colonies. Their shipping
ventures were modest and not always successful, but the
firm remained stable and profitable.[4]

At the time of the American Revolution, they had
enough surplus capital to purchase at least two tracts
of land. They bought a 3,000 acre indigo plantation,
called Orange Grove, in Baton Rouge, and 1,000 acres
of land on the Florida side of the Mississippi, called
the Ionica Estate. The partners lost both tracts in
1783, because the peace treaty awarded the territory
to Spain.[5]

---

[3]Willing to Thomas Willing of London, Mar. 1,
1756, Mar. 30, 1757, To Nathaniel Sharpe, Apr. 17,
1757, Willing Letter Books, HSP.

[4]For the scope of the firm's activities, see
Ver Steeg, Morris, p. 201, n. 5.

[5]Robert Morris, In the Account of Property, in
Account of Robert Morris' Property (Philadelphia, n.d.), pp.
19-20; Balch, Willing, p. 20.

Little is known of the firm's operations until
the outbreak of the American Revolution. Documents
and letters for this period of Morris' career are
rare, but the firm must have prospered. By the
mid-1760's, Morris and Willing had assumed leading
roles in the commercial and political activities of
Philadelphia.

As a colonial merchant, Morris objected to the
mercantile policies of Great Britain reflected in
the Grenville program and the Townshend Acts. He
opposed the Stamp Act and signed the nonimportation
agreement in 1765.[6] Nevertheless, he reluctantly
signed the Declaration of Independence. He not only
thought that demands for a separation from Britain
were premature, he also had to consider the effect
of a war on his trading connections in that nation.
Although he committed himself to fight for the
colonies if war came, he continually hoped for a
reconciliation between the colonies and the mother
country.[7] As late as December 9, 1775, he wrote to an

[6]The agreement is printed in Balch, _Willing_,
pp. 29-40.

[7]RM to Henry Lee, Jan. 24, 1776, RMP, HSP.

unnamed correspondent: "I am now a Member of the Continental
Congress and if I have any influence or should hereafter
gain any it shall be exerted in favour of every measure
that has a tendency to procure Accomodation on terms
Consistant with our just Claims and if I thought there was
any thing ask'd on this side not founded on the Constitution
in reason and Justice I would oppose it."[8] On July
20, 1776, he shared his thoughts with Colonel Joseph Reed:

> I am not for making any sacrifice of dignity, but
> I would hear them [the British Commissioners] if
> possible; because, if they can offer peace on
> admissible terms, I believe the great majority
> of America would still be for accepting it....
> I have uniformly voted against and opposed the
> Declaration of Independence, because in my
> poor opinion, it was an improper time, and will
> neither promote interest nor redound to the honor
> of America; for it has caused division when we
> wanted union, and will be ascribed to very different
> principles than those which ought to give rise to
> such an important measure.[9]

But war came, and Morris was to reap more of its
benefits than any other businessman. He turned
enthusiastically to politics, and he played the game
skillfully. This flair for politics blended well with
his business acumen, and brought him to the peak of his
career as Financier of the American Revolution.

In fact, the Revolution created many careers and
many fortunes. The idea that government office is a
public trust was novel; perhaps it still is. The

---

[8]Burnett, Letters, I, 271.

[9]American Archives, 5th ser., I (1848), 468.

Continental Congress appointed merchants to positions
in the Quartermaster and Commissary Departments because
of their applicable skills and their business contacts
in the states and abroad. These merchants saw no
conflict of interest in using their public office to
increase their personal wealth and to benefit their
partners and friends. Most were commission agents,
not salaried employees. Jeremiah Wadsworth of Connecticut,
for example, became Commissary General of the Revolutionary
Army in 1778. In that capacity, he received a commission
of one and one-half per cent on all goods that he bought
for the army.[10] As a result of this contract system,
merchants in government positions remained in private
trade, often using government funds to finance their
privateers and transporting their private cargoes in
public vessels. They formed partnerships with merchants
who sold goods to the government, and they awarded
government contracts to their business associates or to
firms with which they hoped to establish good relations
for the benefit of their private companies. Their public
accounts, which were inseparable from their private
accounts, remained unsettled after the war ended.[11]

---

[10]Margaret E. Martin, Merchants and Trade of the
Connecticut River Valley, 1750-1820 (Northampton, 1939),
pp. 76-79.

[11]This discussion is based on information in E. James
Ferguson, The Power of the Purse: A History of American
Public Finance, 1776-1790 (Chapel Hill, 1961), pp. 72-75;
Ver Steeg, Morris, pp. 13-15; Martin, Connecticut River
Valley, pp. 78-79; Robert A. East, Business Enterprise in
the American Revolutionary Era (New York, 1938), pp. 47-48.

In this environment, opportunities were numerous.
So, of course, were the risks. Morris, however, gam-
bled on high profits. During his first year in Congress
in 1776, he was a member of the Executive Committee at
Philadelphia, the Marine Committee, the Secret Committee
of Commerce, and the Secret Committee of Correspondence.[12]
His most lucrative opportunities came from the Secret
Committee of Commerce, which bought foreign products
for the army and paid for them with American goods. Congress frequently advanced money to mercantile firms to
initiate the importation of vital supplies. All firms
to which contracts had been awarded were expected to
produce vouchers. Approximately one-fourth of the Committee's disbursements from 1775 to 1777 went to Willing
and Morris.[13]

In addition, on February 19, 1776, Morris and three
New York City merchants, John Alsop, Philip Livingston,
and Francis Lewis, contracted with the Secret Committee
to export American products to France and to import
goods "suitable for the Indians." Silas Deane, a
Connecticut merchant and a Committee member, was to be

_____

[12]A list of the members of the Congressional com-
mittees is in the Journals of the Continental Congress
(34 vols; Washington, D. C., 1906), V, 1063-67.

[13]These statistics come from Ferguson, Power of
the Purse, p. 77 and n. 12.

their European agent. The Committee advanced $200,000

to the merchants, who were

> allowed five per. ct. for purchasing the cargo
> here; and also to such of said contractors as shall
> go personally to Europe to execute and superintend
> this business - exclusive of the charges of selling
> the produce and manufactures of these Colonies,
> to be exported as aforesaid, and for shipping the
> remittances, besides the duties, a clear commission
> of five per. ct. on the original cost of such remittances
> in Europe, the said United Colonies running the
> whole risk of the said adventure ... and also
> insuring such vessels against all British seizures
> and captures.[14]

Morris and Deane also invested in several privateering

expeditions with four Philadelphia merchants, John Ross, John

Maxwell Nesbitt, David Hayfield Conyngham, and William

Hodge. Paul Wentworth, an English spy, informed Henry

Howard, Lord of Suffolk, that Deane had contracted for

Willing and Morris to trade with France in clothing,

shoes, blankets, and drugs. The capital was to be

£400,000 sterling and the cargoes were to be shipped

as French property with American passes.[15] Thus,

by April 27, 1776, John Adams, in a now famous quote,

could write to Horatio Gates:

> You ask me what you are to think of Robert
> Morris? I will tell you what I think of him.
> I think he was a masterly Understanding, of
> an open Temper and an honest Heart: and if
> he does not always vote for what you and I should
> think proper, it is because he thinks that a large

---

[14]The Secret Committee to Deane, Mar. 1, 1776, with
the contract enclosed, in Burnett, Letters, I, 372-74.

[15]William G. Sumner, The Financier and the Finances
of the American Revolution (2 vols; New York, 1891), I,
207; East, Business Enterprise, pp. 132-34.

Body of People remains, who are not yet of his Mind.
He has vast designs in a mercantile way. And no doubt
pursues mercantile ends, which are always gain; but he
is an excellent Member of our Body.[16]

In 1778, Morris turned his attention to the expansion
of his private business. He not only left Congress, he
also dissolved his partnership with Willing.[17] He immediately formed loose, but generally effective, partnerships with almost all of the prominent merchants in
the colonies. He engaged in privateering with William
Bingham at Martinique and with the Philadelphia mercantile firm of David Conyngham and John Nesbitt. He purchased European goods with John Ross and Isaac Hazlehurst,
both Philadelphians. He dealt in securities and supplies
for the French with John Holker, the French agent for
purchasing supplies for the Royal Marine. His efforts
to profit from the tobacco trade involved partnerships
with Jonathan Hudson of Baltimore, Carter Braxton of
Virginia, and Hewes and Smith of North Carolina.[18]
Most important for this study, however, Morris became
intrigued by the profits to be made from the sale of the
nation's vacant lands. In 1780, he signed Articles

---

[16]Burnett, Letters, I, 433.

[17]Ver Steeg, Morris, pp. 28-29.

[18]East, Business Enterprise, pp. 126-48; Ver Steeg,
Morris, pp. 29-36.

of Agreement with Samuel Beall and John May for buying
lands in Virginia, and with Silas Deane to sell lands
in Europe.[19] Although the latter deal collapsed
because Deane switched over to the British, Deane wrote
to James Wilson, on July 24, 1783, about the benefits
to be derived from investments in American land:

> It clearly appears to me that the two
> great objects of America must be the settlement
> and cultivation of good lands and the establishment
> of manufactures. If we review the rise and progress
> of private fortunes in America, we shall find that
> a very small proportion of them has arisen or
> been acquired by commerce, compared with those made
> by prudent purchases and management of lands.[20]

By 1781 Morris was the most influential merchant
in the former colonies. Not all of his enterprises were
successful, but his investments were diversified and
involved so many different partners that risks
were minimized and losses easily absorbed. Morris
forgot this lesson in the 1790's. Then he put almost
all his money into lands and his most damaging purchases
were made with the same two men, John Nicholson and
James Greenleaf. Morris had profited during the
Revolutionary years from his complicated and simultaneous
investments in numerous enterprises. Perhaps,
he thought in the 1790's that he could similarly

---

[19]Ver Steeg, Morris, p. 35.

[20]Quoted in A. M. Sakolski, The Great American
Land Bubble: The Amazing Story of Land-Grabbing, Speculations,
and Booms from Colonial Days to the Present Time (New
York, 1932), pp. 29-30.

handle the financing and management of large land
purchases in thirteen different regions. He was a
self-confident, inveterate optimist. His success in the
early years of the war inflated this self-confidence to
a potentially dangerous level. His experiences as
Financier raised it to a level that dulled his perception
regarding the limits of his personal credit.

As the war progressed, the nation's financial
outlook darkened. Up to 1781, Congress had financed
the war with bills of credit, domestic and foreign
loans, and requisitions from the states.[21] By 1781,
inflation was rampant, and these sources failed to
provide enough revenue to continue the war effort.
As the government moved towards bankruptcy, Congress
resolved, on February 7, 1781, to create the office
of Superintendent of Finance, and Morris was the
most qualified man for the new post.[22] Before he
accepted, Morris insisted that Congress clarify the
powers of this new position. He explained that if Congress
believed "that the office ... is incompatible with
commercial concerns and connexions, the point is
settled; for I can not on any consideration consent
to violate engagements or depart from those principles

---

[21]A discussion of each of these sources of income
is in Ver Steeg, Morris, pp. 43-44; Ferguson, Power
of the Purse, pp. 29-47.

[22]JCC, XIX, 126.

of honor which it is my pride to be governed by."
To protect himself from criticism and charges of
corruption, he demanded that "If, on the contrary,
Congress have elected me to this office under the
expectation that my mercantile connexions and engagements
were to continue, an express declaration of their
sentiments should appear on the minutes, that no
doubt may arise or reflections be cast on this score
hereafter."[23] Morris also insisted on the right to appoint
all employees in his office and "the absolute power of
dismissing from office or employment all persons
whatever that are concerned in the official expenditure
of public moneys...." Congress hesitated, but finally
agreed to his terms.[24]

As Financier, Morris concentrated on the immediate
problems of supply of the army and restoring the credit
of the United States. He also developed long-range
plans for national economic development. Recent scholars have
praised such accomplishments as the formation of the Bank

[23]Francis Wharton, ed., The Revolutionary Diplomatic
Correspondence of the United States (8 vols; Washington,
D. C., 1889), IV, 297-99, 379-80.

[24]Ibid., pp. 412-14.

of North America, his relative success in supplying the
troops, his proposals for the restitution of public
credit, and his reorganization of the Treasury administration.[25]

But these same years nurtured the seeds of his
downfall in the neglect of his mercantile operations
and the glorification of his personal credit in the
issuance of "Morris notes." The former resulted in
part in his financial losses of the 1780's; the latter
in the growth of his overwhelming sense of financial
security.

Once he assumed office, he took control of almost
all important business, because almost all questions
facing Congress involved the issue of finance. Even
before he began his official duties, he presented to
the President of Congress his plan for a national bank,
to be called the Bank of North America.[26] The capi-
talization was $400,000, which would be divided into
shares of $400. The Government would accept bank notes,
which would serve as specie, as payment for duties and
taxes. Although privately owned, the Superintendent
of Finance had the authority to regularly examine
the Bank's books.[27] On May 25, Congress finally

[25]Ver Steeg, Morris; Ferguson, Power of the Purse.

[26]Wharton, Diplomatic Correspondence, IV, 421.

[27]Ibid., p. 565.

approved the plan, but in spite of general enthusiasm
for the idea, few people subscribed.[28]

Instead, the war forced Morris to direct his energies
to the problem of supplying the continental army. Although he was encouraged by the Congressional resolution
of May 28, 1781, which empowered General George Washington to impress supplies, the results were still disappointing.[29] Morris again turned to friends, such as
Holker, Hudson, Jonathan and William Turnbull, and William
Duer, to provide for the army.[30] After the American victory at Yorktown, the Financier was reasonably successful in supplying the troops by contract. He believed that
"in all countries engaged in war, experience has sooner or
later pointed out contracts with private men of substance
and talents equal to the undertaking as the cheapest, most
certain, and consequently the best mode of obtaining those
articles which are necessary for the subsistence, covering,
clothing, and moving of an army."[31]

Actually, the termination of fighting in 1781 freed
Morris to develop his own program for economic growth,
and he presented his plans for funding the national

[28]JCC, XX, 545-47.

[29]Ibid., 555-56.

[30]Ver Steeg, Morris, pp. 73-74.

[31]Morris to Oliver Phelps, Mar. 30, 1782, in
Wharton, Diplomatic Correspondence, V, 286-87.

debt to Congress in two letters on November 5, 1781
and July 29, 1782.[32] The first letter stressed the
necessity of settling the accounts between the states
and the national government. In the second, he presented
a cogent program for funding the debt. He pointed out
the value of domestic and foreign loans. Domestic
loans, although they "diverted [money] from those channels
in which it would otherwise have flowed," had the advantage
of giving "stability to Government by combining together
the interests of moneyed men for its support...." Foreign
loans, which were also desirable, would bevdifficult to obtain
until the United States had reestablished its public credit
at home. In addition to the restitution of such credit,
funding would achieve three objectives: the return of
funds to creditors, the encouragement of foreign speculation
in American securities, and the restoration of confidence
by which "not only the Government (being more respectable)
would be more respected, and consequently better obeyed,
but the mutual dealings among men on private credit would
be facilitated." Morris repeated his request for a five
per cent impost, a land tax, a poll tax, and an excise
on liquor.

Ironically, for a future land speculator, the
Financier expressed contempt for the methods of large

---

[32]Wharton, Diplomatic Correspondence, IV, 822-25,
V, 619-34.

landholders and proposed a program of land development
that favored the small farmer. In his July 29 letter,
he wrote:

> The land of America may, as to the proprietors, be
> divided into two kinds; that which belongs to the
> great landowners, and that which is owned and
> occupied by the industrious cultivators. This
> latter class of citizens is, generally speaking,
> the most numerous and most valuable part of a
> community. The artisan may, under any government,
> minister to the luxuries of the rich, and the rich
> may, under any government, obtain the luxuries
> they covet. But the free husbandman is the natural
> guardian of his country's freedom. A land tax
> will probably, aat the first mention, startle this
> order of men; but it can only be from the want of
> reflection, or the delusion must be kept up by the
> artifice of others. To him who cultigates from one
> to five hundred acres, a dollar per hundred is a
> trifling object, but to him who owns a hundred
> thousand it is important. Yet a large proportion of
> America is the property of great landholders; they
> monopolise it without cultivation; they are, for
> the most part, at no expense either of money or
> personal service to defend it, and keeping the price
> higher by monopoly than otherwise it would be, they
> impede the settlement and culture of the country.
> A land tax, therefore, would have the salutary
> operation of an agrarian law without the iniquity.
> It would relieve the indigent, and aggrandize the
> State by bringing property into the hands of those
> who would use it for the benefit of society.

Morris then explained why the sale of back lands would
not raise sufficient funds to pay the public creditors:

> If these lands were now in the hands of Congress,
> and they were willing to mortgage them to their
> present creditors, unless this were accompanied
> with a due provision for the interest it would
> bring no relief. If these lands were to be sold
> for the public debts they would go off for almost
> nothing. Those who want money could not afford
> to buy lands. Their certificates would be bought
> up for a trifle. Very few moneyed men would become
> possessed of them, because very little money would
> be invested in so remote a speculation. The small

number of purchasers would easily and readily combine;
of consequence they would acquire the lands for
almost nothing, and effectually defeat the intentions
of Government, leaving it still under the necessity
of making further provision, after having needlessly
squandered an immense property.

How quickly Morris altered his attitude when the economic
advantage of land speculation appeared to promise
him relief from his own financial difficulties!

In his reorganization of the Treasury, Morris'
most significant appointment was that of Gouverneur
Morris as his assistant.[33] Gouverneur, a member of the
prominent New York-New Jersey family and no relation
to Robert, was talented and popular. Although
several of his relatives were loyalists, Gouverneur
adopted the patriot cause. He was a member of the New
York Provincial Congress from 1775 to 1777 and the
Continental Congress from 1778 to 1779. A close
friendship developed between the Financier and his
assistant, and throughout the 1790's Gouverneur,
who was in Europe, was Robert's harshest critic and
most perceptive adviser. If Gouverneur had been in the
United States during this decade, he might have exercised
a restraining influence on his former superior. But
communications were slow, and the Financier responded
sensitively to the slightest criticism. Gouverneur's

[33]Wharton, Diplomatic Correspondence, IV, 622. The
relationship between Robert and Gouverneur is presented
in Mary-Jo Kline, "Gouverneur Morris and the New Nation,
1775-1778" (Unpublished Ph.D. dissertation, Columbia
University, 1970).

letters, increasingly frustrated in tone, had little
effect on Robert.

Most damaging to Morris' later career was the psycho-
logical impact of the power he wielded and the flattery
he received as Financier. Congress had accepted him on
his own terms and made few decisions without his approval.
Before he resigned he was to learn that his personal credit
rating was higher than that of the United States government. In 1781 Morris began to issue "Morris notes" to
replace the now worthless continental currency. The notes,
payable to the "Bearer" at sight in periods of thirty to
sixty days, were usually drawn on John Swanwick, who served
as the cashier to the Office of Finance, and were in de-
nominations of from twenty to one hundred dollars. These
notes, plus those of the Bank of North America, were hopefully to provide a circulating currency and ease the tax
burden.[34]

In 1783 the soldiers' demands for current and back
pay placed an additional strain on the Continental Congress. To some extent, Morris welcomed these new demands.
If he could channel the soldiers' activities, they would
form a pressure group which Morris wanted to use to influence and ultimately convince Congress to implement
his funding proposals.[35] Morris correctly sensed that the

---

[34]RM to Governors, Sept. 4 1781, in Wharton,
Diplomatic Correspondence, IV, 693. See also Ver
Steeg, Morris, pp. 87-88.

[35]Ver Steeg, Morris, p. 166.

approaching peace would weaken his hand in Congress.[36]
As he believed that his personal credit was vital to
the nation's economy, the Financier tried to prod
Congress into action by submitting a letter of
resignation on January 24, which read in part:

> Congress will recollect that I expressly
> stipulated to take no part in past transactions.
> My attention to the public debts, therefore, arose
> from the conviction that funding them on solid
> revenues was the last essential work of our
> glorious Revolution. The accomplishment of this
> necessary work is among the objects nearest my
> heart, and to effect it I would sacrifice time,
> property, and domestic bliss.

> Many late circumstances have so far lessened
> our apprehensions from the common enemy that my
> original motives have almost ceased to operate.
> But other circumstances have postponed the
> establishment of public credit in such a manner
> that I fear it will never be made. To increase our
> debts while the prospect of paying them diminishes,
> does not consist with my ideas of integrity. I must,
> therefore, quit a station which becomes utterly
> insupportable. But lest the public measures might
> be deranged by any precipitation, I will continue to
> serve until the end of May. If effentual measures
> are not taken by that period to make permanent
> provision for the public debts of every kind,
> Congress will be pleased to appoint some other man
> to be the superintendent of their finances. I should
> be unworthy of the confidence reposed in me by my
> fellow citizens if I did not explicitly declare that
> I will never be the minister of injustice.[37]

In spite of this tactic, Morris was disappointed and
discouraged by the cautious program approved by Congress
on April 18, 1783.[38] He agreed to remain in office

---

[36]Ver Steeg, Morris, p. 169.

[37]Wharton, Diplomatic Correspondence, VI, 228-29.

[38]JCC, XXIV, 256-62.

until the army had been paid. The only funds available
to pay the troops consisted of "Morris notes." If the
Financier resigned, the redemption of these notes would
depend on the program of his successor. To fulfill
his obligation to the soldiers, he stayed in office.[39]
According to Ver Steeg, the Financier issued a total of
$1,000,000 in "Morris notes."[40] Although he had not
secured the adoption of his funding proposals, his broad
plan provides a now recognized bridge to Hamilton's
program of 1790.

Morris finally resigned in November, 1784, and
returned to nurse his sorely neglected mercantile
business. The economic effect of the war on the
Financier's private business is almost impossible
to calculate as his account books for the period of the
Confederation have hot been located. At first his
credit rating was high, but by the late 1780's he had
suffered a major, but not a fatal, breakdown in his
commercial network. According to his son Thomas, Morris'
"pecuniary losses were not owing to his public engagements
in the war of Independence. Heavy as those engagements
were, (the last two years of the war having been

[39]RM to Committee of Congress, Apr. 14, 1783, in
Wharton, Diplomatic Correspondence, VI, 429-32.

[40] Morris, p. 179.

supported almost entirely by his advances and by his
credits,) he was eventually reimbursed by the public."[41]

Throughout the Confederation, Morris conducted his most
significant activities as a partner in the New York City
firm of William Constable, John Rucker, and Company, which
was established in 1784. Gouverneur Morris was also a
member of this firm. The Company was capitalized at
£20,000, New York currency, with Robert putting up £10,000
to cover his as well as Gouverneur's share. Rucker became
the firm's European representative.[42]

The foreign operations of Constable, Rucker, and
Company were tied to one of Morris' pet schemes: a monopoly
of the tobacco trade between the United States and France.
Americans had begun to carry tobacco to France in 1775, in
violation of British mercantile laws, in return for arms.
After the war Charles Gravier, comte de Vergennes, informed
the farmers-general, which controlled the tobacco monopoly,
that it could purchase the commodity directly in the United
States. Morris' initial attempts to secure the commission for
these purchases collapsed because he was still Superintendent
of Finance. But, with the support of Benjamin Franklin
and the powerful Paris and Rouen banking firm of
Le Couteulx and Company, Morris signed a contract

---

[41]Quoted in Orsamus Turner, Pioneer Period of the Holland
Purchase of Western New York (Buffalo, 1849), pp. 355-56.

[42]Donald G. Tailby, "Chapters from the Business Career
of William Constable: A Merchant of Post-Revolutionary
New York" (unpublished Ph.D. dissertation, Rutgers, The
State University, 1961), p. 177.

with Le Normand d'Etoiles, the agent of the farmers-general,
in April, 1785.[43] Morris agreed to ship and deliver 20,000
hogsheads of Virginia tobacco annually in 1785, 1786, and
1787 to the ports of Bourdeaux, Havre-de-Grace, Dieppe,
and Morlaix. The farmers-general would pay him 36 livres
per hundredweight, which would be remitted to Le Couteulx
and Company in Paris for the Financier's account. Le Normand
advanced Morris 1,000,000 livres and the farmers-general
promised not to make any additional purchases of tobacco
in the United States.[44]

Morris, on the basis of Le Normand's advance, began
to manipulate the tobacco market in the United States. The
further he drove the price of tobacco per hundredweight
below 36 livres, the greater would be his profit and the
more certain the French would be of a steady supply of the
commodity. Morris succeeded in lowering the domestic price
from 40 to 22 shillings, Virginia currency, per hundredweight,
by issuing his own private bank notes for his agents to
use in purchasing tobacco. The notes were redeemable
at his Philadelphia office in gold, silver, or foreign
bills of exchange.[45]

---

[43]Jacob M. Price, France and the Chesapeake: A History of
the French Tobacco Monopoly, 1674-1791, and of Its Relationship
to the British and American Tobacco Trades (2 vols; Ann
Arbor, 1973), II, 741.

[44]A copy of the contract is in the Thomas Jefferson
Papers, DLC. See also Price, French Tobacco Monopoly, II, 753.

[45]Price, French Tobacco Monopoly, II, 755; Frederick L.
Nussbaum, "American Tobacco and French Politics, 1783-1789,'
Political Science Quarterly, XL (Dec., 1925), 497-516; Tailby,
"Constable," p. 189; William A. Davis, "William Constable: New
York Merchant and Land Speculator, 1772-1803" (unpublished
Ph.D. dissertation, Harvard University, 1955), p. 103.

Almost immediately, Morris' monopoly met serious opposition from Thomas Jefferson, Vergennes, the Marquis de La Fayette, and Simon Berard. They achieved a partial victory in 1786 with the Decision of Bernais. The French Comptroller-General, Calonne, agreed that no similar monopolies would be awarded in the future. Although Morris' contract would be fulfilled, the farmers-general would, during the same years, purchase an additional twelve to fifteen thousand hogsheads of tobacco yearly on the same terms as provided for in its agreement with the Financier.[46]

The success of Constable, Rucker, and Company depended on the success of Morris' tobacco contract, because Rucker was expected to purchase cargoes to ship to New York and to pay all of Morris' bills in Europe by drawing on the Financier's account with Le Couteulx.[47] In 1786 Rucker's behavior became erratic. At first he refused to honor any of Morris' notes. Although he changed his mind later in 1786, he disappeared in 1787 and died the next year.[48] On December 1, 1787, Constable informed Gouverneur Morris that Rucker had left £80,000 sterling of Morris' bills unpaid.[49] Morris never fully recovered from the loss.

---

[46]Price, French Tobacco Monopoly, pp. 756-69; Nussbaum, "American Tobacco," pp. 504-10.

[47]Tailby, "Constable," p. 190.

[48]Ibid., pp. 195-203.

[49]Constable Papers, NYPL.

As a merchant and a politician, Morris had earned
the respect, and often the envy, of most of his contemporaries. Few men, William Duer excepted, could
rival the diversity of his activities or the scope of
his investments. Yet, on November 17, 1787, Constable,
expressing a view that would have then seemed heretical,
wrote to Gouverneur: "I have a very bad opinion of
Robert Morris Talents...."[50]

The Confederation and early national periods offered men with surplus capital two areas of investment:
foreign trade and land.[51] Morris was unsuccessful at
the first in the 1780's; the latter ruined him in the
1790's. To recover from his losses during the Confederation, Morris turned his back on all new mercantile
activities. Instead, he decided that the cure for his
financial ills was the expanding land market. He engaged in land speculation with his usual unbounded
enthusiasm and optimism. As with the tobacco contracts,
he was not willing to settle for a small piece of the
market. He bought huge tracts, comprising millions of
acres, and counted heavily on his European contacts to
provide an endless market for the sale of his lands.
With the tightening of the money market in 1796, he

[50]Constable Papers, NYPL. See also Sumner,
Financier, II, 277.

[51]Sakolski, The Great American Land Bubble, p. 29.

assumed that his credit was as limitless as it had been
during his years as Financier. He was shocked, and even
offended, by his creditors' efforts to collect the debts
he owed them.

Morris' sanguine expectations for the land market
rested heavily on his belief that American back lands would
always be attractive to Europeans for investments or
settlements. Precedent existed to support Morris' theory.
Colonists had begun to speculate in land shortly after they
arrived. One could always sell cleared or developed land
at a profit and then move further into the back lands and
repeat the process. Without stocks or extensive shipping
activities, land was the only form of speculation available
to the early settlers. As early as 1618, the London Company
attracted colonists to Virginia by promising them a headright
of fifty acres and additional land for all settlers they
brought with them. Eventually all of the colonies adopted
some form of this system. In addition, discontented
Europeans had always looked to the United States as a
refuge and a place in which they could establish settlements
on their own terms. This was true of the Puritans, the
Quakers, and the Palatine Germans. Americans, such as
William Duer, shared Morris' assumptions about the European
demand for land in the United States. In 1789, Duer sent
Joel Barlow to France to sell shares in the "Scioto Company,"
which held an option on Ohio lands. Both Morris and Duer
would be disappointed in the efforts of their European agents.

Morris' land purchases in the 1790's are incredibly

complicated. His own confusion about his holdings stemmed
from faulty titles, unclear or indefinite boundaries,
conflicting surveys, Indian claims, and increasingly, from
his efforts to satisfy creditors by mortgaging land to them.
He mortgaged overlapping tracts to different creditors,
formed four unsuccessful land companies, and found that
his failure to diversify his investments left him without
any alternative source of income after the land market
collapsed.

In studying the Financier's land empire, scholars
face one additional problem. This is the third period
in Morris' life for which important sources are missing.
His ledger, journal, and letter book for the early
1790's have not been found. No carefully preserved
collection of incoming correspondence exists. Moreover,
Morris purchased so many tracts that to attempt to trace
each one is impossible and would have little bearing
on the pattern established by his major acquisitions.
The best single source for a description of Morris'
holdings is a pamphlet entitled Account of Robert
Morris' Property, which the Financier prepared for his
bankruptcy proceedings in 1801.[52]

The Financier's later career sheds light on an
unexplored side of the land boom. Several excellent
works exist on the development and settlement of land
in the 1790's, but Morris viewed the land as an

---

[52]Philadelphia, n.d.

investment in itself, as a commodity to be bought and
sold for profit.[53] He looked to dispose of his land
quickly and at a large profit to other speculators.
He had too many simultaneous investments to concentrate
on the intensive development of any one, and he lacked the
surplus capital necessary to offer credit to individual
settlers.

As one of the leading land speculators of the 1790's,
Morris serves as an excellent focal point for a study
of land investment during the Federalist period. His
extensive purchases during this decade explain the
dethronement of Philadelphia's merchant prince.

---

[53]See, for example, Helen I. Cowan, _Charles
Williamson: Genesee Promoter, Friend of Anglo-American
Rapprochement_ (Rochester, 1941); Paul D. Evans, _The
Holland Land Company_ (Buffalo, 1924).

CHAPTER II[*]

THE GENESEE COUNTRY

Throughout the Confederation and Federalist periods, the national and state governments, financially drained by the struggle with Great Britain, recognized that the sale of their back lands was their largest potential source of revenue. Congress, by the sale of the public domain, and the states, by the sale of their western lands, fostered the growth of land speculation in the post war period. Instead of selling small parcels to individual settlers, governments on all levels first offered the land as payment for revolutionary debts. They then sold the remainder in large tracts to speculators for an immediate profit. The speculator had three options. He could hold on to the land until prices rose, sell the entire tract to another purchaser for a quick return, or develop the land and sell it, on credit if necessary, to prospective settlers. Both the governments and the speculators treated the western lands as an article of trade to be bought and sold as any other commodity. Businessmen, eager for new fields of investment, after

---

[*]This chapter has been published, in slighly different form, as obert Morris: Genesee Land Speculator," New York History, LVIII pril, 1977), 197-220.

Fig. 1.

Reprinted by permission from Ruth L. Higgins, <u>Expansion</u>
<u>in New York with Especial Reference to the Eighteenth</u>
<u>Century</u> (Columbus, 1931).

the war, purchased vast tracts of land for only a few cents per acre.[1]

On October 10, 1780, the Continental Congress resolved to receive all unappropriated lands ceded by the states to the national government. By 1790, New York, Virginia, Massachusetts, Connecticut, South Carolina, and North Carolina had relinquished 228,081,867 acres to the United States government.[2] After the cessions by New York and Massachusetts in 1781 and 1785, approximately 6,000,000 acres of land remained in dispute between the two states. The land, located west of the Preemption line in New York, began at Sodus Bay on Lake Ontario and passed through Seneca Lake to the Pennsylvania boundary line. Massachusetts derived its title to the land from the Plymouth Company's Charter of 1620. New York claimed that the 1620 Charter was invalid because of the prior occupation of the land by the Dutch, and based its claims on two grants, dated February 29, 1664 and June 29, 1674, from Charles II to his brother, the

---

[1]Thomas Abernathy, Western Lands and the American Revolution (New York, 1959), p. 216; Curtis P. Nettels, The Emergence of a National Economy, 1775-1815 (New York, 1962), pp. 149-50; A. M. Sakolski, The Great American Land Bubble: The Amazing Story of Land-Grabbing, Speculations, and Booms from Colonial Days to the Present Time (New York, 1932), pp. 31-32; Payson Jackson Treat, The National Land System, 1785-1820 (New York, 1910), p. 14.

[2]JCC, XVIII, 915; Thomas Donaldson, The National Domain: Its History with Statistics (Washington, D. C., 1884), pp. 10-11.

Duke of York.3

In 1784 Massachusetts officials, determined to secure a clear title to the land in order to sell it, petitioned Congress to appoint commissioners to settle the dispute. Congress ordered the agents of the states involved to agree on a panel of judges to decide the issue. The agents were unsuccessful in their efforts to find impartial arbiters, and the two states agreed to settle the question without recourse to Congress or the courts.4 On December 16, 1786, the states signed the Hartford Convention, which granted Massachusetts the preemption rights to the land, which included the right to purchase the Indian title and sell the lands, and awarded New York governmental jurisdiction over the area.5

3Miers Fisher, Brief of the Titles of Robert Morris, Esquire, to a Tract of Country in the County of Ontario, in the State of New-York, One of the United States of America (Philadelphia, 1791), p. 1; Howard L. Osgood, "History of the Title of the Phelps and Gorham Purchase," Publications of the Rochester Historical Society, I (1892), 21-31.

4JCC, XXVII, 547-50, XXIX, 865; James Duane, John Jay, Robert R. Livingston, Egbert Benson, and Walter Livingston represented New York; John Lowell and James Sullivan represented Massachusetts.

5At these negotiations, the agents for New York were Duane, Benson, Robert R. Livingston, Robert Yates, John Haring, and Melancton Smith; the agents for Massachusetts were Lowell, Sullivan, Theophilus Parsons, and Rufus King. For the text of the Hartford Agreement, see Deeds, Misc. Rec., NYSSO. For a 1915 court case between the Senecas and the State of New York, which involved the constitutionality of the Hartford Convention, see The People of the State of New York ex rel. Walter S. Kennedy, Plaintiff in Error, v. Frederick W. Becker, as Sheriff of Erie County, New York, Defendant in Error, 92 U.S. 7 (1915).

39

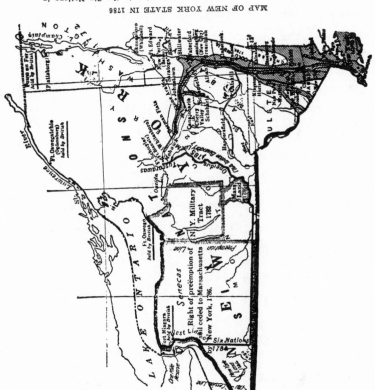

MAP OF NEW YORK STATE IN 1786

Showing 13,000,000 acres of land belonging to the Six Nations in 1786, with an Indian population of about 17,000. State's white population was then about 190,000 and occupied the shaded area on the Mohawk-Hudson and Long Island.

Fig. 2.
Reprinted from Charles F. Milliken, "The Phelps and Gorham Purchase," in History of the Genesee Country, ed., by Lockwood R. Doty (4 vols.; Chicago, 1925), I, 369.

At the time of this agreement the label
"western New York" referred to what is now Ontario, Genesee,
Steuben, Allegany, Niagara, Chautauque, Cattaraugus,
Monroe, Livingston, Erie, Yates, Wayne, Orleans, and
Wyoming Counties. Soldiers who had participated in
General John Sullivan's ruthless expedition against
the Iroquois Indians at Newtown in 1779 returned home
with glowing reports about the fertility of the region.
In particular, they stressed the cultivation of wheat,
grass, and grains, and the growth of timber.[6] As a
result, Massachusetts easily found purchasers for the
entire tract.

Desperately in need of funds, the state agreed
to sell at least part of the tract, and the best offer
came from Oliver Phelps and Nathaniel Gorham. Both were
prominent men. Phelps, a native of New Windsor, Connecticut,
had served in the commissary department during the Revolution.
After the war he lived in Sheffield, Massachusetts, and was
a member of the state assembly, the state senate, and the
governor's council. Gorham, originally from Charlestown,
Massachusetts, was a delegate to the Continental Congress

---

[6]Thomas F. Gordon, Gazetteer of the State of New York
(Philadelphia, 1836), p. 587; John W. Barber, Historical
Collections of the State of New York (New York, 1851), p. 256;
Chipman P. Turner, The Pioneer Period of Western New York
(Buffalo, 1888), p. 51; Joseph H. Mather and L. P. Brockett,
Geography of the State of New York (Hartford, 1847), pp. 220,
299-300; Percy W. Bidwell and John I. Falconer, History of
Agriculture in the Northern United States: 1620-1860
(Washington, D. C., 1925), p. 171; Neil A. McNall, An
Agricultural History of the Genesee Valley, 1790-1860
(Philadelphia, 1952), pp. 1-4; 15, 240-42; Turner,
Pioneer History, pp. 570-83; Royal L. Garff, "Social
and Economic Conditions in the Genesee Country, 1787-1812"
(unpublished Ph.D. dissertation, Northwestern University,
1939), pp. 53-54.

from 1782 to 1783 and again from 1785 to 1787.[7] In
1788 these two businessmen, who had joined together
to outbid their competitors, offered to purchase the
entire tract of approximately 6,000,000 acres for
"two hundred and thirty thousand pounds, in the
consolidated securities of this Commonwealth, to be
paid in three equal annual payments, with interest in
like securities, after one year, and ample security
to be given for the repayment of the same...." On March
21, 1788, a Committee of the House of Representatives
of the state legislature reported "that the sum aforementioned
is not adequate to the value of the abovesaid right...."[8]
Then on March 31 of the same session, Gorham, Phelps
and their associates proposed to purchase the same
tract for "three hundred thousand pounds in the consolidated
State Securities or two hundred and ninety thousand pounds
in the sd. securities and two thousand pounds in specie."[9]

[7]Samuel H. Wandell, "Oliver Phelps," New York History,
XXIII (July, 1942), 275-82; George H. Humphrey, "Nathaniel
Gorham," Publications of the Rochester Historical Society,
VI (1927), 297-99.

[8]MS Journal of the House of Representatives of the
Commonwealth of Massachusetts, Microfilm Collection of
Early State Records, DLC.

[9]Ibid. See also Osgood, "Phelps and Gorham Purchase,"
p. 35. Phelps and Gorham's associates included Judge
James Sullivan, Thomas Skinner, Israel Chapin, and
William Walker.

On April 1 the legislature agreed to sell the land
to the Phelps-Gorham syndicate for £300,000 in consolidated
securities, payable in three installments, on the
condition that the speculators extinguish the Indian
title by purchasing the land from the natives.[10]
At the time of this sale, Massachusetts securities
were at twenty per cent of their face value. The
legislature had thus sold the land for £60,000
or $200,000, which was less than three cents per
acre. In fact, Phelps and Gorham paid more for
the land because in 1789 the value of these securities
rose to thirty three per cent.[11]

The Phelps-Gorham group was not the only prospective
purchaser of the Indian title. In the autumn of 1787,
in Hudson, New York, John Livingston formed the New
York Genesee Land Company with Caleb Benton, Peter
Schuyler, Ezekial Gilbert, Jared Coffin, and Robert
Troup.[12] To eliminate any competition, Livingston

---

[10]Deeds, Misc. Rec., NYSSO; MS Journal of the House
of Representatives of the Commonwealth of Massachusetts,
Microfilm Collection of Early State Records, DLC.

[11]Ferguson, Power of the Purse, p. 270; Osgood,
"Phelps and Gorham Purchase," p. 36; Clayton Mau, The
Development of Central and Western New York: From the
Arrival of the White Man to the Eve of the Civil War as
Portrayed Chronologically in Contemporary Accounts
(Rochester, 1944), p. 68; Robert W. Silsby, "Credit and
Creditors in the Phelps-Gorham Purchase" (unpublished Ph.D.
dissertation, Cornell University, 1958), p. 1.

[12]Shaw Livermore, Early American Land Companies: Their
Influence on Corporate Development (New York, 1939),
p. 198.

allied his group with the Niagara Genesee Land Company,
which had been organized by Colonel John Butler, Samuel
Street, and John P. Johnson, all British citizens of
Canada, and Benjamin Barton, an American.[13] As article
37 of the New York constitution forbade treaties with
and purchases from the Indians without the direct
sanction of the state, Livingston's company met with
the Six Nations in 1787 at Kanadesaga and secured a
999 year lease to all of the Indians' claims in the
Genesee.[14] In return, the natives received an immediate
payment of 20,000 Spanish milled dollars and an annual
rental of 2,000 Spanish milled dollars. In January,
1788, Livingston concluded a similar agreement with the
Oneidas. As a result of these leases, Livingston controlled
twelve million acres in New York. Governor George Clinton,
who had planned to hold a treaty with the Indians to secure
formal cession of their lands to the state, immediately
used his influence to have the legislature nullify
Livingston's agreements with the natives. On March 1,

---

[13]Charles F. Milliken, "The Phelps and Gorham
Purchase," in History of the Genesee Country, ed. by
Lockwood R. Doty (4 vols.; Chicago, 1925), I, 359;
Paul D. Evans, "The Frontier Pushed Westward," in
Conquering the Wilderness, ed. by Alexander Flick
(New York, 1934), pp. 7-16.

[14]Milliken, "The Phelps and Gorham Purchase,"
pp. 356-59; Evans, "The Frontier Pushed Westward,"
pp. 7-16; Osgood, "The Phelps and Gorham Purchase,"
pp. 36-38.

1788, the legislature invalidated the leases on the
grounds that they were really purchases in violation
of the state constitution.[15]

Although Phelps and Gorham were now free to negotiate
with the Indians, they knew that Livingston's influence
with the Indians could be of assistance to them. When
Phelps arrived to meet with the natives at Kanadesaga,
he learned that Livingston and his associates were holding
a council with them at Buffalo Creek. Phelps decided
to buy Livingston's support. On April 19, 1788,
they signed an agreement by which Livingston's group
received 23 shares in the Phelps-Gorham enterprise and
£5,400, Massachusetts currency, in return for their
assistance in securing the Indian title for the
Massachusetts speculators.[16]

---

[15]"An Act for appointing Commissioners to hold Treaties
with the Indians, within this State" (New York Laws, 11th
Sess., Ch. XLVII [Microfilm Collection of Early State
Records, DLC]); "Transcript of Proceedings of the Legislature
of New York in the matter of Livingston's Petition," Feb.
20, 1788, HLCP, NYSL; Evans, "The Frontier Pushed
Westward," pp. 7-16; Osgood, "Phelps and Gorham Purchase,"
pp. 36-38; Livermore, Early American Land Companies,
pp. 198-99.

[16]Phelps to Gorham, June 5, 1788, Phelps to _____,
June 6, 1788, "Blank Draft of Phelps' Agreement with
Caleb Benton in behalf of the New York Lessee Company,"
July , 1788, "Account of the Genesee Purchase, 1788-
1790," P-GP, NYSL. In 1789, the lessees withdrew from
the venture and accepted four townships in the Genesee
country as payment for their services (Evans, "The
Frontier Pushed Westward," pp. 7-16).

Finally, on July 8, 1788, Phelps concluded a treaty with the Five Nations. The Indians sold only 2,600,000 of their 4,000,000 acres for £2100, New York currency and an annuity of $500. The land conveyed to Phelps and Gorham was bounded on the south by the northern boundary of Pennsylvania, on the west by a line from the Pennsylvania to the confluence of Canaseraga Creek with the Genesee River to Lake Ontario, on the east by the Preemption line, and on the north by Lake Ontario.[17] As the sale to Phelps and Gorham was conditional until they had purchased the Indian title, the Massachusetts legislature now passed an act confirming their right to the land.[18]

The speculators immediately hired Colonel Hugh Maxwell, a Revolutionary officer from Heath, Massachusetts, to survey the tract. With the help of Augustus Porter, Maxwell completed the survey in 1789 at a cost of £1796.11.6, Massachusetts currency.[19] By the spring of that year,

---

[17]Deed, July 8, 1788, O'Rielly Papers, NYHS.

[18]Fisher, Brief, pp. 11, 31.

[19]"Account of the Genesee Purchase, 1788-1790," P-GP, NYSL. In an account prepared in 1791, Phelps and Gorham entered £4910.17.9, Massachusetts currency, for "sundry expenses surveying, exploring, selling Lands, cutting Roads, treating with the Indians & ca." since 1788 (O'Rielly Papers, NYHS). An interesting, but often inaccurate, account of the purchase and survey is Augustus Porter, "Narrative of Early Years in the Life of Judge Augustus Porter," Publications of the Buffalo Historical Society, VII (1904), 289-91. For a biographical sketch of Porter, see Charles M. Robinson, "The Life of Judge Augustus Porter: A Pioneer in Western New York," Publications of the Buffalo Historical Society, VII (1904), 229-75.

Phelps and Gorham had laid out 40 towns and claimed
to have sold over 500,000 acres.[20]

Although Phelps assured Theodore Sedgwick, a member
of the House of Representatives from Massachusetts, that
"Indisputable security has been given for the payment [to
Massachusetts] in three annual periods," the two
speculators were in financial difficulty by June.
First, they faced the expenses of the surveys and the
cash settlements with the Indians and the two land
companies. In addition, many of the purchasers
were small farmers who needed long extensions of credit
in order to pay for the land. Most damaging to the
speculators, however, was the enactment of Alexander
Hamilton's financial program, which caused an immediate
rise in the value of the depreciated Massachusetts
securities.[21] In June, 1789, Gorham informed the
Council of Massachusetts that no prospect existed of his
paying the first bond before the second became due.
He offered to "relinquish the Bargain," if the
legislature repaid the money he and Phelps had
advanced and provided compensation for their efforts.

---

[20]Phelps to Sedgwick, Mar. 30, 1789, P-GP, NYSL.

[21]Milliken, "Phelps and Gorham Purchase," p. 366;
George S. Conover, ed., History of Ontario County,
New York: With Illustrations and Family Sketches of
Some of the Prominent Men and Families (Syracuse, 1893),
p. 93; Silsby, "Credit and Creditors," p. 3.

The speculators would either reconvey the entire 6,000,000 acre tract to the state, or purchase, at a reasonable price, the 2,600,000 acres to which they had extinguished the Indian title. Instead of accepting this offer, the legislature postponed payment of the first bond until April, 1790. But on June 9, 1790, Phelps and Gorham reconveyed to the Massachusetts two thirds of their original purchase, or 4,000,000 acres, as payment for the two bonds still outstanding.[22]

Phelps and Gorham then sought a purchaser for one of the two million acres still in their possession. By August 7 they had arranged to sell the land to Robert Morris, who signed the articles of agreement three days later.[23] Morris had undoubtedly heard his associate Adam Hoops, who had served with Sullivan in 1779, praise the Genesee country. The Financier also met with Phelps, whom he knew from the commissary department during the Revolution, and with Gorham, who called Morris out of sessions of the United States Senate to discuss the Genesee business.[24]

---

[22]Gorham to Phelps, June 25, 1789, P-GP, NYSL; Fisher, Briefs, pp. 34-37.

[23]RM to Gouverneur Morris, Aug. 8, 1790, GMP, NC; Indenture, Nov. 18, 1790, Deeds, Misc. Rec., NYSSO.

[24]Osgood, "Phelpsaand Gorham Purchase," p. 35; Milliken, "The Phelps and Gorham Purchase," p. 352; William Maclay, The Journal of William Maclay: United States Senator from Pennsylvania, 1789-1791 (New York, 1927), p. 123.

Initially, Morris considered becoming a third partner
in the purchase with Phelps and Gorham, but decided instead
to purchase the land himself. By the indenture, Phelps
and Gorham sold Morris 1,000,000 acres of land, minus
47,000 acres which they reserved for themselves, for
£30,000, Massachusetts currency. Morris agreed to pay
£5,000 by January 10, 1791, £5,000 by June 1, 1791 with
interest from January 10, 1790, one-half the remainder on
December 1, 1791 and the final £10,000 on December
1, 1792. The last two payments included interest from
September 10, 1790.[25]

As soon as Morris decided to purchase the land,
he chose Gouverneur Morris and William Temple Franklin,
the grandson of Benjamin Franklin, as his European agents
for the sale of the entire tract. He informed his former
assistant that this "bargain ... will ... not only be
the means of extricating me from all the embarrassments
in which I have been involved, but alsothe means of making
your Fortune and mine." If Gouverneur succeeded in selling

[25]Indenture, Nov. 18, 1790, Deeds, Misc. Rec., NYSSO; RM
to G. Morris, Aug. 8, 1790, GMP, NC. In Phelps and Gorham's
Journal, under the date of Nov. 18, 1790, there is a partial
list of townships conveyed by them to Morris (P-GP, NYSL). Many
secondary works discuss Morris and his role in the Genesee
country. See, for example, in addition to the works already cited,
Turner, Pioneer History; Orsamus Turner, History of the Pioneer
Settlement of Phelps and Gorham's Purchase, and Morris' Reserve
(Rochester, 1851); Henry O'Rielly, Sketches of Rochester; With
Incidental Notices of Western New-York (Rochester, 1851);
Elisha W. Vanderhoof, Historical Sketches of Western New York
(Buffalo, 1907); John Kennedy, Robert Morris and the Holland
Purchase (Batavia, 1894); Nina M. and Francis Tiffany, Harm
Jan Huidekoper (Cambridge, 1904); James H. Hotchkin, A History
of the Purchase and Settlement of Western New York, and of the
Rise, Progress, and Present State of the Presbyterian Church
in that Section (New York, 1848); Ruth L. Higgins, Expansion
in New York: With Especial Reference to the Eighteenth Century
(Columbus, 1931).

the land in Europe, then Morris would purchase at least
two of the four million acres reconveyed to Massachusetts
by Phelps and Gorham. Hopefully, the purchasers would be
a specific company, which would then sell the land to
prospective emigrants in France and the Low countries.
Always overeager about a new enterprise, Morris bragged
"that this is the best tract of Country now remaining
in a body (unoccupied) within the limits of the United
States of America for the settlement of Foreigners who
wish to live contiguous to each other." The land was
fertile, the Indian danger nil, and because of some
sales by Phelps and Gorham, settlers already lived on
the land under the protection of the state government.[26]

Morris, in fact, was so certain of the European
demand for American lands, that he expected to pay
all but the first installment to Phelps and Gorham out
of the proceeds of such sales. To meet these payments,
the Financier intended to draw on Gouverneur for 100,000
livres in January and June in bills of exchange payable
in sixty or ninety days. In Europe, Le Couteulx and
Company served as Morris' bankers. If Gouverneur sold
800,000 acres at 6 livres per acre and then deducted his
expenses, Robert estimated his profit, after he
completed the payments to Phelps and Gorham at
2,200,000 livres or $330,000.[27]

---

[26]RM to G. Morris, Aug. 8, 1790, GMP, NC.

[27]Ibid.

In these instructions to Gouverneur, Morris established the pattern for his speculative activities. He
would purchase large tracts for immediate sale to other
speculators, with part of the profits from such resales
paying for the original purchase. He would rely heavily
on his growing number of European agents, his previous
connections with European banking houses, and his belief
in the steady European demand for American lands as an
investment and for settlement.

Wisely, Gouverneur declined serving as Morris' primary agent. As an informal representative of the United
States government in Britain, Gouverneur realized that
any role he might play as a private entrepreneur would
have "excited all kind of Suspicion [and] Materially
Injured every other Operations."[28]

Morris thus pinned his hopes on William Temple Franklin. As early as September, 1790, Morris had approached
Franklin with the prospect of travelling to Europe to sell
the Genesee land. To insure Franklin's acceptance of this
commission, Morris offered him an unusually generous arrangement. First, the Financier purchased Franklin's
three New Jersey farms for £5,000, Pennsylvania currency,
with £500 payable immediately. For the remainder of the
purchase money, Morris decided to execute a bond

---

[28]G. Morris to RM, Nov. 29, 1790, GMP, DLC.

and a mortgage to Franklin for $4,500 payable in 18
months with interest payments every 6 months. In addition,
Morris promised Franklin a 10 per cent commission on all
sales, 600 guineas yearly, travelling expenses, and
payments for copying and printing expenses and bankers'
commissions.[29]

Before Franklin sailed, Morris gave him detailed
instructions for the sale of the Genesee land in Paris
or London. Although he would accept two livres per
acre, Morris hoped that the land would sell for double
that price. He urged Franklin to sell all of the land
to a single company for "Ready Money." If a company
could not be formed for this purpose, the land should
be sold for three million livres at a lottery. If the
lottery scheme also failed, the agent could advertise
the lands and sell to anyone who would purchase at
least fifty acres at six livres per acre, with one-half
down and the remainder in three or five years at five
per cent interest paid annually. In the event that a single
purchaser bought one thousand acres, Morris would reduce
the price to four or five livres per acre. Franklin
had to deposit all money received with Le Couteulx and Company
in Paris or Bourdieu, Chollet, and Bourdieu in London.

---

[29]RM to Franklin, Sept. 21, 22, 1790, Franklin to
RM, Sept. 16, 21, 23, 1790, GMP, NC.

As soon as the deposits totalled £45,000 or 120,000 Mexican
dollars, Morris would discharge his mortgage to Phelps
and Gorham, who had arranged to receive payment on the
last three installments through William Burgess, a London
merchant. As for Gouverneur's role in any sale, Morris
explained:

> Mr. G. Morris is my most particular friend, that
> I respect and esteem him exceedingly, and that
> he possesses as he is justly entitled to, my
> utmost confidence.... Altho' I do not say that
> he is to have a controuling Power over your
> Operations, yet it will be very agreeable to
> me that his Opinion and yours should coincide
> upon the important points....30

In his effort to reach all potential purchasers of
American land, Morris also authorized Benjamin Van Pradelles
to sell five townships, totalling 115,400 acres, in Flanders.
According to their arrangement, Van Pradelles was to receive
a commission of 8 per cent on the first 60,000 acres
sold, 6 per cent on the next 40,000, and 4 per cent
on all subsequent sales. In addition, he would receive
a cash payment of 600 Spanish dollars. As with Franklin,
Morris encouraged Van Pradelles to sell either the
entire tract to one company, or if necessary, each
township to a different company for at least 4 livres
per acre. If these plans failed, individual
settlers could purchase lots of from fifty to one

30RM to Franklin, Oct. 28, 1790, to G. Morris, Dec.
3‰, 1790, GMP, NC. On November 1, Morris executed a power
of attorney to Franklin, vesting in him "full powers &
authorities to effect sales of whole or parts of tract...."
(Franklin's Journal, 1790-1791," OCHS)

undred acres at six livres per acre, with four livres
down and the remainder payable in from three to five years
at five per cent annual interest. Morris' Amsterdam
bankers were Wilhem and Jan Willink, who were also the
United States' bankers. If Van Pradelles sold all
five townships, Franklin would assign him additional
lands.[31]

Gouverneur reacted pessimistically to Van Pradelles'
mission. He informed Morris that the wealthy people
in Flanders would not emigrate as long as the possibility
of restoring the emperor existed, and the poor did not
yet feel oppressed enough to leave. By January, 1791,
Van Pradelles had requested a change in his instructions
because of the difficulties he had experienced in finding
purchasers. Gouverneur later referred to him as a
"Poor Creature."[32]

The failure of Morris' agents to conclude any sales
in Paris and Flanders proved unimportant. Success greeted
Franklin quickly, and rather unexpectedly, in London. He
established contact with Patrick Colquhoun, who was the
representative of Sir William Johnstone Pulteney and William
Hornby. Pulteney, Britain's most influential land speculator,
had served in Parliament from Shrewsbury. Hornby had been

[31]RM to Van Pradelles, Oct. 29, 30, 1790, to G. Morris,
Aug. 8, 1790, Van Pradelles to RM, Oct. 29, 1790, GMP, NC.

[32]G. Morris to RM, Nov. 21, 1791, GMLB, DLC; Van
Pradelles to G. Morris, Jan. 24, 1791, GMP, NC; Gouverneur
Morris, A Diary of the French Revolution, ed. by Beatrice
C. Davenport (2 vols; Boston, 1939), I, 48-49.

Governor of Bombay, and Patrick Colquhoun, who had worked for
a mercantile house in Virginia, founded the Glasgow Chamber
of Commerce on his return to Scotland. In the negotiations
between Franklin and Pulteney, Colquhoun served as the
middleman, and on February 15, 1791, Franklin and Colquhoun
signed the preliminary articles of agreement.33

Although the terms of the sale were favorable to
Morris, the Financier had hoped for an even larger profit.
The Pulteney Associates agreed to pay £75,000 sterling
by January 1, 1797 for 1,000,000 acres of Genesee land.
Morris was responsible for surveying the land and for
extinguishing the claims of Indians and squatters. If the
survey revealed more than 1, 000, 000 acres in the tract,
the surplus would belong to the purchasers. Because
the final articles, dated March 17, 1791, provided for
advances to Morris in yearly installments, the last two
payments from the Associates were discounted five per cent.
The Associates promised to pay £10,000 yearly from 1791
to 1795 and £12,000 in 1796 and 1797. As New York
prohibited alien ownership of land, the final articles
bound Franklin to grant to the purchasers, by December
31, 1792, "a conveyance as shall entitle them to
hold the said lands in fee simple, notwithstanding any
Law which now Exists concerning Alienage or other Disabilities."
In the meantime Franklin was to "Execute a Mortgage in
favour of the said Associated Purchasers and to such other

33Franklin to RM, Feb. 1, 18, 1791, Colquhoun to RM,
Feb. 18, 1791, Franklin to G. Morris, Feb. 21, 1791, GMP,
NC; Pulteney and Hornby to Colquhoun, Feb. 15, 1791, "Franklin's
Journal," 1790-1791," OCHS. A typescript of the preliminary
articles of agreement is in the OCHS.

persons as they shall name being citizens of America."[34]

Of all of Morris' land sales, this was undoubtedly
the most profitable. At par £75,000 sterling equalled
$330,000. As Morris paid £35,000, Massachusetts currency,
or $116,872, for the tract, he netted close to $216,128.

In accordance with the articles, Morris arranged
for a survey of the tract. In 1788, Morris employed
Benjamin Ellicott to correct any errors in Colonel Hugh
Maxwell's running of the Preemption line. His survey,
completed in December, 1792, was officially adopted
by the state.[35] Morris also engaged Adam Hoops,
and three assistant surveyors, Frederick Saxton, John
Adlum, and Augustus Porter, to resurvey the entire purchase.
This survey, finished early in 1793, showed that Morris
had actually purchased 1,264,569 acres from Phelps and Gorham.
By special arrangement he paid the two Massachusetts

---

[34]A copy of the final articles is in the GMP, NC.

[35]RM to Andrew Ellicott, requesting Benjamin's
assistance, May 14, 1792, OCHS; "An Act supplementary
to the act entitled "An act authorizing the Surveyor General
to ascertain the Eastern Boundary line of the lands ceded
by this state to the commonwealth of Massachusetts,' and
for other purposes herein mentioned" (New York Laws, 19th Sess.,
Ch. XLCII [Apr. 2, 1796]). The Ellicott brothers, Andrew,
Benjamin, and Joseph, were all famous surveyors. See Sally
K. Alexander, "A Sketch of the Life of Major Andrew Ellicott,"
Records of the Columbia Historical Society, II (1889)
158-202; Catharine Van Cortlandt Mathews, ed., Andrew
Ellicott: His Life and Letters (New York, 1908); Warren
S. Ely, "Andrew Ellicott, the Great Surveyor," Collections
of the Bucks County Historical Society, V (1926), 745-51;
G. Hunter Bartlett, "Andrew and Joseph Ellicott," Publications
of the Buffalo Historical Society, XXVI (1922), 1-48.

speculators £9476.8.0, Massachusetts currency, for the surplus.[36]

In spite of this sale to Pulteney, Morris remained in debt because of the French tobacco contracts. On March 21, 1791, Colquhoun drew on Pulteney's banker, Sir Robert Herries, for the first installment. Through Franklin, Morris requested additional advances on the payments due to him from the Associates. On June 10, the British group advanced the Financier another £3750, with a promise to move forward the remaining payments. Between September, 1791, and October, 1792, the Pulteney Associates paid Morris £27,661.0.5, and Morris received the final installments in January and July, 1793. As a result of the discounting, the Englishmen figured that the land cost them only £63,779.14.8. From that sum, Morris had to deduct Franklin's commission of £7752.17.11. His net profit, reduced by approximately £11,000, or $50,000, thus amountdd to $166.128.[37]

The only remaining difficulty--New York's ban on alien ownership of land--was easily resolved. On April 26 Charles Williamson of Scotland, who had been a British prisoner-of-war during the American Revolution, agreed to move to the United States, become a naturalized citizen, and manage the Association's lands, in return for a two and one-half percent commission. Early

[36]RM to Hoops, June 12, 1791, O'Rielly Papers, NYHS; Hoops's "Return of Survey," Feb. 4, 1793, in George S. Conover, The Genesee Tract: Cessions Between New York and Massachusetts. The Phelps and Gorham Purchase. Captain Charles Williamson and The Pulteney Estate (Geneva, 1889), pp. 8-10; Agreement, Morris, Phelps, Gorham, Feb. 16, 1793, in Conover, Genesee Tract, p. 10.

[37]For these payments, see "Franklin's Journal, 1790-1791," OCHS.

in 1792, Williamson acquired American citizenship, and Morris
officially conveyed the tract to him in April.[38]

Unlike Morris, Williamson and the Associates adopted
specific plans for the development and settlement of
their land. Back in 1791, Franklin had prepared a
pamphlet for the Association to be distributed in
Europe to promote the sale of the Pulteney purchase.
In this pamphlet, Franklin emphasized the stability of
the United States government and the steady increase in
population, which he predicted would double every twenty
years. Lands in America were described as secure, cheap,
and fertile. Now is the time to invest, he wrote,
because in a few years all available capital will be
invested in lands and the profits will be smaller.[39]

The only significant group of foreigners to
emigrate from Europe to the Pulteney lands arrived

---

[38]"Franklin's Journal, 1790-1791," OCHS; Deeds,
Misc. Rec., NYSSO. For Williamson's agency, see Cowan,
Williamson; Arthur C. Parker, "Charles Williamson:
Builder of the Genesee Country," Publications of the
Rochester Historical Society, VI (1927), 1-34; Paul D.
Evans, "The Pulteney Purchase," Quarterly Journal of the
New York State Historical Association, III (Apr., 1922),
83-104; Wendell Tripp, "Robert Troup: A Quest for Order
and Security, 1757-1832" (unpublished Ph.D. dissertation,
Columbia University, 1973), pp. 178-79, 133-62, 182-214;
Robert W. Silsby, "Mortgage Credit in the Phelps-Gorham
Purchase," New York History, XLI (June, 1960), 3-34.

[39]Observations on the Present Situation of Landed
Property in America (London, 1792).

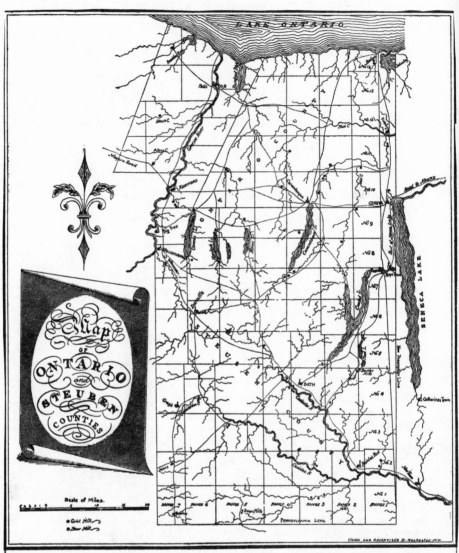

THIS IS A REDUCED FACSIMILE OF THE ORIGINAL MAP APPEARING IN THE EXCESSIVELY RARE FIRST EDITION (1798) OF CAPTAIN CHARLES WILLIAMSON'S LETTERS "DESCRIPTION OF THE GENESEE COUNTRY." IT IS THE MOST CORRECT MAP OF PHELPS AND GORHAM'S PURCHASE.

Fig. 3.

in 1792. Led by Wilhelm Von Moll de Berezy, this group of
discontented Germans from Hamburg was lured to America by
Berezy's promises of great wealth. Their settlement at
Williamsburgh failed because of imprudent management and
the disorderly behavior of the immigrants. Berezy asserted
the supremacy of his authority over Williamson's and
contracted large debts, often by drawing on Morris. After
a riot at Williamsburgh, Berezy and some of his followers
fled to Philadelphia where they solicited aid from Morris.
In 1794 he and his supporters moved their settlement to
Canada.[40]

On the whole, Morris was more than satisfied with
the handsome profit he received from his dealings with
the Pulteney Associates. Gouverneur, on the other hand,
openly expressed his dissatisfaction with Franklin's
handling of his agency. In spite of an explanatory letter
from Franklin, Gouverneur refused to approve of the terms
of the sale.[41] Morris had instructed Franklin to sell

---

[40]RM to Williamson, Aug. 9, 1792, Mar. 30, Apr. 11,
Sept. 15, 1793, Osgood Papers, RPL; RM to Benjamin Walker,
Aug. 22, 1792, Misc. MSS., NYSL: RM to T. Morris, Jan. 18,
1793, RMP, CHHL; T. Morris to RM, Feb. 4, 1793, O'Rielly
Papers, NYHS. For Berezy's defense of his actions, see
A. J. H. Richardson and Helen I. Cowan, ed., "William
Berezy's Williamsburgh Documents," Publications of the
Rochester Historical Society, XX (1942). Additional
information on Berezy is available in Helen I. Cowan,
"Williamsburgh: Lost Village on the Genesee," Rochester
History, III (July, 1942), 5-24; Parker, "Williamson,"
pp. 7-11. For Berezy's reception in Canada, see John G.
Simcoe to Lord Dorchester, Mar. 16, June 17, 1794, in E. A.
Cruikshank, ed., The Correspondence of Lieut. Governor
John Graves Simcoe, With Allied Documents relating to his
Administration of Upper Canada, II (Toronto, 1924), 190, 278.

[41]Franklin to G. Morris, Mar. 25, 1791, GMP, NC;
G. Morris to Franklin, Apr. 7, 1791, to RM, Apr. 11, 1791,
GMLB, DLC.

for a minimum of 2,000,000 livres. At the current rate
of exchange, the £75,000 sterling paid by the Pulteney
Associates equalled at most 2,250,000. As Robert Morris
correctly assumed that 6 livres were worth 5 shillings,
Gouverneur reasoned that the Financier had expected
Franklin to sell for not less than £90,000. Although
Gouverneur suggested legal loopholes by which Morris
could void the agreement, he understood the Financier's
financial needs and did nothing to jeopardize the sale.[42]

As for Morris' profit, Gouverneur applied the money
to satisfy some of Robert's European creditors. He planned
to pay 240,000 livres to Le Couteulx and Company, and then
use part of Pulteney's second, third, and fourth installments
to pay Phelps and Gorham. Robert, who wanted to draw on
these proceeds for his investments in the United States,
was never completely satisfied with these arrangements.[43]

For Morris, this purchase and sale of one million
acres was only the first of his Genesee speculations.
He never wavered in his opinion of the high quality
of the lands or in his belief that he could immediately
resell the land at a great profit. Before he even knew

[42]G. Morris to RM, May 20, 1791, to Franklin, Feb.
27, 1791, GMLB, DLC.

[43]G. Morris to RM, June 28, Sept. 1, 16, 29, Oct. 13,
Nov. 21, 1791, to Franklin, Sept. 7, Oct. 5, 1791, to
Le Couteulx and Co., Oct. 5, 1791, GMLB, DLC; Franklin
to G. Morris, Sept. 8, Oct. 6, 1791, GMP, NC.

of Franklin's activities, the Financier planned to purchase from Massachusetts the remaining two-thirds of the original Phelps-Gorham purchase, which the latter reconveyed to the state on June 9.

According to the original arrangements, Gorham, Phelps, and Morris were partners in this new purchase, and in December, 1790, they signed an agreement authorizing Samuel Ogden, Gouverneur's brother-in-law, to purchase the tract of approximately 4,000,000.[44] Morris offered up to $400,000 for the land, with $40,000 in six months and the remainder, without interest, in annual installments of $40,000. If Massachusetts officials insisted on interest, Morris could make such payments no sooner than two years after the date of purchase. Since Morris knew that the price he proposed exceeded the limit set by Phelps and Gorham for their participation in the purchase, he expected them to back out. Indeed they did, and Morris instructed Ogden to purchase the tract on Morris' account, but in his own name. As none of Morris' competitors could match his offer, Massachusetts sold the land to Ogden on March 12, 1791 for £100,000, Massachusetts currency, or approximately $366,333.33. Then on May 11, Ogden

[44]RM to Ogden, Jan. 20, 1791, to Phelps and Gorham, Jan. 20, 1791, O'Rielly Papers, NYHS.

[45]RM to Ogden, Jan. 21, 1791, to Thomas Russell, Jan. 20, 1791, O'Rielly Papers, NYHS; Indenture between Ogden and the Commonwealth of Massachusetts, Deeds, Misc. Rec., NYSSO.

assigned the tract to Morris, to whom the state officially conveyed the land as five separate tracts.[46]

Of the five tracts, Morris eventually sold four to six Dutch banking houses formally organized as the Holland Land Company on February 13, 1796. The firms involved were Nicholas and Jacob Van Staphorst and Nicholas Hubbard, Wilhem and Jan Willink, Pieter Stadnitski and Son, Pieter and Christian Van Eeghen, Isaac Ten Cate and Hendrick Vollenhoven, and Rutger Jan Schimmelpenninck. In 1789, four of these Dutch houses (Stadnitski, Van Staphorst and Hubbard, Van Eeghen, and Ten Cate and Vollenhoven) appointed Théophile Cazenove to investigate the advisability of speculating in American securities. Cazenove, who had conducted a brokerage and commercial business in Amsterdam from 1763 to 1788, was the brother of J. Henry Cazenove, a successful London banker. Cazenove was especially grateful to Stadnitski, who had helped him to recover from earlier financial difficulties.[48]

Although he landed in New York in 1790, Cazenove immediately established himself in Philadelphia. He

---

[46]Deeds, May 11, 1791, "Resolution of the Massachusetts Senate," Mar. 12, 1791, HLCP, NYSL. See also Fisher, Brief, pp. 21-22, 44-45; Frederick W. Beers, Gazetteer and Biographical Record of Genesee County, N.Y., 1788-1890 (Syracuse, 1890), p. 22.

[47]Evans, The Holland Land Company, pp. 4-5.

wanted to observe first hand the activities of the
national government and to form friendships with men
who were influential in the decision-making process.
On behalf of his Dutch principals, he speculated in
the national debt and purchased shares in the stock
of the Bank of the United States.[48] As he arrived
in the United States with ready cash to invest,
Cazenove attracted all types of speculators, many of
whom convinced him of the soundness of their schemes.
He invested unsuccessfully in the Potomac Canal Company, the James River Company, the Santee Canal Company, the New York Lock Navigation Companies, and the
Connecticut Canal Company. In 1791 he subscribed
twenty-five thousand dollars worth of stock in Alexander Hamilton's Society for Establishing Useful Manu-
factures.[49]

By the end of 1791 the number of cheap securities
for sale had decreased, and speculation in public securities no longer offered an opportunity for profit.
Cazenove, who was impressed by the potential profits of
land speculation, pointed to Morris' sale to the Pulteney

---

[48]Cazenove to the Four Houses, Aug. 23, 1791,
CLB, GA.

[49]Evans, The Holland Land Company, pp. 7-9.

Associates as evidence of the profits to be expected
from such purchases. He convinced three of his principals
to invest in western lands. For that purpose, the Willinks
and Schimmelpenninck joined with their fellow bankers.
The Van Staphorsts stayed out of the land market until
February, 1792.[50] Along with Cazenove, the Dutch
employed Gerrit Boon and John Lincklaen as agents. The
three men made several small purchases for the Amsterdam
bankers, but their main investment came through Robert
Morris.[51]

From the outset of their negotiations, Cazenove
knew that Morris could sell only two of the five
tracts he had recently purchased from Massachusetts.
The Financier had reserved one tract for himself and had
assigned the remaining two to his son, Robert Morris, Jr.,
for sale or mortgage in Europe. On December 24, 1792,
the two speculators reached an agreement. Unlike the
clear-cut sale to the Pulteney Associates, this agreement
contained provisions that kept Morris entangled with the
Holland Company until well into the year 1801. The
Amsterdam bankers agreed to pay £75,000 sterling in cash
for the 1,000,000 acre tract with the option that, if by
December 24, 1795, the Company decided not to purchase

---

[50]Cazenove to the Four Houses, Aug. 23, 1791,
CLB, GA.

[51]Evans, The Holland Land Company, pp. 15-19; Helen L.
Fairchild, ed., Journals of John Lincklaen: Travels in
the Years 1791 and 1792 in Pennsylvania, New York, and
Vermont (New York, 1897).

the land, the cash advance would become a loan. In that
case, the conveyance of title to the land would become a
mortgage for securing repayment from Morris in four annual
installments beginning on December 24, 1798. Until the
Dutch firms decided on the option, they held a mortgage on
the 500,000 acre tract in case Morris defaulted. If
they agreed to purchase the first tract, they would then
pay Morris an additional £37,500 sterling for the second.
The Company, however, could withhold payment of the
£37,500 until Morris completed all of the necessary
surveys and extinguished all Indian claims to the land.
To eliminate the problem presented by New York's restriction
on alien ownership of land, Morris conveyed the tracts
in trust to the New York City mercantile firm of Herman
LeRoy, William Bayard, and James McEvers.[52]

As he had received £75,000 from this arrangement,
Morris wanted to hold on to the remaining three Genesee
tracts until land prices rose. To do this, he had to
prevent his son from concluding any sales in Europe.
The Financier did not know that in December, 1792, the
younger Morris had already reached an agreement for the
sale of the two tracts entrusted to him.

Robert Morris, Jr., had travelled to Europe
as an agent for his father, who authorized him

---

[52]Cazenove to the Four Houses, Nov. 16, Dec. 2, 20,
1792, CLB, GA; Articles of Agreement, Dec. 24, 1792, O'Rielly
Papers, NYHS, Deeds, Misc. Rec., NYSSO, HLCP, NYSL; Indenture,
Dec. 24, 1792, Deeds, Misc. Rec., NYSSO, HLCP, NYSL, RMP,
NYPL. See Turner, Pioneer History, p. 646; Morris, Account
of Property, p. 5.

to offer two of the Genesee tracts as security for a loan of £100,000 sterling. Under Gouverneur's influence, the younger Morris decided instead to sell the land. After an unsuccessful stay in London he went to Amsterdam, where he learned that the Holland Company was interested in new speculations in American lands.[53] He had not yet received his father's letter, written after the sale to Cazenove, which instructed Robert Jr. that "it is unnecessary for you to sell any more Genesee lands, but any bargains you made previous to the receipt of this letter shall be fulfilled.... Neither are you to mortgage any part of my property as I do not now want a loan of Money...." By the time this letter reached Europe early in 1793, his son had concluded his own sale to the same Dutch firms.[54] In December, Robert Jr. had sold to the Dutch bankers 1,000,000 acres in the eastern tract of the Genesee country for 650,000 florins, or $260,000, and he gave the Company an option to purchase an additional 800,000 acres in the west tract for 600,000 florins, or $240,000, payable in six months. The agreement stipulated that Morris had to survey the land into

---

[53] G. Morris to Rm, Apr. 25, June 25, 1792, to RM, Jr., May 20, June 27, July 18, August 27, Sept. 9, 1792, to Willinks, Apr. 23, 1792, GMLB, DLC; Willinks to G. Morris, May 4, 1792, GMP, NC.

[54] RM to RM, Jr., Dec. 19, 1792, RMP, CHML: G. Morris to RM, Feb. 14, 1793, GMLB, DLC.

lots of 450 to 500 acres and extinguish the Indian title.
LeRoy, Lincklaen, and Boon received these lands in
trust for the Company.[55] The news of this sale
reached the United States in February, 1793.[56]

The decision by the Dutch bankers to invest so
heavily in New York lands was due largely to the efforts
of Stadnitski. In 1792 he published a plan for speculating
in American lands. After the purchase from Morris the
Six Houses formed a joint stock company, capitalized at
3,000,000 florins. The Dutch agreed to pay an annual
interest of 5 per cent on each of the 3,000 shares. As
security, the Company offered 1,000,000 acres of
Genesee land. When the Company received the news of
Cazenove's purchase, they proposed to accept 3,450,000
florins worth of additional subscriptions, which they
secured against another 1,000,000 Genesee acres.[57]

---

[55]Articles of Agreement, Feb. 27, 1793, O'Rielly
Papers, NYHS, HLCP, NYSL, HLCP, GA; Indenture, Feb. 27,
1793, RMP, NYPL, Deeds, Misc. Rec., NYSSO, HLCP, NYSL.
See Evans, The Holland Land Company, p. 26; Turner,
Pioneer History, p. 647; Morris, Account of Property,
p. 6. See also "Journal B," f. 214, RMP, HSP.

[56]Cazenove to the Six Houses, Feb. 23, 1793,
CLB, GA.

[57]Pieter Stadnitski, Voorafgaand Bericht wegens
eene Negotiatie op Landen in America (Amsterdam, 1792).
See Evans, The Holland Land Company, pp. 28-30; Tiffany,
Huidekoper, pp. 98-100.

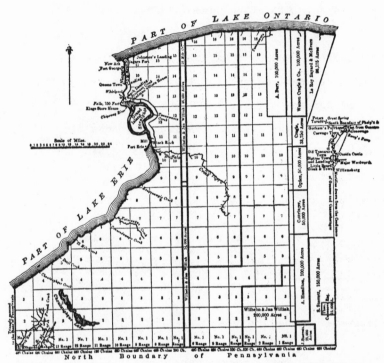

MAP OF HOLLAND LAND COMPANY'S PRELIMINARY SURVEY 1797

Fig. 4.
Reprinted from Charles F. Milliken, "The Phelps
and Gorham Purchase," in History of the Genesee
Country, ed. by Lockwood R. Doty (4 vols.; Chicago,
1925), I, 391.

The success of these negotiations led the Dutch to purchase
the two tracts on which they held options. Accordingly,
on July 20, 1793 Morris conveyed 800,000 acres to LeRoy,
Lincklaen, and Boon and 500,000 acres to LeRoy, Bayard,
and Matthew Clarkson.[58]

Before Morris could fulfill his obligations to the
Holland Land Company by surveying their land and purchasing
the Indian title, he ran into financial difficulty because
of his mismanagement of the fifth Genesee tract known as
tract number 1; or the Morris Reserve. In August, 1791
Morris borrowed $100,000 from William S. Smith, who was in
the United States as the agent of the Pulteney Associates.
The Financier secured this loan by giving Smith a mortgage
on tract number 1. Although Morris agreed to repay Smith
in 6 per cent stock in the funded debt of the United States
in two installments, due on July 1, 1792 and January 1, 1793,
he was unable to meet the second payment.[59]

---

[58]Articles of Agreement and Indenture, July 20, 1793,
RM and LeRoy, Lincklaen, and Boon, Deeds, Misc. Rec., NYSSO,
HLCP, NYSL; Articles of Agreement and Deed, July 20, 1793,
RM and LeRoy, Bayard, and Clarkson, HLCP, NYSL. See Turner,
Pioneer History, pp. 647-48; Morris, Account of Property, p.6.
LeRoy, Bayard, and Clarkson held 300,000 of the 500,000 acre
tract in trust for the Willinks (Articles of Agreement, Aug.
24, 1792, RM, Jr. and Willinks, and Articles of Agreement,
Jan. 11, 1793, RM and Willinks, RMP, NYPL; Articles of
Agreement, July 20, 1793, RM and LeRoy, Bayard, and Clarkson,
O'Rielly Papers, NYHS, HLCP, NYSL; Deed, July 20, 1793, RM
and LeRoy, Bayard, and Clarkson, Deeds, Misc. Rec., NYSSO,
HLCP, NYSL). See Turner, Pioneer History, pp. 402, 648;
Morris, Account of Property, p. 6.

[59]Indenture, August 13, 1791, Deeds, Misc. Rec., NYSSO,
Hamilton Papers, DLC; Defeasance, Aug. 13, 1791, RMP, DLC;
Hamilton Papers, DLC; Bill, Walker v. Morris, filed Oct. 24,
1795, New York Chancery Decrees before 1800, W-174, Historical
Documents Collection, Queens College of The City University
of New York.

In spite of the mortgage to Smith, Morris sold two tracts
in the Reserve without informing the Pulteney Association.
On February 18, 1792 he sold James Watson, Andrew Craigie
and James Greenleaf 100,000 acres for £15,000, New York
currency, or $37,500.[60] Then, on January 11, 1793 he
conveyed the so-called Triangle Tract, containing 86,793
acres, to LeRoy and Bayard for £12,000, New York currency,
or $30,000.[61]

In 1795 Benjamin Walker, who had succeeded Smith
as the agent of the Pulteney Association, learned of
Morris' sales in the Reserve and threatened to take legal
action. Morris immediately searched for a way to pay the
$50,000 due to the Associates, but he had no funds to draw
on. In July he asked LeRoy and Bayard to advance him
$50,000 worth of 6 per cent stock on credit or to
purchase an additional $50,000 worth of land adjoining
the tract they already owned. The merchants accepted
neither proposal.[62]

As Morris moved closer and closer to bankruptcy, he
developed a high-handed attitude towards his more persistent
creditors. He never apologized for his inability to pay,
but rather snapped at their impatience. He thus informed
Walker that he was not to blame for the difficulties

---

[60]Indenture, Feb. 18, 1792, Deeds, Misc. Rec., NYSSO;
"Journal B," f. 46, RMP, MSP. Watson and Greenleaf were
partners in a New York City mercantile firm; Craigie was a
Massachusetts businessman. For Morris' grants in the Reserve,
see The Genesee Pioneer Association. A History of Its
Organization, List of Officers and Members, and the Annual
Address delivered June 11, 1878, by Hon. Norman Seymour
(Batavia, 1879), p. 17.

[61]Indenture, Jan. 11, 1793, Deeds, Misc. Rec., NYSSO;
"Journal B," f. 236, 237, 298, RMP, MSP.

[62]RM to LeRoy and Bayard, July 22, 1795, RMLB, DLC.

stemming from this "innocent Transaction." Although he
lacked "Ready Money," he owned extensive property. He
wanted to pay Pulteney as soon as possible because Pulteney "asked me to do so and because I wish to free that
Tract of Country from the Incumbrance."[63]

By October, 1795, Morris had not paid Walker, and
the latter filed a bill in the New York Court of Chancery
requesting an injunction that would prohibit Morris from
selling any additional lands in the Reserve.[64] By the
time the Court issued the injunction in May, Morris had
taken definite steps to repay Pulteney. The Financier
agreed to sell 50,000 acres through his agent, Samuel Ogden, and to use the bonds he received to repay Pulteney.
In May, Ogden conveyed the land to Othniel Taylor and Asa
Danforth for $57,000. Morris informed Walker of this de-
velopment and offered to assign Ogden's contract to him.
Walker could discharge the mortgage and pay Morris the
small sum that would be due to him. Walker refused to
accept this arrangement.[65]

Walker's rejection created new problems for Morris.
Not only was the Financier unable to repay Pulteney, but
as long as the injunction stood, he could not use the Reserve to secure his debt to John B. Church. Church was
the English brother-in-law of Alexander Hamilton's wife,
and Hamilton served as Church's attorney in the States.

---

[63]RM to Walker, July 30, 1795, RMLB, DLC.

[64]Bill, Walker v. Morris, Historical Documents
Collection, Queens College.

[65]RM to Ogden, Apr. 27, May 11, 1796, RMLB, DLC.

Prior to March, 1793, Morris purchased 100 shares of
bank stock from Church for £100 sterling per share.
As security, Morris mortgaged to Church one of his
Philadelphia estates. In May, 1793, Morris paid
part of this debt by selling Hamilton 20,290 acres in
Luzerne County, Pennsylvania for £4565.5.0 sterling.
Efforts to pay the remaining sum proved futile, and in
1794 Morris cancelled the mortgage on his Philadelphia
estate. Instead, he agreed to pay Church with $100,000
of deferred debt payable in February, 1795 at an
annual interest of 6 per cent.[66] When Morris
discovered that he could not meet this obligation,
he transferred to Church 750 shares in the newly formed
North American Land Company. Church refused this stock.
So, in April, 1796, Morris mortgaged 100,000 Genesee
acres in the Reserve to Hamilton as security for the
remainder of the debt. Although the land was tied up
by Walker's suit, the Court allowed Morris to execute
the mortgage to Hamilton, along with a bond for $81,679.44
payable by January 1, 1801.[67]

Walker's refusal to accept payment of Pulteney's
loan on Morris' terms delayed the execution of the
Mortgage to Hamilton. The tracts involved in

---

[66]For this debt, see Harold C. Syrett, ed., The Papers
of Alexander Hamilton (New York, 1973), XVIII, 359-70;
"Journal B," f. 200, 374, RMP, HSP; RM to Church, May 17,
1796, RMLB, DLC.

[67]RM to Church, May 28, Oct. 9, 1795, to Hamilton,
Apr. 27, 1796, RMLB, DLC: MS Minutes of the N. Y. Court
of Chancery, May 14, 1796, HR, NYC; Bill, Church v. Morris
and Hamilton, filed July 1, 1797, New York Chancery Decrees
before 1800, C-180, Historical Documents Collection, Queens
College.

Ogden's sale to Taylor and Danforth and the mortgage to
Church had a common border. Morris had to cancel the sale
to Taylor and Danforth, convey the tract to Garrett
Cottringer, a Philadelphia merchant who was also Morris'
bookkeeper, and insert Cottringer's name in the mortgage
to Hamilton. Morris thus temporarily quieted his problems
with Church.[68]

Church, however, returned to the United States from
England in the spring of 1797 and filed a suit to force
Morris to pay the interest he owed or to have the Court
foreclose the mortgage. On November 14, 1797, Chancellor
Robert R. Livingston ordered the seizure of all of Morris'
New York property. With the help of Samuel Sterett, a
Philadelphia merchant, Morris paid Church $10,821.63,
and the suit was dismissed early in 1798. But in 1799,
Church successfully brought another suit against Morris
to foreclose the mortgage to pay the principal of the
debt. Livingston ordered a sale of the tract, and in
1800, Philip Church attended the sale and purchased the
tract for his father.[69]

---

[68]RM to Hamilton, May 31, 1796, RMLB, DLC; Morris,
Account of Property, p. 3.

[69]Bill, Church v. Morris and Hamilton, filed July
1, 1797, New York Chancery Decrees before 1800, C-180,
Historical Documents Collection, Queens College; Bill,
Church v. LeRoy, Bayard, and McEvers, filed June 26,
1806, New York Chancery Papers, BM-716-C, HR, NYC; MS
Minutes of the N.Y. Court of Chancery, Nov. 7, 27,
Dec. 18, 1797, Feb. 20, Mar. 2, 1798, May 17, Aug. 12,
1799, HR, NYC; RM to Richard Harison, one of his attorneys,
Feb. 17, 1798, PMLB, DLC.

During the time that Morris was settling his account
with Church, he was also trying to satisfy his debt to
Pulteney. Morris finally conveyed the 50,000 acres in
Cottringer's name to Charles Williamson, who in turn
reconveyed to Morris the land in the Reserve held by
Pulteney as security for the loan from Smith, his special
agent, to Morris. On June 6, 1798, the Chancery Court
dismissed Walker's suit.[70]

In addition to these transactions, Morris conveyed
other parts of the Reserve to several creditors. In
August, 1795, for example, he sold 33,750 acres to Andrew
Craigie for £12,234 to satisfy a debt.[71] He conveyed
another 175,000 to Samuel Sterett to secure his debt of
approximately $350,000 to the firm of George Harrison
and Sterett.[72] He also gave half of a tract known as
Mount Morris to his son Thomas, and the second half to
Thomas FitzSimons as partial security for still another
debt.[73]

All of these incumbrances intruded on Morris' efforts
to fulfill his obligations to the Holland Land Company.
Moreover, until 1796, a treaty with the Indians was an
impossibility, due to the hostility between the United States

---

[70]RM to Hamilton, Jan. 7, 1797, to Williamson, June 3,
July 20, 1797, to James Marshall, his son-in-law, May 31,
1797, RMLB, DLC; Morris, Account of Property, pp. 2-3;
MS Minutes of the N.Y. Court of Chancery, HR, NYC.

[71]Indenture, Apr. 5, 1797, Deeds, Misc. Rec., NYSSO;
RM to Ogden, Jan. 8, 1796, RMLB, DLC; Morris, Account of
Property, p. 2.

[72]Indenture, May 4, 1797, Deeds, Misc. Rec., NYSSO;
Morris, Account of Property, p. 3.

[73]"Journal C," f. 370, RMP, HSP; Morris, Account of
Property, p. 3.

and the northwest tribes. The British, who still retained
the northwest posts, encouraged the Indians' opposition
to the national government. Anthony Wayne's victory
over the Indians at Fallen Timbers in 1794, which led
to the Treaty of Greenville in 1795, solved the main
problem; the Jay Treaty, ratified in 1796, eliminated
the British complication.[74]

Thus, in 1796, Morris began preparations for
a meeting with the Indians. Unfortunately, by that
time, he was well on his way to debtors' prison and
he lacked the funds necessary for such negotiations.
The Holland Land Company, anxious to clear its title
in order to begin selling the land, advanced Morris
£9,000 out of the £37,500 originally retained as
security for Morris' promise to extinguish all Indian
claims to its Genesee tract. As security for the advance,
Morris gave the Dutch a mortgage on 40,000 Genesee acres
to which he miraculously still held a clear title.[75]

Next, each interested party appointed representatives
to the talks with the Senecas. On August 25, Morris asked

[74]RM to T. Morris, Mar. 26, 1796, RMLB, DLC; T. Morris
to RM, May 13, 1796, O'Rielly Papers, NYHS; Cazenove to the
Six Houses, May 23, 1796, HLCP, GA.

[75]Indenture, Dec. 28, 1796, RM and LeRoy, Lincklaen,
and Boon, Misc. Rec., NYSSO, HLCP, NYSL. A few days later,
Morris assigned this same tract to the Willinks for the
balance due them on Morris' pledge, in 1793, to deliver to
them 215 shares of stock in the Bank of the United States
(Indenture, Dec. 31, 1796, RM and LeRoy, Bayard, and McEvers,
Deeds, Misc. Rec., NYSSO, HLCP, NYSL; RM to Willinks, May 24,
1797, RMLB, DLC; Cazenove to Bayard, Lincklaen, and Boon,
July 31, 1797, HLCP, GA; Morris, Account of Property, p. 3).

George Washington to appoint a commissioner to represent
the United States at the proposed meetings. The President
consulted Attorney General Charles Lee, who explained that
such an appointment required the approval of the Senate.[76]
At the December session of Congress, Washington nominated
Isaac Smith, a former New Jersey congressman who was now
a Judge of the New Jersey Supreme Court. Smith declined
and Washington chose Colonel Jeremiah Wadsworth of
Connecticut. By the provisions of the Hartford Convention,
Massachusetts could appoint a commissioner to any talks with
the Indians, and state officials chose General William
Shephard. William Bayard and a nephew of the Van Staphorsts
represented the Dutch.[77]

On August 1 Morris sent a power of attorney to his
own negotiators, Thomas Morris and Charles Williamson.

---

[76] RM to Washington, Aug. 25, Dec. 23, 1796, O'Rielly
Papers, NYHS (the letter of Dec. 23 was never sent); Charles
Lee to Secretary of State Timothy Pickering, May 26, 1796,
RG 60, Letters from and Opinions of Attorneys General, 1791-
1811, DNA: Pickering to RM, August 27, 1796, to Washington,
Aug. 27, 1796, RG 59, Domestic Letters of the Department of
State, Vol. 9, Oct. 12, 1795-Feb. 28, 1797, DNA.

[77] Journal of the Executive Proceedings of the Senate
(Washington, D.C., 1828), I, 229, 232. For the President's
stipulation that the treaty be held only with the consent
of the Indians, see Executive Journal, I, 229, Captain
James Bruff, the Commander of Fort Niagara, to Secretary
at War James McHenry, Sept. 25, 1796, O'Rielly Papers,
NYHS, RM to T. Morris, May 29, 1797, RMLB, DLC. See also
RM to Cazenove, May 24, July 18, 1797, to T. Morris, June 30,
July 20 (two letters), 1797, to Shephard, July 8, 1797, to
Wadsworth, July 20, 1797, RMLB, DLC; Cazenove to the Van Eeghens,
Mar. 11, Aug. 7, 1797, to the Six Houses, May 22, 1797, to
Bayard, July 19, 1797, HLCP, GA; T. Morris, "Narrative of
Events in the History and Settlement of Western New York,"
The Historical Magazine, 2nd ser., V (June, 1869), 379-80.

In his instructions to them, he proposed to offer the
Indians a perpetual annuity of no more than $4,500 for
all of their Genesee lands. If necessary, his agents
could award special annuities of $250 to $300 to the
Seneca Chiefs and to Joseph Brant, the powerful Mohawk
leader. If the Indians refused an annuity, Morris offered to pay them $75,000 for the tract.[78]

Morris was to be disappointed in the results of
these talks, which were held in August and September
at what is now Geneseo. The Indians were neither as
anxious to sell nor as naive about the value of their
lands as Morris had hoped. Under the influence of Corn-
planter, they demanded larger reserves than their prospective purchasers wanted to grant. To overcome the
opposition of the Chiefs to the sale, Thomas Morris
successfully offered them bribes. On September 15 the
parties signed the Treaty of Big Tree, by which Morris
paid the Indians $100,000 worth of stock in the Bank
of the United States. The President of the United States
was to hold the stock for the Indians, who would receive
the interest in yearly payments. In addition to stock,

---

[78]Power of Attorney, Aug. 1, 1797, Deeds, Misc. Rec.,
NYSSO, O'Rielly Papers, NYHS, RMP, CHHL, HLCP, NYSL; RM
to T. Morris and Williamson, Aug. 1, 1797, O'Rielly Papers,
NYHS. Williamson declined serving (T. Morris, "Narrative,"
p. 381).

the natives obtained reservations of 200,000 acres.[79] Morris considered the terms of the treaty far too generous.[80]

The Financier was now ready to complete the necessary survey of the land granted to the Dutch bankers. He directed Adam Hoops to survey ten specific tracts, including those in the Morris Reserve that bordered on the Company's land.[81] Cazenove, in turn, ordered his surveyor, Joseph Ellicott, to ascertain the boundary lines of the Indian reservations, of the land reserved by New York State, and of the tracts sold to the Company and

---

[79]Treaty of Big Tree, Sept. 15, 1797, Deeds, Misc. Rec., NYSSO. The standard sources for information on the Treaty are T. Morris, "Narrative," pp. 381-84, Normal B. Wilkinson, "Robert Morris and the Treaty of Big Tree," MVHR, XL (Sept., 1953), 257-78, A History of the Treaty of Big Tree and an Account of the Celebration of the One Hundredth Anniversary of the Making of the Treaty, Held at Geneseo, N.Y., September the Fifteenth Eighteen Hundred Ninety-Seven. Published by the Livingston County Historical Society (Dansville, 1897). The diaries of T. Morris and Wadsworth at the negotiations are printed in People of the State of N.Y. v. Frederick W. Becker, 92 U.S. 7 (1917). See also T. Morris, "Rough Notes of a Speech to Seneca Indians," Misc. MSS., RM, NYHS; RM to T. Morris, Sept. 15, 29, 1797, O'Rielly Papers, NYHS; RM to T. Morris, Aug. 15, 1797, to McHenry, Aug. 11, 1797, to Ogden, Sept. 30, 1797 to Wadsworth, Aug. 12, 15, 1797, to P. Busti, Sept. 15, 1797, to Cazenove, Sept. 23, Nov. 1, 1797, to Secretary of the Treasury Oliver Wolcott, Jr., Oct. 25, 1797, RMLB, DLC; Cazenove to the Van Eeghens, Sept. 28, 1797, HLCP, GA; William L. Stone, The Life and Times of Sa-Go-Ye-Wat-Ha, or Red Jacket (Albany, 1866), pp. 237-49.

[80]RM to LeRoy, Bayard, and McEvers, Jan. 27, 1798, RMLB, DLC; Evans, The Holland Land Company, pp. 193-95; Wilkinson, 'Treaty of Big Tree," pp. 276-78.

[81]"Extracts from Instructions from Rbt. Morris to Major Adam Hoops," RMP, NYPL; Morris, Account of Property, pp. 2-4.

the Willinks, as well as to survey the tracts owned by the Dutch bankers and determine the course of the Genesee River.[82]

By 1798, Morris was in debtors' prison, where he saw all of his land being sold to satisfy his creditors. On February 14, 1798 he conveyed 110,258 acres of the Morris Reserve to FitzSimons, R. Morris, Jr., and Joseph Higbee, in trust, to secure certain specified debts.[84] But the end of Morris' involvement in New York's western lands proved protracted and complicated.

By a New York law, passed on April 2, 1798, aliens could own land within the state, and the legal process of transferring titles from the trustees of the Company to

---

[82]May 10, 1798, in Robert W. Bingham, ed., Holland Land Company's Papers: Reports of Joseph Ellicott as Chief of Survey (1797-1800) and as Agent (1800-1821) of The Holland Land Company's Purchase in Western New York, in Publications of the Buffalo Historical Society, XXXII (1937), 21-26.

[83]Detailed documentary material is available on the survey. See RM to T. Morris, Sept. 29, 1797, O'Rielly Papers, NYHS; RM to Hoops, Sept. 25, Oct. 4, 5, Nov. 5, Dec. 23, 1797, to Craigie, Oct. 19, 1797, to Cazenove, Oct. 2, 4, 5, 1797, RMLB, DLC; RM to Hoops, Sept. 25, Oct. 6, 1797, June 2, 3, 5, 6, 1798, to T. Morris, June 6, 1798, "Conversation between A. Hoops and Joseph Ellicott, June 11, 1798, Hoops to Porter, June 12, 13, 1798, RMP, NYPL; Ellicott to Hoops, June 11, 12, 1798, Cazenove to Ellicott, July 25, Oct. 6, 16, 1797, May 10, 1798, Ellicott to Cazenove, Sept. 25, Nov. 19, 1797, Aug. 16, 29, 1798, "Report of Joseph Ellicott for the Year 1797," "Report of Mr. Joseph Ellicott concerning the State of the Survey of the Genesee Lands Made in 1798," 1800, in Bingham, Reports of Joseph Ellicott," pp. 3-9, 11-15, 21-26, 35-36, 38-39, 49-125; Cazenove to Ellicott [July 25-Oct. 18] 1797, Oct. 18, 1797, Ellicott to Busti, Nov. 20, 1800, in "Extracts from Joseph Ellicott's Letter Books and Early Correspondence," Publications of the Buffalo Historical Society, XXVI (1922), 50-57, 76-78; Cazenove to the Van Eeghens, Feb. 22, May 21, 1798, May 4, 1799, HLCP, GA; Porter, "Narrative," p. 316.

[84]RM to Hoops, June 6, 1798, "Extracts from Instructions from Rbt. Morris to Major Adam Hoops," RMP, NYPL; Morris, Account of Property, pp. 3-4.

its Dutch principals began.[85] At the suggestion of James
Marshall, Morris devised a new scheme, of questionable
legality, to raise funds. His son-in-law indicated that
the option given to the Dutch, in the December 24, 1792'
contract, of either purchasing the land or considering
it as security for a loan, was also Morris' option. The
Financier thus decided to consider the contract a mortgage
and planned to sell the two western tracts involved.
His attorney, Edward Livingston, supported this new
maneuver. Livingston had developed his own scheme to
buy up all of Morris' outstanding notes, and then, if
the Court accepted Morris' new theory, attach all of
the Financier's Genesee property.[86]

In his efforts to purchase all of the judgments
against Morris' New York lands, Livingston met two obstacles.
In June, 1797, Talbot and Allum had obtained a judgment
against Morris for $6,000, which Morris declared to be
the oldest judgment against him in New York. Gouverneur
Morris, who returned to the United States in 1798,
purchased this judgment for Morris' family.[87] The second

---

[85]"An Act to enable Aliens to purchase and hold real
Estates within this State, under certain restrictions therein
mentioned" (New York Laws, 21st Sess., Ch. LXXII [April 2,
1796]); Evans, The Holland Land Company, pp. 211-13;
Turner, Pioneer History, pp. 646-50; "J.J. Vander Kemp's
List of Papers," HLCP, NYSL. Copies of all of the deeds
of transfer are in Deeds, Misc. Rec., NYSSO, HLCP, NYSL.

[86]RM to Cazenove and Busti, Feb. 9, 1799, RMP, CHHL;
"Opinion of Messrs. R. Harison, A. Hamilton, B. Livingston,
Robt. Troup, David A. Ogden, Lawyers of New York, concerning
the Pretensions of Robert Morris," Apr. 17, 1799, HLCP, GA.

[87]Ogden and others to Busti, Apr. 16, 1800, HLCP, GA;
Morris, Account of Property, p. 4. For a full discussion
of this suit, see FitzSimons & Others v. Ogden & Others,
7 Cranch (U.S.) 2 (1812).

problem was a judgment for $50,000, obtained by Aaron
Burr in 1798 for Solomon Townsend. Townsend was the agent
for Paschal Hollingsworth of Philadelphia, one of Morris'
creditors. In March, 1799, Thomas Mather, acting with Burr,
purchased the title to Morris' four million Genesee acres
at a sheriff's sale. Livingston, who was unaware of Talbot
and Allum's judgment, had concluded an agreement with
Mather and his associates for one-fourth of the profit from
the sale of this land.[88]

Besides Livingston and Mather, the Dutch bankers
decided to purchase all claims against Morris. Faced with
the technical error of having failed to record the articles
of agreement for the 1,500,000 acre tract at both Albany
and the Ontario County Clerk's Office, they needed to
purchase all conflicting claims before anyone learned
of their oversight. In the summer of 1799, Ogden, as
attorney for the Amsterdam bankers, offered Livingston
$5,000 for Mather's claim, but Livingston refused to
accept less than $15,000. Then, in January, 1800,
Ogden learned of Talbot and Allum's judgment, which had
preceded Townsend's. If a sale was effected under
Talbot and Allum's judgment, any titles obtained at the
1799 sale would be invalidated. In the meantime, the
error in recording the articles would be corrected. At
a sale held in February Ogden's plan failed, and he
blamed Adam Hoops, who was Gouverneur's agent. Hoops

[88]Ogden and others to Busti, Apr. 16, 1800, HLCP,
GA; RM to T. Morris, Feb. 26, Sept. 7, 1799, RMP, CHML;
Morris was unsuccessful in his efforts to convince James
Rees to purchase the land at this sale, after which Morris
would have found "Persons to take it off your hands allowing
you a reasonable compensation for your Trouble." (RM to Rees,
Dec. 31, 1798, Apr. 23, 1799, RMP, NYPL).

pressured the sheriff to adjourn the sale after he was
outbid by John Dickenson, who represented the Mather-
Burr group. Dickenson offered $34,000 for the land.[89]

Ogden then returned to his original plan of
purchasing all conflicting claims. To secure Townsend's
judgment, Ogden allowed Hollingsworth to think that the
Company was bringing suit to have the judgment invalidated.
At the same time, Ogden convinced Philip Church to propose
to purchase the tract for $5,000 at any new sale ordered
by the Court. When Hollingsworth heard of Church's
modest offer, he agreed to sell to the Company for
$10,000. Busti, who had replaced Cazenove, accepted
these terms.[90]

Now that the Burr group was out of the picture, Ogden
and Gouverneur negotiated for the sale of Talbot and Allum's
judgment to the Company. Attorneys for the Dutch also
knew that the eastern line of the Company's land conflicted
with the ill-defined boundaries of Morris' grants in the
Reserve. If Ogden enlisted the assistance of the landowners
in the Reserve to buy up Talbot and Allum's judgment,
they could redefine the boundary lines at a shared
expense. Gouverneur agreed and on April 22, 1800

---

[89]FitzSimmons v. Ogden, p. 6.

[90]The information in this and the next two paragraphs
comes from Ogden to Busti, Apr. 16, 1800, Apr. 10, 1801,
"The Award," Jan. 22, 1801. HLCP, GA; FitzSimmons v.
Ogden, pp. 2-22; Agreement between G. Morris and the
Company, Apr. 22, 1800, HLCP, NYSL; Agreement between
G. Morris and the Company, Jan., 1801, discussed in
Busti to the Van Eeghens, Jan. 28, 1801, HLCP, GA. See
also Evans, The Holland Land Company, pp. 178-85.

he sold Talbot and Allum's judgment to the Dutch for
$7,000. To settle the boundary disputes, the landholders
appointed Hamilton, Ogden, and Thomas Cooper to study
the various claims. Their award, presented early in 1801,
did not satisfy all of the parties involved. Church and
Morris' Genesee trustees unsuccessfully brought suit
against Ogden for the recovery of land they had lost
under the award.

As a result of the alien land act of 1798, the Dutch
principals could now hold title to their Genesee lands
in their own names. They requested confirmation deeds
from Morris of the Company's title to the 1,500,000 acre
tract. In January, 1800, Gouverneur arranged to surrender
the land to the Company in return for an annuity of
$1,500 to Mary Morris, Robert's wife.

All of these Genesee purchases, sales, and suits
occurred amidst the confusion of Morris' speculative
activities throughout the United States. If Morris had
held on to his New York lands until the early 1800's when
land values rose, he would have netted a handsome profit.
But, because of his other land investments and because
of the debts he owed from the French tobacco contracts,
he either sold his Genesee lands for immediate funds or
mortgaged them to satisfy his creditors. In preparing
for his bankruptcy proceedings he wrote: "I shall begin
with the Lands purchased in the Genesee Country,

acknowledging that if I had contented myself with those
purchases, and employed my time and attention in disposing
of the land to the best advantage, I have every reason to
believe, that at this day I should have been the wealthiest
citizen of the United States...."[91]

Morris had miscalculated the demand for American lands
both in Europe and the United States. The fact remains
that in spite of heavy promotional literature encouraging
investment and immigration, the developmental policies
of the Pulteney Association and the Holland Company did not
yield great profits for their principals. The pamphlets
by Franklin and Stadnitski related to Morris' holdings,
but other pamphleteers were also active.

For example, Gilbert Imlay, a veteran of the American
Revolution, published a pamphlet in 1792, which stressed
the fertility of the Genesee soil, the abundance of game
and fish, the agreeable climate, and the advantages of
its navigable lakes and rivers. He claimed that in two and
one-half years the population rose from 1,070 to 7,000.
To help newly arrived settlers, Imlay prepared a five-
year plan for farming. Written specifically for a British
audience, he asserted that "The overflowings of Germany
and France are now emigrating to America; and it might,
in the course of a few years, be matter of serious regret
if Britons and Irelanders, who have a much better right, did
not endeavour to cement, by this intimate connexion and

---

[91]Morris, Account of Property, p. 1

a natural alliance, countries which are by nature designed
for the mutual aggrandizement and support of each other."[92]

Even after Morris' failure, Williamson published
two pamphlets on the advantages of settling in the Genesee.
In 1799, he published a series of letters to "a friend,"
who was considering immigrating to the Genesee. According
to the Pulteney agent, three thousand people per year
arrived in western New York from Pennsylvania, Maryland,
New Jersey and New England, and their settlements presented
"an appearance of respectability never before instanced
in so new a country."[93]   A second pamphlet, published
anonymously in 1803 or 1804, described the region's
natural resources, climate, population, and topography,
and asserted that "Lands that are now selling at four
dollars an acre, were sold twelve years ago at only the
same number of shillings an acre, and the advance of their
value in the course of 10 or 15 years hence will most
probably be very considerable."[94]

---

[92]An account of the soil, growing timber, and other
productions, of the lands in the countries situated in the
back parts of the states of New-York and Pennsylvania, in
North America; and particularly the land in the county of
Ontario, known by the name of the Genesee tract, lately
located, and now in the progress of being settled, in Gilbert
Imlay, A Topographical Description of the Western Territory
of North America (3d ed., London, 1797), pp. 458-481.

[93]Description of the Settlement of the Genesee Country,
in the State of New-York. In a Series of Letters from a
Gentleman to His Friend (New York, 1799), in E. B. O'Callaghan,
ed., The Documentary History of the State of New York (Albany,
1849), II, 1127-68. The pamphlet included a smaller pamphlet
published in 1798.

[94]Robert Munro [Charles Williamson], A Description of
the Genesee Country, in the State of New York (New York,
1804), in O'Callaghan, Documentary History, II, 1169-89.

Throughout this entire period of optimism and wild speculation, perhaps the only cautious voice belonged to Gouverneur Morris. Although his confidence in the gains to be made from land speculation was limited, he admitted that the Genesee lands were "among the few Tracts of back lands in which I have faith."[95] Still, he warned Robert that the European wars would negatively affect all foreign investment in the United States.[96] By the end of 1794, Gouverneur, shocked at the extent of Morris' investment in the Federal City, implored:

> But in the name of Friendship and of common Sense, let me ask you to what Purpose all this Accumulation of Property with so much Trouble and Labor and Anxiety? Why not pay off every thing & every Body and enjoy quietly?...when I consider how easy it is for you to liquidate all your affairs and preserve an immense Property more than a wise Man would wish to be plagued with the Care of much more, I own to you that I stand in Admiration of that Inconsistency in human nature from which the best of its members are so far from being exempted.[97]

Even though Morris ignored his advice, Gouverneur remained loyal. In fact, Gouverneur's more practical judgment led him to arrange for the small pension Mary Morris received from the Holland Company. Without this money, the Morris' had absolutely no funds.

The Financier had bankrupted himself by 1798. He began his land speculations after he had already overextended himself with the French contracts. If he expected to profit from these new investments, he had to hold on to the bulk of his land long enough for prices to rise.

---

[95]G. Morris to RM, Aug. 14, 1792, GMLB, DLC.

[96]Dec. 24, 1792, GMLB, DLC.

[97]Dec. 28, 1794, GMLB, DLC.

Undeveloped land rarely affords its owners an immediate
profit. Instead, Morris neglected his mercantile business
and left himself no alternative source of income with
which to extinguish his debts or provide for his personal
expenses. He used his land to pay his debts, but when
the land bubble burst in 1796, the immense property
he possessed had little value.

In the 1790's, Morris latched on to land speculation
as the answer to his financial problems. All would be
well, he reasoned, when his lands paid off. He had
invested too much too early and refused to admit his
error. Still, the Genesee country was not the cause of
his failure. If anything, his use of this land to
satisfy certain creditors prolonged his financial life.

CHAPTER III

PENNSYLVANIA

Morris' purchases in his home state were more varied
than his speculations in New York. Although he acquired
large tracts of Pennsylvania back lands, he also owned
smaller, well-developed estates in Philadelphia, the
Northern Liberties, and Bucks County. More important,
Pennsylvania land formed the sold basis for all but one
of Morris' land companies and colonization schemes.

In 1783, Pennsylvania's most pressing problem was
the settlement of its revolutionary war debt, which consisted mainly of depreciation certificates. In 1780 the
Continental Congress, in need of financial support, requested that each state pay its soldiers in the Continental Army for back and current pay and for losses in-
curred because of pay issued in depreciated continental
currency. In response, the states issued depreciation
certificates to their soldiers.[1] To redeem these cer-
tificiates, Pennsylvania, in 1783, reserved a continuous

---

[1]JCC, XIV, 975, XVI, 344. For example, "An Act
to Settle and Adjust the Accounts of the Troops of this
State and for Other Purposes Therein Mentioned" (James
T. Mitchell and Henry Flanders, ed., The Statutes at
Large of Pennsylvania from 1682 to 1801 [Philadelphia,
1904], X, 233-38). See also Joseph C. Ruddy, "The
Policy of Land Distribution in Pennsylvania Since 1779,"
(unpublished M.A. thesis, Pennsylvania State College,
1933), pp. 60-61.

tract of 720,000 acres in Beaver, Allegheny, Armstrong,
and Butler Counties. The statute divided the depreciation
tract into five districts, which deputy surveyors
subdivided into lots of 200 to 350 acres. By 1789
the state had sold only 316,935 acres, for which it had
received only partial payments totalling $87,805.33.
This same act also set aside donation lands, which were
awarded to officers and soldiers of the Pennsylvania
line according to their rank.[2]

The state's land laws resulted in rampant speculation.[3]
Merchants, who had purchased depreciation certificates at
prices below par, now used them to buy large tracts of land.
The surveyors, appointed under the 1783 act, were Daniel
Leet, Nathaniel Breading, William Alexander, Ephraim Douglass,
Samuel Jones, James Cunningham, Joshua Elder, and Samuel
Nicholson, the brother of John Nicholson. These men, who
associated with Pennsylvania's merchants and speculators,

[2]"An Act for the Sale of Certain Lands Therein Mentioned
for the Purpose of Redeeming and Paying Off the Certificates
of Depreciation Given to the Officers and Soldiers of the
Pennsylvania Line, or their Representatives, and for
Appropriating Certain Other Lands therein Mentioned for
the Use of the Said Officers and Soldiers to be Divided
Off to Them Severally at the End of the War" (Mitchell,
Pennsylvania Statutes, XI, 32-36). See also Ruddy, "Land
Distribution," pp. 60-62; Report of the Secretary of
Internal Affairs (Harrisburg, 1892), pp. 30, 33; R. Nelson
Hale, "Pennsylvania Population Company," (unpublished Ph.D.
dissertation, University of Pittsburgh, 1950), pp. 10-11.

[3]The best discussion of Pennsylvania's land policy
is in Norman B. Wilkinson, "Land Policy and Speculation
in Pennsylvania, 1779-1800" (unpublished Ph.D. dissertation,
University of Pennsylvania, 1958).

91

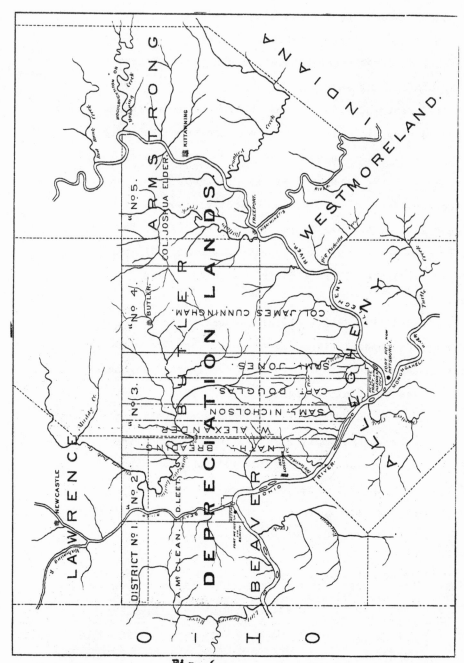

Fig. 6.
Reprinted from the **Report of the Secretary of Internal Affairs** (Harrisburg, 1892).

prepared inaccurate surveys that awarded additional
choice lands to their friends and benefactors. As a
result, disputes arose between speculators and settlers
over conflicting surveys, the sales of the same tract
to different individuals, and the purchaser's responsibility
to determine, in advance, if the lands he wanted were
unoccupied. All disputes came before the Board of
Property, whose members were the President and
Vice-President of the Supreme Executive Council of
Pennsylvania, the Secretary of the Land Office, the
Surveyor-General, and the Receiver-General. Claimants
could appeal the Board's decisions to the state
courts.[4]

In addition, state officials used their offices
for private speculation, and at this, John Nicholson was
the unquestioned champion. Like Morris and Duer, he was
one of the speculative giants of the 1790's. First, he
had served as an auditor for issuing depreciation certificates.
In 1781, he became auditor to settle the pay of the
Pennsylvania troops. All of the auditors' functions
fell to him in 1782, when he became Pennsylvania's
first Comptroller-General. In that capacity, Nicholson
freely used his public office for private gain. He was in

[4]The Board of Property was created by "An Act to
Vest Certain Powers in the President of this State, Together
with the Other Officers Therein Named, and for Other Purposes
Therein Mentioned" (Mitchell, Pennsylvania Statutes, X,
408-11 [Apr. 5, 1782]). See also Wilkinson, "Land Policy,"
pp. 84-85; Report, p. 27; Charles Huston, An Essay on the
History and Nature of Original Titles to Land in the Province
and State of Pennsylvania (Philadelphia, 1849), pp. 443-44.

an ideal position to take advantage of the state's land
laws, because his functions included the validation of
depreciation and donation claims. Since the surveyors
worked for Nicholson, he always knew the locations of the
most valuable lots. In 1787 he also became Escheator-
General and was thus responsible for the disposition of
confiscated estates. Nicholson first met Morris in
December, 1782, about one month after Nicholson had become
Comptroller-General. Although he and Morris opposed each
other politically in the 1780's, by the early 1790's, they
had been partners in several Pennsylvania land deals.[5]

Nicholson was also friendly with his fellow state officers
on the Board of Property. In particular, he cultivated
Daniel Brodhead, who was the Surveyor-General from 1789 to
1800. With Brodhead's assistance, Nicholson inserted
fictitious names on depreciation and donation lists or paid
others to buy certificates for him from soldiers who were
unaware of the value of the land. After the speculators
had acquired the certificates, the surveyors awarded them
only the best tracts. Soldiers could bring grievances to the
county courts, but the judges, whose salaries were
controlled by Nicholson, favored the large landowners. In

---

[5]"An Act for Methodizing the Department of Accounts of
this Commonwealth and for the More Effectual Settlement of the
Same" (Mitchell, Pennsylvania Statutes, X, 448-57 [Apr.
13, 1782]). See Robert D. Arbuckle, "John Nicholson, 1757-
1800: A Case Study of an Early American Land Speculator,
Financier and Entrepreneur" (unpublished Ph.D. dissertation,
The Pennsylvania State University, 1972), pp. 30-32, 44,
53-55. See also RM Diary, Dec. 5-6, 1782, RMP, DLC;
"John Nicholson's Account Current Book with Robert Morris,"
WRHS; Nicholson-Cottringer correspondence in JNP, PHMC.

1794 the state legislature impeached Nicholson for
speculating in new loan certificates, which could also be
exchanged for land. Although acquitted, Nicholson resigned.[6]

Unlike Nicholson, Morris' full-scale participation
in the Pennsylvania land boom did not begin until
after the passage of the Land Act of April 3, 1792.[7]
Supposedly designed to benefit and protect the
individual settler, speculators easily evaded its
provisions. Under this act, individuals paid 50
shillings for every 100 acres located in the tract acquired
from the Indians in 1768, £5 per 100 acres in the land
purchased from the Indians in 1784, and £7.10.0
for every 100 acres in the territory north and west
of the rivers Ohio and Allegheny and Conewango creek.
The statute offered two different methods of purchasing
land. Any person "who may have settled and improved,
or is desirous to settle and improve" the land applied
to the secretary of the land office and gave him a

---

[6]Arbuckle, "Nicholson," pp. 57-72; Wilkinson, "Land
Policy," pp. 179-231; Edmund Hogan, The Pennsylvania State
Trials: Containing the Impeachment, Trial, and Acquittal
of Francis Hopkinson and John Nicholson, Esquires (Philadelphia,
1794), I. See also "An Act for Furnishing the Quota of this
State Towards Paying the Annual Interest of the Debts of the
United States and for Funding and Paying the Interest of the
Public Debts of this State" (Mitchell, Pennsylvania Statutes,
XI, 454-86 [Mar. 16, 1785]).

[7]"An Act for the Sale of the Vacant Lands Within
this Commonwealth" (Mitchell, Pennsylvania Statutes,
XIV, 232-39. See also Ruddy, "Land Distribution," pp. 67-72.

description of the particular acres he desired. The
Secretary then granted a warrant to the purchaser for a
maximum of 400 acres, which required the surveyor-general
to complete a survey of the tract within 6 months.
Any person, however, who had already made a settlement
and improvements on land "lying north and west of (the)
rivers Ohio and Allegheny, and Conewango creek,"
could request a survey and "by a virtue of such settlement
and improvement" be entitled to not more than 400 acres.
The act further provided that

> no warrant or survey be issued ... for lands
> lying north and west of the rivers Ohio and
> Allegheny, and Conewango creek ... unless the
> grantee has, prior to the date of such warrant,
> made, or caused to be made, or shall, within the
> space of two years next ... make ... an actual
> settlement thereon, by clearing, fencing and
> cultivating at least two acres for every
> hundred acres ... erecting thereon a messuage
> for the habitation of man, and residing or
> causing a family to reside thereon, for the
> space of five years ... and that in default
> of such actual settlement and residence ... it
> shall and may be lawful to and for this
> commonwealth to issue new warrants to other
> settlers for the said lands....

The only exception to this provision was if the
settler "shall, by force of arms of the enemies
of the United States, be prevented from making such
actual settlement, or be driven therefrom...."
From 1792 to 1794, the Commonwealth issued 5,000
warrants for a total of 5,000,000 acres.[8]

In spite of this act, speculators acquired
large tracts of land. To evade the 400 acre limit

---

[8]Ruddy, "Land Distribution," p. 71.

they took out warrants in other people's names or even in fictitious ones. The warrantee then assigned the tract to the speculator for 5 shillings by signing a deed poll, which entitled the holder to a patent for the land described as long as a survey was returned according to law. As a result of the hostilities between the United States and the northwest Indians, the speculators claimed exemption from the settlement and improvement requirements of the 1792 act. Until such improvements were effected, the land office refused to issue patents.[9]

Since Morris had acquired the bulk of his Pennsylvania holdings, most of which were never patented, by deed poll, an exact list of his lands is almost impossible to reconstruct. Extant lists are incomplete, and some of the entries, many of which are vague and state only the number of acres and the counties in which they were located, may be duplicates of tracts described more specifically in surviving deed polls. Still, records do exist, and the known minimum of Morris' holdings is impressive. These included at least 100,000 acres in Luzerne County, 100,000 in Northumberland, 80,000 in Northampton, 45,000 in Westmoreland, 11,000 in Bedford,

---

[9]RM to Hamilton, Mar. 14, 1796, RMLB, DLC. According to Henry C. Black, a deed poll "was originally so called because the edge of the paper or parchment was polled or cut in a straight line, wherein it was distinguished from a deed indented or indenture" (Black's Law Dictionary [4th ed., St. Paul, 1951], p. 503).

4,000 in Dauphin, 2,000 in Huntington, and 1,500 in Fayette. According to a pamphlet entitled Robert Morris' Property, the Financier owned 660,000 acres in Washington, Allegheny, Northumberland, Luzerne, Bedford, Huntington, Cumberland, Wayne, Northampton, Mifflin, and Bucks Counties.[10]

In addition to these holdings, Morris also concluded joint purchases of Pennsylvania lands with Nicholson. From 1792 to 1794 they acquired 1,721,327 acres at a cost of $487,375.45. Then, in 1795, in an effort to ease his financial situation, Morris sold his interest in these lands to Nicholson at cost.[11]

Morris also owned other estates throughout Pennsylvania for his personal use. His first such purchase had been a practical one. In 1777, he acquired a house and several lots in Manheim,

---

[10]Robert Morris' Property, in Morris, Account of Property, pp. 1-18, 19-45; "Deed Poll List," RMP, HSP; Robert Morris Deeds, HSP; Mifflin, Northumberland, Luzerne, and Westmoreland Counties, Deeds, JNP, PHMC.

[11]Articles of Agreement, Jan. 18, 1793, RM, Nicholson, and William Stedman, Articles of Agreement, June 10, 1794, James Moore, Nicholson, and RM, Covenant and Articles of Agreement, Feb. 24, 1794, Abraham Witmer, Nicholson, and RM, Articles of Agreement, Mar. 31, 1794, John Barrows, Jr., Nicholson, and RM, Articles of Agreement, Aug. 15, 1793, John Battin, Nicholson, and RM, Articles of Agreement, Mar. 31, 1794, Ephraim Blaine, Nicholson, and RM, Articles of Agreement, Feb. 11, 1794, Watterman Baldwin, Nicholson, Andrew Norney, and RM, JNP, PHMC. See also Nicholson's Account with RM, Jan. 30, 1796, RMP, HSP; RM to Nicholson, Feb. 10, 1796, RMLB, DLC; "John Nicholson's Account Current Book with Robert Morris," WRHS.

Lancaster County, from William Bausman. The Morris'
lived in this house, which had been built by the
glass manufacturer, Henry William Stiegel, during
the British occupation of Philadelphia from 1777 to
1778. In July, 1781, he sold this estate to James
Jenkins for $1200, which represented a loss of $770 to
the Financier. During the same period, he also leased
2 lots in Manheim from Francis Hopkinson of Bordentown,
New Jersey for £5 per year. Unlike his other purchases,
Morris used this land to fill an immediate need and
disposed of the lots as soon as practicable.[12]

The reverse is true of Morris' acres in
Bucks County. After Congress rejected this estate,
known as Morrisville or the "Delaware Works," for the
nation's capital, Morris mortgaged parts of it to
secure his debts. In one case, he mortgaged the
Works to the Bank of North America to cover a debt
of £37,500, Pennsylvania currency. In September,
1794, William Linton, as attorney for the Bank,
acknowledged full satisfaction for the money due.[13]

---

[12]George L. Heiges, "Robert Morris in Manheim,"
Papers Read before the Lancaster County Historical
Society, XXXIV (June, 1930), 121-33; Stan V. Henkels, ed.,
The Confidential Correspondence of Robert Morris the
Great Financier of the Revolution, being Letters from the
Leading Statesmen, Military and Naval Heroes and Patriots
of that Time (Philadelphia, 1917), pp. 28, 29.

[13]Two Indentures, Dec. 9, 1791, RM and the President,
Directors, and Company of the Bank of North America, BCRD.
For other mortgages on this estate, see Indenture, Nov. 15,
1792, RM and P. Colvin, Indenture, Nov. 28, 1791, RM and
John Ashley, BCRD. The debate over the selection of a
capital city is discussed in chapter 4.

Morris' Bucks County property was one of the few
estates that the Financier carefully planned and
developed. He divided the estate into fourteen farms,
each with a house for a tenant. On a creek in
the Delaware River, he built a dam, iron works, and
several mills. Two ferries operated, and he could have
easily reinstituted a third. On the main island, near
the iron works, Morris constructed houses for a
manager, millers, bakers, smithies, carpenters,
coopers, saw manufacturers, and candle makers.
Robert Morris, Jr., who was his father's agent at
Morrisville, lived on a lot that included a garden,
an ice house, stables, and carriage houses. On the
property, Morris founded a quarry and two shad fisheries.
In describing the value and potential of this land,
Morris wrote:

> The town of Morrisville is admirable
> well calculated for a manufacturing place,
> situated between Philadelphia and New York
> the great road passing through it, the
> intercourse with those great markets may be
> daily had, and the transportation of articles
> by navigable water can at all times be
> commanded, so that a little encouragement
> to mechanics and manufacturers would enliven
> and give value to this town. The site is a
> delightful one on the banks of the Delaware,
> twenty nine miles distant from Philadelphia,
> one mile from Trenton, and one from Lamberton
> [Lambertville]. The surrounding country thickly
> inhabitated, health and abounding in all the articles

necessary for the supply of a town.
In short, this estate is so well known
that it is needless to add that its value
is and must be continued progressive.[14]

For his private residences, Morris owned land
in Philadelphia and the Northern Liberties, an area
just outside of the city. In the temporary capital, the
Morris' lived in a house on Market Street, between Fifth
and Sixth Streets, which the Financier purchased on August
25, 1785 for £3,750 sterling from Mary and Sarah
Masters and Richard Penn and his wife. On this land,
Morris built one of the finest homes in Philadelphia,
complete with stables and gardens. After Congress
selected Philadelphia as the temporary seat of
government, Morris turned the house over to President
Washington, For this, the Corporation of Philadelphia,
in 1796, paid Morris £3,000, Pennsylvania currency.

-----

[14] A Schedule of Property Within the State of
Pennsylvania Conveyed by Robert Morris to the Honorable
James Biddle, Esq., and Mr. William Bell in Trust for
the Use and Account of the Pennsylvania Property Company,"
Mar. 18, 1797, RMP, HSP, RMP, DLC, BCHS. See also "Robert
Morris Envisioned Bucks County Development: Document in
State Land Office gives Early Statesman's Views," Bulletin
of the Department of Internal Affairs of the Commonwealth
of Pennsylvania, XX (July, 1952), 7-9; W. W. H. Davis,
The History of Bucks County, Pennsylvania, from the
Discovery of the Delaware to the Present Time (Doylestown,
1876), pp. 657-61; Robert S. Dana, "Morrisville and Its
Vicinity," Collections of the Bucks County Historical
Society, III (1909), 244-57; Richard H. S. Osborne,
"Historic Summerseat," Collections of the Bucks County
Historical Society, III (1909), 237-38; William C. Ryan,
"Founding of Morrisville," Collections of the Bucks County
Historical Society, III (1909), 363-66; D. K. Turner,
"Robert Morris, the Financier of the Revolution,"
Collections of the Bucks County Historical Society,
II (1909), 170-71.

Although Washington occupied the home from November,
1790 until the spring of 1797, Morris agreed in 1795
to sell the lot to Andrew Kennedy for $37,500, after
the expiration of Washington's term. The Financier's
family moved into an adjoining lot on the southeast
corner of Sixth and Market Streets, which Morris
had purchases in 1787. This house, which was the
sequestered home of loyalist Joseph Galloway, had been
the official residence of the Supreme Executive Council
of Philadelphia.[15]

Galloway's house, however, was too simple for
Morris' taste. In 1790 he purchased another lot
between Chestnut and Walnut Streets and Seventh and
Eighth Streets from John Dickinson. As payment,
Dickinson accepted £7,000 and Morris' estate at
Brandywine Hundred.[16] In 1795 shortly before Morris'
affairs plunged downward, he engaged Pierre Charles

---

[15]"Address of Nathaniel Burt, February 12, 1875, on
the Washington Mansion in Philadelphia," Miscellaneous
Papers of the Pennsylvania Historical Society, I (1875),
12, 31-33; Armine N. Hart, "Robert Morris," in Annals
of Philadelphia, and Pennsylvania, ed., John F. Watson,
III (1887), 260-61; List of RM"s Property in Philadelphia
and the Northern Liberties, n.d., RMP, NYPL; "Journal B,"
f. 355, RMP, HSP.

[16]Articles of Agreement, Oct. 9, 1790, RM and
Dickinson, RM to Dickinson, Oct. 10, 1790, Logan Papers,
HSP; "Memorandum of Agreement between Robert Morris and
John Dickinson, for the lot on Chestnut Street, in
Manuscript Department, Historical Society of Pennsylvania,"
Pennsylvania Magazine of History and Biography, XXXIV
(Apr., 1910), 237-38; "Journal B," f. 157, RMP, HSP.

L'Enfant to plan and build a magnificent home on this site.
For this mansion Morris imported glassware and furniture
from all over Europe. L'Enfant, who was given a free hand
in the undertaking, immediately expanded on Morris' original
proposal. Although L'Enfant assured Morris that his family
could move into the house by the autumn of 1795, L'Enfant
never completed the mansion and the Morris' never lived in
it. In anticipation of L'Enfant's promise, Morris sold
his Market Street property and home in February, 1795, to
Robert Kidd and William Bell for $25,533. As temporary
quarters, he rented a home across the street from L'Enfant's
work on Chestnut Street for £2,000 yearly. This grand,
but never finished structure, was dubbed "Morris' Folly."
In 1797 the Financier complained to Gustavus Scott: "I have
expended ten times the sum I was told my house was to cost
& the Roof is not compleat, the south Front not carried up
nor a single floor laid or Wall plaistered and now I am out
of money and Credit, so that all stands still, and unless
Times change the Work cannot be resumed by me. Thus you
may judge how sufficiently I am Chastized for my folly."[17]

In the Northern Liberties, Morris purchased two
estates, known as "Springetsbury" and "The Hills." The
former he purchased from John Penn, Jr., on October
15, 1787 for £5,620. As late as August, 1795, Morris

---

[17]"Journal C," f. 135, RMP, HSP; RM to L'Enfant,
Sept. 24, 25, 1795, Aug. 15, 17, 1796, to Scott, May
10, 1797, RMLB, DLC; Morris, Account of Property, p. 11;
Turner, "Morris," p. 170.

had not paid for these 142 acres.[18]

"The Hills" was Morris' favorite retreat. He
purchased the land from Tench Francis in July, 1770.
Located three miles from Philadelphia on the eastern
bank of the Schuylkill River, Morris added 220 acres
to his original purchase of only 80. During the
Revolution, the British ruined the estate by using the
buildings as barracks. After the War, Morris rebuilt
the property to include

> a large and elegant green House ... with an excellent
> Vault ... and a covered Room for preserving tools
> & ca. in Winter, the whole being a strong Stone
> building with the necessary Glasses, casements,
> Fruit Trees, Plants shrubbs & ca. in good order;
> a well of excellent water.... The whole enclosed
> with fruit Trees of the best kinds.... Adjoining
> to this Garden is a farm House and Kitchen, a
> spring House and a Granary or store room over
> it, a coach House Barn and stables, large cow House
> with arched Doorways, and Hay lofts over the whole;
> a brew House and Pig Pen....

He hoped to divide the land on either side of a canal
that ran through the estate into tracts of from 4 to 10
acres for Philadelphians who desired summer residences.
Morris retired to "The Hills" in 1797 in an effort
to escape from the sheriff and his creditors.[19]

Other Pennsylvania properties belonging to the
Financier included the Ton Alley, Minor Street, Front

---

[18]"John Penn, Junr. Esqr ... in Account with Robert
Morris," n.d., RMP, CHHL; "Journal B," f. 22, RMP, HSP.

[19]Benjamin Harrison to RM, Aug. 18, 1778, in Henkels,
Confidential Correspondence, p. 19; "Schedule of Property
... of the Pennsylvania Property Company," Mar. 18, 1797,
RMP, HSP, RMP, DLC, BCHS; Hart, "Robert Morris," p. 261.

Street, and Water Street lots in Philadelphia, 160 acres,
known as "Trout Spring" in Montgomery County, and a 10,000
acre estate in Chester County, held jointly by Morris and
Thomas Willing.[20]

Still, the bulk of Morris' Pennsylvania land was in
undeveloped back lands. To encourage sales, and thereby
raise money, Morris and Nicholson formed a total of six
land companies during the 1790's. Although the North American Land Company was the most famous, they had formed two
earlier companies in Pennsylvania.

The first, in which Morris was only minimally involved,
was the Pennsylvania Population Company. Formed on May 4,
1792, its alleged purpose was to "establish a barrier to
the frontiers and enable the settlement of other lands to
be made in safety," and to "promote and expedite the population of the same." The Company's capital consisted of
2,500 shares of stock, worth 200 acres each, or $200. The
managers, all of whom were familiar faces in land speculation, were Théophile Cazenove, the Holland Land Company's
agent, General William Irvine, the commander at Fort Pitt,
Daniel Leet and John Hoge, two deputy surveyors, George Mead,
a merchant, and General Walter Stewart, the inspector of
the revenue and surveyor of the port of Philadelphia.[21]

---

[20]Morris, Account of Property, pp. 11, 15, 22; "Schedule
of Property ... of the Pennsylvania Property Company," Mar. 18,
1797, RMP, HSP, RMP, DLC, BCHS; "Ledger C," f. 102, "Journal C,"
f. 162, RMP, HSP.

[21]The plan of association of the Pennsylvania Population
Company is in the Pennsylvania Population Company Minute
Books, I, 1-8, CCHS.

The Company's lands were in northwestern Pennsylvania, north of the Ohio River and west of the Allegheny River and Conewango Creek. Immediately after the passage of the 1792 land act, Nicholson, by deed poll, took out 640 warrants in the region.[22] At the first Company meeting on May 11, 1430 shares had been subscribed, and by December 22, all 2500 shares had been purchased.[23] The President and managers held title to all the lands in trust for the Company, and they were responsible for dividing the net proceeds from land sales among the stockholders in proportion to the number of shares each owned. After fifteen years, the shareholders would vote to continue or liquidate the Company. If liquidated, the shareholders would divide proportionately the remaining lands and funds. To defray Company expenses, the President and managers could levy a maximum of $10.00 assessment on each share. Levies up to $40.00 required the support of a majority of the stockholders, and a levy of more than $40.00 required their unanimous approval. Nicholson, the first President, was alsotthe largest stockholder,

---

[22]Hale, "Pennsylvania Population Company,' pp. 27-28; Joseph H. Bausman, History of Beaver County, Pennsylvania and Its Centennial Celebration (New York, 1904), I, 287.

[23]Minute Books, I, 14, CCHS. A list of subscribers is in the Minute Books, I, 8-11, CCHS and is printed in Hale, "Pennsylvania Population Company," p. 34.

[24]Minute Books, I, 1-8, CCHS.

with 400 shares. He subscribed 100 shares for Morris, who
did not become a manager until January 25, 1793.

In order to promote sales, the managers appointed a
committee to prepare a plan of settlement. The first 50
families would receive 150 free acres and the next 100
would receive 100 acres. The Company agreed to sell a total
of 30,000 acres, but no more than 300 acres to any one
settler, for $1.00 per acre payable in three installments,
the first without interest, at 2, 3, and 4 years. All of
these settlements were at Beaver Creek, French Creek, and in
the Erie Triangle. Unless prevented by Indian hostilities,
settlers had to clear 10 acres and build a house on their
lots within two years of settlement in order to fulfill the
requirements of the 1792 land act and receive their deeds.[26]

Efforts to attract settlers failed. Before 1794,
the Company claimed that Indian raids had prevented
any settlement of their lands. Undeterred by the alleged
danger, squatters, however, had settled on Company lands,
justifying their actions by claiming that the speculators
had not fulfilled the two year settlement requirement.
After Wayne eliminated the Indian threat by defeating
the natives at Fallen Timbers in 1794, more and more

[25]Minute Books, I, 8-11, CCHS. Arbuckle claims that
Nicholson subscribed 535 shares, including 347 to be paid
for in money and 188 in Donation lands ("Nicholson,"
p. 231). See also Walter J. McClintock, "Title Difficulties
of the Holland Land Company in Northwestern Pennsylvania,"
The Western Pennsylvania Historical Magazine, XXI (June,
1938), 123-24.

[26]Minute Books, I, 46-48, CCHS.

settlers moved on to Company lands. As a result of the pressure these squatters brought to bear against the state legislature in 1794, two laws were passed to prohibit the land office from receiving any additional applications for unimproved land.[27] Under the provisions of the new legislation, the Company had to pay immediately for all its warrants or forfeit them.

Thus, the Company had netted little money. Early in 1795 Morris accepted Nicholson's offer to purchase his shares for $20,000, which was the cost price. As Nicholson had no ready money, Morris extended his associate credit. Here, Morris' connection with the Company ended.[28]

In 1800 the Republicans gained control of the state government. Because their land policy favored the individual owner, the Pennsylvania Population Company and the Holland Land Company faced numerous suits. As aliens, the Holland Company's principals could appeal decisions to the Federal Courts, which eventually ruled

---

[27]"An Act to prevent the receiving any more applications, or issuing any more warrants, except in certain cases, for land within this commonwealth" (Pennsylvania Laws, 1794 Sess., Ch. CCXLVI [April 22, 1794], Microfilm Collection of Early State Records, DLC) and "A Supplement to the Act, entitled "An Act to prevent the receiving any more applications or issuing any more warrants, except in certain cases, for land within this commonwealth" (Pennsylvania Laws, 1794, Sess., Ch. CCLXIV [Sept. 22, 1794], Microfilm Collection of Early State Records, DLC).

[28]RM to Nicholson, Jan. 17, 1795, RMLB, DLC; "Journal B," f. 139, 163, 298, "Journal C," f. 109, 126, 137, RMP, HSP.

in their favor. In 1812, the stockholders in the
Population Company, which was experiencing difficulties
with unfriendly state courts, decided to liquidate.
For this purpose, the managers borrowed $500 to conduct
an auction. Money from the sale totalled $70,739, of which
$44,715.94 went to pay outstanding debts. The shareholders
then divided the remainder.[29]

As with his other holdings, Morris tried to
peddle his Pennsylvania lands throughout Europe.
In 1790, before Franklin sailed as Morris' agent for
the sale of the Genesee land, the Financier also deeded
to Franklin six tracts in Northampton County, totalling
10,000 acres, for sale abroad. Morris explained that this
rich timber land had not yet been settled because of
difficulties with the Indians and conflicing claims to
part of the land by inhabitants of Connecticut. Although
the lands now sold for 15 shillings per acre, Morris boasted
that in two or three years, the price per acre would
average £3 to £5. The Financier admitted that he was selling
the tracts to help settle his debts, and believed that those
in Northampton County were likely to sell at a good price
for ready money. He asked at least half a guinea per acre.
Once again, sanguine expectations were not borne out by
events. At least four of the tracts were in the Financiers'

[29]Minute Books, II, 293-94, CCHS; Hale, "Pennsylvania
Population Company," pp. 207, 223-24, 251; McClintock,
"Holland Land Company," pp. 12-16.

possession at the time of his bankruptcy.[30] Morris
and Nicholson did manage to sell 3465 acres in 1795,
but it brought only 9 pence per acre.[31]

The two speculators did enjoy a degree of success,
however, in selling Pennsylvania lands to Europeans.
Because Pennsylvania permitted aliens to own land,
the state attracted French and English exiles.[32] The
most famous settlement, known as "Asylum," represented
the efforts of French Revolutionary émigrés to establish
a colony on the Susquehanna River.

The French Revolution produced two waves of emigrants
to England, Germany, and the United States. Those
who came to America formed their pictures of the New
World from pamphlets circulated in Europe by American land

---

[30]RM to Franklin, Sept. 30, 1790, RMP, NC; Morris,
Account of Property, pp. 7-8.

[31]"Lands in Northampton and Luzerne Counties Dr.
to Thomas Wright," n.d. and "Patents for Robert Morris
and John Nicholson for Eight Tracts in Northampton
County," n.d., RMP, HSP.

[32]See "An Act to enable Aliens to purchase and hold
real Estates within this Commonwealth (Pennsylvania Laws,
1789 Sess., Ch. VI [Feb. 11, 1789]), "An Act to revive
and continue in force, for a limited time, an Act,
entituled 'An Act to enable aliens to purchase and hold
real estates within this commonwealth (Pennsylvania
Laws, 1791-1792 Sess., Ch. LXXXVII [Mar. 8, 1792]), and
"An Act to extend an act, entituled 'An Act to enable
aliens to purchase and hold real estates within this
commonwealth" (Pennsylvania Laws, 1795 Sess., Ch. CCLXXV,
[Feb. 12, 1795]).

promoters.[33] The first group, composed of aristocrats who supported the old régime, fled France in 1789 to escape the guillotine. The second group, composed of members of the nobility and bourgeoisie, left France only after the excesses of the September massacres in 1792.[34]

Morris and Nicholson seized the opportunity to sell a large tract to the prospective settlers in this second group. Louis Marie, Vicomte de Noailles, and Omer Antoine Talon negotiated for the French. Noailles, who was Lafayette's brother-in-law, had fought in the American Revolution. In 1789 he became a member of the Estates-General. Talon had been the criminal prosecutor of Paris in 1789. In 1792 he angered the Jacobins as royal judge at the Châtelet and as a member of King Louis'

---

[33]Francis S. Childs, *French Refugee Life in the United States, 1790-1800: An American Chapter of the French Revolution* (Baltimore, 1940), pp. 5-7.

[34]Childs, *French Refugee Life*, pp. 7-11; J. G. Rosengarten, *French Colonists and Exiles in the United States* (Philadelphia, 1907), pp. 106-07.

secret service.[35] In 1793 these two Frenchmen selected
Charles-Felix Bué Boulogne, a French attorney associated
with Duer's Scioto Company, and John Keating, an
interpreter, as their American agents. At first,
Nicholson agreed to sell only 60,000 acres at $1.00 per
acre, with one-half down and the remainder in two
installments. Boulogne insisted on additional land, and
Nicholson then offered him from 160,000 to 300,000 acres
at the same price in the area between the Delaware River
and the eastern branch of the Susquehanna.[36] Before he
accepted these terms, Boulogne toured this land in
Northumberland County with Adam Hoops. On his return, he
purchased 200,000 acres in the Bradford-Wyoming section
of Pennsylvania. The colony would be located on the
Susquehanna, near the present town of Towanda.[37]

Unfortunately for Morris and Nicholson, the
conflicting claims of settlers from Connecticut and
Pennsylvania clouded their title to the lands that
Boulogne chose. The Susquehanna Company, formed in 1753,
sold land in the Wyoming Valley to Connecticut settlers

[35]Childs, French Refugee Life, pp. 31, 33; David J.
Jeremy, ed., Henry Wansey and His American Journal: 1794
(Philadelphia, 1970), p. 106, note 82.

[36]Arbuckle, "Nicholson," p. 270.

[37]Childs, French Refugee Life, p. 70; David Craft, "The
French at Asylum," Proceedings and Collections of the
Wyoming Historical and Geological Society, V (1900),
81; Louise W. Murray, The Story of Some French Refugees
and their "Azilum," 1793-1800 (Athens, 1903), pp. 19-20.

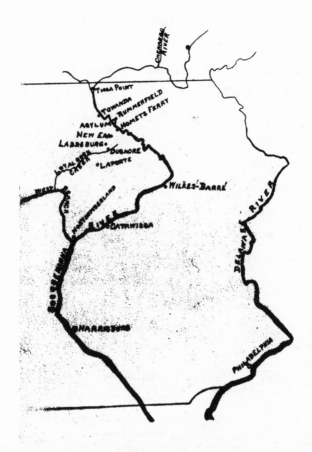

Fig. 7. - Asylum
Reprinted from Louise W. Murray, <u>The Story of Some
French Refugees and Their "Azilum," 1793-1800</u> (Athens,
1903), p. 21.

under the authority of Connecticut's colonial charter.
Pennsylvania, however, had received title to the land
by the 1782 Decree of Trenton. In 1793 settlers from
both states engaged in legal battles over their titles.
Before Noailles and Talon accepted Nicholson and Morris'
proposal, they insisted on securing title to the land
fromm the claimants of both states. Matthias Hollenback,
a proprietor of stóres and trading posts along the
Susquehanna, agreed to negotiate with the Connecticut
claimants, while Hoops, as Morris' agent, settled with
the Pennsylvanians. Hoops was successful, but Morris
thought that Hollenback was paying too much for the
Connecticut claims. Morris suggested that if the
claimants demanded too much money, Hollenback should
threaten them with legal action. Instead, Hollenback
paid from $133 to $800 for these lots out of his own
funds, and Morris and Nicholson never fully reimbursed
him.[38]

Early in 1794, the French were unable to meet
their payments to the two speculators for the land because

_____

[38]L. W. Murray, Azilum, pp. 24-26; Craft, "The
French at Asylum," pp. 83-85; Elsie Murray, "French
Experiments in Pioneering in Northern Pennsylvania,"
Pennsylvania Magazine of History and Biography, LXVIII
(Apr., 1944), 179-80; Elsie Murray, "Early Land
Companies and Titles of Northumberland County,
Proceedings of the Northumberland County Historical
Society, XX (1954), 25; T. Wood Clarke, Emigres in the
Wilderness (New York, 1941), p. 60.

they had not received enough money from prospective
émigrés. Still in France, these future settlers
faced increasing guillotinings and new property
laws that drained their reserves.[39]

In order to save the settlement, and hopefully,
raise the value of Pennsylvania lands, Morris and
Nicholson formed the Asylum Company on April 22, 1794.
The basis for the Company's capital of $2,500,000 was
1,000,000 acres, which was divided into 200 acre
shares. A subscriber could purchase a share for $500.
The Board of Managers could purchase additional lands
for the Company and employ any necessary surveyors
and land agents. The Board also had the authority to
sell land to settlers. During the first year,
settlers would pay the Company a minimum of $2.00 per
acre, with five years credit. Interest payments began
after the third year of settlement at the rate of six
per cent per annum. At first, the Board would apply
all funds to pay existing debts or purchase additional
lands. Then, the Company would pay shareholders yearly
dividends. Morris, as the first President of the Board,
held the title to all lands in trust for the Company.
After fifteen years, the Board would sell the Company's
assets for cash at a public auction, and divide the

---

[39]E. Murray, "French Experiments," p. 181.

balance proportionately among the shareholders.[40]   In February, 1795, Morris and Nicholson guaranteed a yearly dividend of 6 per cent per share, even if the Company had to borrow to pay it. After 3 years, the Board would buy back shares at $500 each from any shareholder who wished to sell. In April, 1795, after Morris was no longer associated with the Company, revised articles annulled the February resolutions. Instead, Nicholson promised a dividend of $30.00 per share, and pledged one-third of the total share as security.[41] According to Shaw Livermore, this Company was, in effect, an unchartered joint stock company, intended "to be [a] business entit[y], functioning under centralized managerial control for the benefit of scattered, non-partner stockholders whose control was to be general and to whom impersonal reports were to be made."[42]

In the spring of 1795, Francois Alexandre Frédéric, Duc de La Rochefoucauld-Liancourt, one of the most astute observers among the travellers of the period, visited the Asylum colony. La Rochefoucauld had supported the French constitution of 1791 and favored the preservation of the royal

---

[40]Plan of Association of the Asylum Company. As Established April 22d. 1794, And Improved April 25. 1795 (Philadelphia, 1795), pp. 3-11. See also Arbuckle, "Nicholson," p. 277; Wilkinson, "Land Policy," p. 113.

[41]Plan of ... the Asylum Company, pp. 11-24.

[42]Early American Land Companies, pp. 171-74.

perogative. After the insurrection in June, 1792,
he supported the King and succeeded in emigrating
first to England and then to the United States.[43]
When he reached Asylum, the settlement consisted
of "Thirty houses ... some inns and two shops...."
To promote sales and agricultural development, the
Company allotted 25,000 acres, divided into town shares
of 400 acres each, for sale. Purchasers of these
shares could settle on the land or entrust its
improvement to a farmer. The subscriber earned
$9.00 for every acre he owned if ten acres were cleared,
with five acres enclosed by a fence. On the whole,
La Rochefoucauld found that the location of the colony
"fits it in a peculiar manner for an emporium of the
inland trade. French activity, supported with money,
will certainly accelerate its growth; and this will
doubtless in time convince the world, that the
enterprise and assiduity of Frenchmen are equally
conspicuous in prosperous and adverse circumstances."[44]

---

[43]Childs, French Refugee Life, pp. 30-31.

[44]La Rochefoucauld-Liancourt, Travels through
the United States of North America, the Country of
the Iroquois, and Upper Canada, in the Years
1795, 1796, and 1797; With an Authentic Account
of Lower Canada, trans. by H. Neuman (London, 1799),
I, 86-95.

Shortly after Nicholson purchased Morris'
interest in the Pennsylvania Population Company, he
offered to buy his partners' Asylum shares. Morris,
in need of cash or a promise of cash on which he
could secure credit, agreed to sell his shares in
the Company to Nicholson for $135,377.61.[45] Since
Nicholson had already purchased Talon and Noailles'
shares, he was the leading stockholder in 1796.[46]

For Morris, the Asylum Company became another
entry in the loss column as he saw his financial
world beginning to crack in 1795. Another French

---

[45]"John Nicholson's Account Current Book with
Robert Morris," n.d., WRHS. Arbuckle incorrectly
states that Morris sold Nicholson his shares in the
Company for $487,375.45, but because Morris owed
Nicholson some money, the Financier netted only
$464,479.84 ("Nicholson," p. 282). On February 10,
1796, Morris sent Nicholson his account current "up
to the 30 Jany 1796 together with several subordinate
accounts..." (RMLB, DLC). The $487,375.45 figure refers,
in fact, to a "subordinate account" dealing with Nicholson's
purchase of Morris' share of their joint Pennsylvania
landholdings. The figure $464,799.84 refers to Nicholson's
total indebtedness to Morris as of Jan. 30, 1796. By
combining the Asylum entries in the general account
of Jan. 30, 1796 with the later entries in the "subordinate
account" relating to Asylum, the correct figure becomes
$135,377.61. Copies of all of the accounts mentioned
in Morris' letter of Feb. 10 to Nicholson are in "John
Nicholson's Account Current Book with Robert Morris,"
n.d., WRHS. See also RM to Nicholson, Apr. 23, 1795, RMLB,
DLC; Nicholson to RM, Apr. 28, 1795, JNLB, HSP.

[46]Arbuckle, "Nicholson," p. 283.

visitor, Charles Maurice Talleyrand-Périgord, who
travelled through the United States in 1794, presented
the most concise explanation for the colony's failure.
He pessimistically predicted that émigrés, who came to
the United States for political reasons, would return to
France with the first general amnesty. The planners
developed the colony on too large a scale. Not enough
colonists existed to occupy all that land. In addition,
English domination of the seas inhibited French oceanic
voyages, and French domestic policy reduced the aristicrats'
property holdings. The settlement violated the basic
concept of supply and demand.[47]

Even more idealistic and even less successful
than the Asylum colony was Joseph Priestley's efforts
to establish a colony for British exiles in Northumberland
County. As a nonconformist, Priestley opposed the
Established Church and supported the repeal of the
Test and Corporation Acts. In 1791 Birmingham

---

[47]Talleyrand's comments are discussed in
E. Murray, "French Experiments," p. 183; Childs,
Refugee Life, p. 186; Lucille L. Zoller, "The French
Settlement at Asylum, Pennsylvania" (unpublished M.A.
thesis, University of Pittsburgh, 1936), p. 43. See
also David Craft, "A Day at Asylum" Proceedings of the
Wyoming Historical and Geological Society, VIII (1904),
46-86; Elsie Murray, French Exiles of 1793 in Northern
Pennsylvania (New York, 1935); Louise W. Murray,
A History of Old Tioga Point and Early Athens Pennsylvania
(Athens, 1908).

rioters, who destroyed Priestley's house, indicated the
growing strength of the opposition to him and his views.
The next year Priestley developed his first ideas for a
colony in the United States founded as a pantisocracy,
which was a utopian community in which everyone was to
exercise equal authority. As pressure mounted against
Priestley in 1793, he sent his son, Joseph, and his
son-in-law, Thomas Cooper, to the United States to
investigate the possibility of establishing a refuge
in Pennsylvania. The two agents journeyed up the
Schuylkill to Sunbury and then up the Susquehanna
to Loyalsock Creek. After this tour, Priestley, Jr.,
along with John Vaughan and Abel Humphries, signed
articles of agreement with Morris and Nicholson early
in 1794. They established a land company, capitalized
at $300,000, which was divided into 100 shares. Morris
and Nicholson accepted 34. The two speculators also
provided 300,000 acres on Loyalsock, Muncy, and
Fishing Creeks in Northumberland County for the
British colony. Land in the colony would sell
for $1.00 per acre, and Priestley guaranteed investors a
6 per cent return per annum. Following the
conclusion of this sale to Priestley, Cooper returned
to England, where in 1794 he published a prospectus
for the Company. He described the colony as "an asylum
from civil persecution and religious intolerance," and "a
rallying-point for the English...." He and Priestley favored

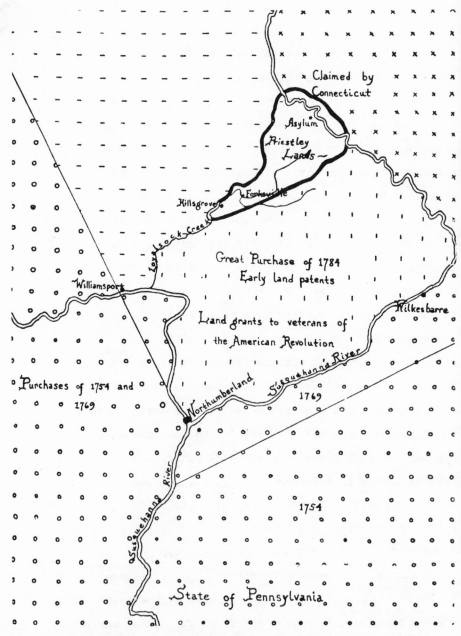

Fig. 8. - Priestley's Lands
Reprinted from Mary C. Park, "Joseph Priestley
and the Problem of Pantisocracy," <u>Proceedings</u>
<u>of the Delaware County Institute of Science</u>,
XI (1947), 13.

Pennsylvania because of its prosperity, temperate climate, abolition of slavery, peace with the Indians, abundance of additional land of good quality, and laws permitting alien ownership of land.[48]

The settlement failed to materialize. Nicholson informed Bird, Savage, and Bird, in London, that although the purchase "had been forfeited on the part of the subscribers yet we held up the land a considerable time in the view that perhaps the Company might come forward with proposals.... The prospects of this accomodation has vanished & our views are no longer turned thereto."[49] Morris and Nicholson later incorporated the land into the North American Land Company.

Priestley arrived in the United States in the summer of 1794 and settled in Northumberland County near the site of the proposed colony. He rationalized the failure of the settlement by explaining that "the generality of Englishmen come to this country with such erroneous ideas, and, unless previously accustomed to a life of labours, are so ill qualified to commence cultivation in a wilderness, that the projectors would

---

[48]Some Information Respecting America (Dublin, 1794).

[49]Apr. 2, 1795, JNLB, HSP.

most probably have been subject to a still more unfound

abuse than they have been...."[50]

Not all foreigners purchased land for colonization.
Some acquired tracts for speculation. Such an investor
was Talleyrand, who arrived in Philadelphia in 1794.
Through Cazenove, Talleyrand met the nation's political
and business leaders, including Morris. Initially
the Frenchman planned to speculate in stocks, but
probably under Cazenove's influence, he increasingly
praised the advantages of land investments.

In fact, at first, Talleyrand wrote negatively
of the prospects of America's land speculators, and
with particular reference to the Financier:

> Although the extravagances of European governments
> are well calculated to persuade reasonable men
> to leave them and take refuge here, I doubt that
> these emigrations are as favorable to the
> speculators as they appear to believe. The men
> arriving from Europe will seek for the most
> part to establish themselves in the sections
> that already are cleared and settled. It seems
> to me, therefore, that the speculators will not
> be able to sell their lands as quickly as they
> have imagined. It is true that these lands
> increase in value by the sole effect of the
> passage of time, but to benefit by this
> increase it would be necessary to be in a
> position to postpone resale for several years
> and most of them are bound by engagements

[50]This discussion of Priestley's settlement is
based on Nicholson to Bird, Savage, and Bird, Apr.
2, 1795, JNLB, HSP; John T. Rutt, ed., Life and
Correspondence of Joseph Priestley (2 vols; London, 1831-32)
II, 238-39; Mary C. Park, "Joseph Priestley and the Problem
of Pantisocracy," Proceedings of the Delaware County
Institute of Science, XI (1947), 1-29, 31-35, 52-57;
Dumas Malone, The Public Life of Thomas Cooper: 1783-1839
(Columbia, S.C., 1961), pp. 76-81; Jeremy, Wansey,
pp. 11, 28-29, 79 and n. 86.

which make it necessary to resell soon,
failing in which, they experience constant
demands for money and are obliged in order
to satisfy them, to have recourse to the expedients
which have soon exhausted their credit. Mr.
Morris, especially, is in this position and as
he is more enterprising than anyone he has
also experienced more difficulties.[51]

But as his speculations in bonds collapsed,
Talleyrand turned to land as a possible source of
profit. He investigated lands in Maine, New York,
and the Federal City before deciding to purchase land
in Pennsylvania from Robert Morris.[52]

In May, 1796, while negotiating with Morris,
Talleyrand prepared an essay on land speculation
in the United States. In contrast to his 1794
statement, Talleyrand now claimed that European investors
did receive "huge profits" from American land, but that
they do not publicize it in order to avoid arousing
"jealousy or competition." Land was " a merchandise
which has not reached its true value and which one can
buy today with the certain hope of reselling with profit."
Aware of the pitfalls that had trapped Morris, he warned
that "the man who speculates in uncultivated lands
should not expect to enjoy an income, therefore he

[51]Talleyrand to Charles Goring, of London, June
10, 1794, in Hans Huth and Wilma J. Pugh, eds. and trans.,
Talleyrand in America as a Financial Promoter, 1794-1796
(Washington, D.C., 1942), pp. 24-25.

[52]Edwin R. Baldridge, Jr., "Talleyrand in the United
States, 1794 to 1796" (unpublished Ph.D. dissertation,
Lehigh University, 1963), pp. 45-82; G. Lacour-Gayet,
Talleyrand, 1754-1838 (Paris, 1928), I, 188-96.

should apply to this use only that part of his capital
which he does not destine for his annual needs and on
which he had at least for a time, no other view than the
project of keeping and increasing it.[53]

On May 24, 1796, Talleyrand and Morris signed
articles of agreement, by which the Financier sold
the Frenchman 108,875 acres in Mifflin, Northumberland,
and Northampton Counties for $142,500.40. If Talleyrand
failed to complete his payments by August 9, 1797, the
sale became null and void. Until that date, Morris could
pledge these lands as security for a loan or debt.[54]

Morris immediately mortgaged these lands. The
Commissioners for settling accounts between the United
States and individuals determined that Morris still
owed the Federal government $93,312.75. This debt
stemmed from a contract between Morris, Willing, and the
Secret Committee of the Continental Congress for the purchase
of goods in France for Congress. John Ross, a Philadelphia
merchant, was Morris and Willing's French representative.
Although the Commissioners evidently tried to be fair,
Morris criticized their ignorance of "mercantile
method and principle," and complained that they had arrived

---

[53]"Observations on speculation in lands in the
United States of America," May, 1796, in Huth,
Talleyrand, pp. 137-75.

[54]Articles of Agreement, RMP, HSP, JNP, PHMC;
Two Indentures, May 24, 1796, RM to Talleyrand, in
Baldridge, "Talleyrand," pp. 135-50; Talleyrand to
RM, May 3, 1796, United States Naval Academy, Annapolis.

at their figure by "charging depreciation" which he
objected to. Morris promised to pay one-half of the
debt by August 9, 1797 and the remainder by Feburary
9, 1799. He proceeded to secure these payments by a
mortgage on the lands sold to Talleyrand.[55] Therefore,
if Talleyrand had met his payments, Morris would have
enjoyed a clear surplus of less than $50,000.

Talleyrand returned to Europe in 1796, and in
1797, reentered politics as the French foreign minister.
As tensions developed between France and the United
States, Morris realized that Talleyrand had no intention
of completing their agreement. On March 18, 1797,
Morris assigned the property to James Biddle and William
Bell in trust for his newly formed Pennsylvania Property
Company.[56] To settle his debt to the United States,
Morris assigned all of his claims on John Ross and
Willing to the Comptroller of the Treasury.[57]

Another European interested in American lands
was James Donatius Le Ray de Chaumont, who came to the

---

[55]Morris, Account of Property, p. 29; Indenture,
May 24, 1796, RM and John Davis, the Comptroller of the
United States Treasury, in Baldridge, "Talleyrand,"
pp. 131-35; Ver Steeg, Morris, pp. 18-20.

[56]Schedule of Property ... of the Pennsylvania
Property Company," Mar. 18, 1797, RMP, HSP, RMP, DLC,
BCHS.

[57]Morris, Account of Property, pp. 29-30.

United States in 1789 to collect debts due to his father
from the Federal Government. Le Ray speculated heavily
in New York State lands before he purchased any tracts
from Morris in Pennsylvania.58 In early 1793,
Morris purchased 86,121 acres between the Susquehanna
and Delaware Rivers in Luzerne County from Samuel
Wallis for £15,000, Pennsylvania currency.59 Later
that year, Robert Morris, Jr., sold approximately
80,830 acres of this land to Le Ray for £27,000. As
security for the title to the lands, for which the
elder Morris had not yet paid, the Financier gave
Le Ray a mortgage on his Springetsbury and Ton Alley
estates and a bond for £30,000. In August, 1795,
Morris conveyed to Le Ray patents to 127 of these
tracts. The remainder was in dispute between Nicholson
and Wallis, but Morris assisted Nicholson in buying
out his competitor.60

    Wherever possible, Morris and Nicholson used their
lands to extend their credit. In December, 1794, for
example, John Bonnet, Morris' agent in Hamburg, sold

58Sakolski, The Great American Land Bubble, pp. 87-94.

59"Journal B," f. 189, RMP, HSP.

60Indenture, Apr. 1, 1793, RM to Le Ray, Misc. MSS,
NYSL; Indenture, Aug. 19, 1795, RM and Nicholson to
Le Ray, Society Collection, HSP; "Journal B," f. 217,
RMP, HSP; Morris, Account of Property, p. 15; RM to
Le Ray, Apr. 6, 1795, to Nicholson, June 11, 1795,
RMLB, DLC.

300,000 acres in Northumberland and Huntington Counties
for £71,250 sterling to Jean Samuel Cordere, the
representative of the two Amsterdam merchant houses of
Cordere, Brantz, and Chanquion, and James Curry and
Company, and the Seville firm of Philip Lom. The
purchasers delayed a final agreement until August, 1795,
when their agent, J. C. Hottinguer, arrived to verify the
quality of the lands. Hottinguer discovered that Morris
and Nicholson had not described 240,000 acres in their
possession, but rather 240,000 belonging to Morris and
General Walter Stewart. The Europeans agreed to accept
these acres along with 60,000 supplied by Nicholson.
The three speculators could draw bills of exchange at
6 months from September 1, 1795, for one-half the purchase
money in proportion to the number of acres each had
furnished. They could draw additional bills, payable
in 6 months, after the scheduled time of payment for
the next one-quarter of the purchase money, and the
remaining one-quarter, payable on December 1, 1798.
The Europeans had until July 1, 1797 to decide to purchase
the land or to accept it as security for the repayment
of any bills already drawn on them by Morris, Stewart,
and Nicholson.[61]

Apparently the European firms decided on
a loan to Morris. On December 9, 1796, James

---

[61]Articles of Agreement, Oct. 1, 1795, RM, Nicholson,
Stewart, and Hottinguer, JNP, PHMC; RM, Nicholson, and
Stewart to Bonnet, Oct. 15, 1795, JNLB, HSP. In 1797,
Hottinguer was agent "X" in the "XYZ" affair.

Marshall and Hottinguer concluded a loan for which
Morris pledged 750 shares of stock in the North American
Land Company. Between October, 1796 and February,
1797, Morris borrowed $52,576.34 from Smith, Cordere,
Brantz, and Chanquion.[62]

Thus, Morris' purchases and sales in Pennsylvania
were varied, but almost invariably disappointing. Land
companies failed because of conflicting claims with
settlers and with other companies, and because of a
lack of subscribers and settlers. Land was a buyer's
commodity.

In the 1790's, Morris invested almost all of his
energy and capital in land. In addition to his
purchases in New York and Pennsylvania, Morris invested
heavily in land in the future capital city of Washington,
D.C. More than any other single purchase, the Federal
City lots were responsible for Morris' decline into
bankruptcy.

----

[62]"Journal C," f. 376, 377, RMP, HSP.

CHAPTER IV

THE FEDERAL CITY

As early as 1783, Morris had been interested in
owning property in and around the city selected by
Congress to be the permanent seat of government. Along
with his contemporaries, he believed that the activities
of the national government assured the city, and the state
in which it was located, political and economic dominance
of the United States. In addition, the increased
population of the region meant additional jobs and a
growing demand for locally produced goods.[1]

Unfortunately, these advantages did not apply to
Washington, D. C., and the purchase of lots in this
capital city bankrupted Morris and his two associates.
Congress, by selecting an undeveloped site for the
capital, hoped to free the national government from
state and local interference and problems.[2]   But, most

---

[1]Kenneth R. Bowling, "Politics in the First Congress,
1789-1791," (unpublished Ph.D. dissertation, University of
Wisconsin, 1968), pp. 155-56; Constance M. Green,
Washington: Village and Capital, 1800-1878 (2 vols; Princeton,
1962-63), I, 7.

[2]Joseph B. Varnum, The Seat of Government of the United
States. A Review of the Discussions, in Congress and
Elsewhere, on the Site and Plans of the Federal City; With
a Sketch of its Present Position and Prospects (New York,
1848), pp. 8-12.

government officials ignored the city until they were
forced by law to convene there in 1800.[3] As the city
would be populated by frequently changing elected
and appointed officers, no one rushed forward to purchase
land for a permanent residence. The city lacked a port
to handle imports and a populated hinterland to supply
exports. As a result, the city attracted few businessmen
and artisans.

For Congress, the selection of a site had been
a difficult decision. As the government moved from
city to city throughout the Revolution and during
the Confederation, the recurring debate over a capital
city remained unsolved.[4] Morris became personally
involved in the discussion on December 23, 1784, when
Congress resolved to appoint three commissioners and
appropriate $100,000 to lay out a federal city on the
banks of the Delaware near Trenton.[5] Not only was the
Financier one of the Commissioners, he also owned land
on the falls of the Delaware, opposite Trenton, in

---

[3]"An Act for establishing the temporary and permanent
seat of Government of the United States" (The Public
Statutes at Large of the United States of America [Boston,
1845], I, 130 [July 16, 1790]).

[4]Congress moved from Philadelphia (Dec. 5, 1774-Dec.
12, 1776) to Baltimore (Dec. 20, 1776-Feb. 26, 1777) to
Philadelphia (Mar. 4, 1777-Sept. 18, 1777) to York (Sept. 30,
1777-June 27, 1778) to Philadelphia (July 2, 1778-June
21, 1783) to Princeton (June 30, 1783-Nov. 4, 1783) to
Annapolis (Nov. 26, 1783-June 3, 1784) to Trenton (Nov. 1,
1784-Dec. 23, 1784) to New York (Jan. 11, 1785-Mar. 4, 1789).

[5]JCC, XXVII, 699-704, XXVIII, 58; Allen C. Clark,
"Origin of the Federal City," Records of the Columbia
Historical Society, XXXV-XXXVI (1935), 1-6.

Bucks County, Pennsylvania. How much land he owned
there in 1784 is difficult to determine, but he had at
least 400 acres in 1787, 850 in 1789, and 2,500 in 1794.[6]

At the first session of Congress in 1789, the selection
of a capital city was a primary issue. Although the 1784
plans had not materialized, Morris still hoped to win
the plum for his Delaware falls property. William Maclay,
Morris' fellow Pennsylvania senator and one of the
Financier's harshest critics, "proposed to Mr. Morris
to bring forward all the places which had been mentioned
for the permanent residence of Congress at one time. He
answered rather roughly: 'Let those that are fond
of them bring them forward; I will bring forward the
Falls of the Delaware.'"[7] As the debate developed,
Morris moved unsuccessfully in and out of deals to

---

[6]"A Draught of Christian Huntsbergers Land ... purchased
from Robert Morris," May 11, 1773; "A Draught of a Tract ...
Sold by Robert Morris to Christian Clemer," May 25, 1774;
"A Draught of a Piece of Land ... being part of Robert
Morris's Tract ... Sold ... to Christian Clymer," Apr. 11,
1787; Deed, Nov. 28, 1791, John Ashley to RM; Deed, Nov. 15,
1792, Patrick Colvin to RM; BCHS; Indenture, Mar. 8, 1787,
John Nixon and RM, Indenture, Dec. 11, 1789, Samuel Ogden
and RM, Indenture, Nov. 28, 1791, John Ashley and RM,
Indenture, Apr. 10, 1792, John Burrows and RM, Indenture,
Nov. 3, 1792, Henry Sheaff and RM, Indenture, Apr. 15, 1793,
Benjamin and Samuel Linton and RM, Indenture, Dec. 4, 1793,
Johseph Vandergrist and RM, Indenture, Sept. 10, 1794,
Joseph Burrows and RM, BCRD.

[7]Maclay, _Journal_, p. 131.

locate the capital on the Delaware, on the Susquehanna,
in Germantown, and in Philadelphia. If the city was
not on his land, at least it would be in his state.

By the opening of the second session, Morris
knew that Pennsylvania, at best, would become only
the temporary residence of the government, and that
Pennsylvania's delegates had to compromise with either
New England or Virginia if they wanted to prevent New
York City from becoming the permanent capital.
Then, in June, Hamilton offered to locate the capital
at Germantown if Morris would help him secure enough
votes to pass the assumption bill. This deal collapsed
when New England and New York refused to accede to Morris'
demand that Philadelphia be the temporary seat of
government. Shortly after Hamilton approached Morris,
Virginia and Pennsylvania agreed to locate the capital
permanently on the Potomac and temporarily in Philadelphia.
This "deal," by which Hamilton secured the votes needed
to pass the assumption bill, is one of the best known and
least documented bargains in American history.[8]

---

[8]For these negotiations, see Maclay, Journal, pp. 131-58;
Bowling, "Politics," pp. 152-85; Sumner, Morris, II, 235-43;
Clark, "Origin of the Federal City," pp. 1-16; Ainsworth
R. Spofford, The Founding of Washington City, With Some
Consideration on the Origins of Cities and Location of
National Capitals (Baltimore, 1881); Harman Yerkes, "Morrisville,
the Capital," Collections of the Bucks County Historical
Society, III (1909), 355-60; Jacob E. Cooke, "The Compromise
of 1790," WMQ, 3d ser., XXVII (Oct., 1970), 523-45; Kenneth
Bowling, "Dinner at Jefferson's: A Note on Jacob E. Cooke's
'The Compromise of 1790,'" WMQ, 3d ser., XXVIII (Oct., 1971),
629-48.

Of the final bill, Morris wrote enthusiastically to
his wife: "I Congratulate you my Dearest Friend upon
our Success, for at length the Senate has passed a
Bill fixing the Temporary Seat of Congress at
Philadelphia...."[9] Feelings on the issue ran high,
and a famous caricature pictured Morris, with Federal
Hall on his back, following the devil from New York
to Philadelphia.[10]

The act empowered Washington to locate the city
between the eastern branch of the Potomac River and
the Conococheaque Creek. On January 22, 1791, the
President established the boundaries of the city, and
appointed General Thomas Johnson, Doctor David Stuart,
and the Honorable Daniel Carroll as "commissioners for
surveying the District."[11] Secretary of State Thomas
Jefferson chose Andrew Ellicott as surveyor and Pierre
Charles L'Enfant as architect. After L'Enfant's dismissal
early in 1792, Ellicott completed the plan of the city.

---

[9]July 2, 1790, RMP, CHHL.

[10]R. W. G. Vail, "A Rare Robert Morris Caricature,"
Pennsylvania Magazine of History and Biography, LX,(Apr.,
1936), 184-86.

[11]Commission, Jan. 22, 1791, in "The Writings of
George Washington Relating to the National Capital,"
Records of the Columbia Historical Society, XVII
(1914), 3; Clark, "Origin of the Federal City,"
pp. 29-31.

He completed his survey in 1793.[12]

The three towns of Carrollsburg, Hamburg, and Georgetown composed the site selected. The last two had no corporeal existence.[13] In March, 1791, the property owners in the District concluded an agreement with the Commissioners for the sale of their land to the United States. The Government paid the owners £25, Maryland currency, or $66.50, per acre "for squares or lands in any form which shall be taken for public buildings or any kind of public improvement or uses," and fair compensation for any woodlands. Holders of lots in Carrollsburg permitted the use of their land in return for one-half the quantity as near as possible to their present holdings. On June 30, fourteen property owners transferred their land to the

---

[12]"Certificate of Survey," Jan. 1, 1793, District of Columbia, DLC; Mathews, Ellicott, pp. 82-102; Bartlett, "Andrew and Joseph Ellicott," pp. 4-14; Ely, "Ellicott," p. 749; Silvio A. Bedini, "Benjamin Banneker and the Survey of the District of Columbia, 1791," Records of the Columbia Historical Society, LXIX-LXX (1969-1970), 7-30; Silvio A. Bedini, The Life of Benjamin Banneker (New York, 1972), pp. 103-36; P. Lee Phillips, "The Negro Benjamin Banneker; Astronomer and Mathematician, Plea for Universal Peace," Records of the Columbia Historical Society, XX (1917), 114-20; Elizabeth S. Kite, ed., L'Enfant and Washington, 1791-1792 (Baltimore, 1929); P. Lee Phillips, The Beginnings of Washington, as Described in Books Maps and Views (Washington, D. C., 1917); Glenn Brown, "The Making of a Plan for Washington City," Records of the Columbia Historical Society, VI (1903), 1-10; Charles Moore, "The Making of a Plan for the City of Washington," Records of the Columbia Historical Society, VI (1903), 11-23.

[13]Arthur Robb, "The Founding of Washington" (typed manuscript, prepared for the United States, Department of Justice, Columbia Law Library, 1936), pp. 9-11.

PROPERTY LINES OF OWNERS OF CITY'S SITE.

Fig. 9.
Reprinted from Wilhelmus B. Bryan, A History of the
National Capital, from Its Foundation through the
Period of the Adoption of the Organic Act (2 vols.;
New York, 1914-1916), I, facing p. 50.

trustees of the city.[14]

The first public sale of lots occurred at Georgetown on October 17, 1791. L'Enfant, who opposed the sale because he thought that speculators would purchase the choice lots at low prices, refused to provide the Commissioners with a map of the city. As a result, they sold only 35 lots at prices ranging from $160 to $534 per lot.[15] After L'Enfant's dismissal, Ellicott completed a plat early in 1792. At a second public sale in October, the results were predictably disappointing as the financial world reacted to the news of William Duer's collapse, the outbreak of the French Revolutionary wars, and the suspension of specie payments by the Bank of England.[16]

At this sale the leading purchaser was Samuel Blodgett, Jr., who then unsuccessfully tried to negotiate a loan in Boston on the Commissioners' unsold lots. He hoped to raise enough funds to enable the Commissioners to complete the construction of all public buildings and thus increase the value of his lots. When this failed, he organized a lottery, at which the first prize would be a hotel in the capital worth

[14]Clark, "Origin of the Federal City," pp. 44-47; Ernest F. M. Faehtz and Frederick W. Pratt, Washington In Embryo or, the National Capital from 1791 to 1800 (Washington, D. C., 1874), pp. 3-4; Agreement, Mar. 30, 1791, PC, June 29, 1791, RG 42, DNA.

[15]PC, Oct. 17, 1791, RG 42, DNA; John B. Osborne, "The First President's Interest in Washington as told by Himself," Records of the Columbia Historical Society, IV (1901), 183-84; Green, Washington, I, 14-15; Clark, "Origin of the Federal City," p. 63; Sakolski, Land Bubble, p. 152.

[16]PC, June 2, 1792, RG 42, DNA; Sakolski, Land Bubble, p. 153.

$50,000, but the Commissioners refused to approve the
scheme. They likewise repudiated Blodgett's second
lottery, which was scheduled to begin in December, 1794,
with a $30,000 house as the grand prize. As Blodgett
had pledged his Washington lots to secure the prizes,
the winners obtained judgments against him and he
lost his Federal City property.[17]

In the meantime, the Commissioners announced a third
sale of lots for September 17, 1793. As an added
inducement, they published along with the advertisement
for the sale a copy of the Maryland law permitting
aliens to own property in the District.[18] Again
few purchasers appeared, even though Washington attended
and bought four lots.[19]

As a result of the poor showing at these sales, the
Commissioners lacked the necessary funds to continue the
construction of the public buildings. This, combined with the
lack of public interest in the growth of the city, opened
the field to speculators. As soon as Washington
authorized the Commissioners to sell lots privately,

---

[17] John C. Fitzpatrick, ed., The Writings of George
Washington (39 vols.; Washington, D. C., 1931-44), XXXIII,
2, 250-52, 293, 359; Wilhelmus B. Bryan, A History of the
National Capital from Its Foundation through the Period of
the Adoption of the Organic Act (2 vols.; New York, 1914-16),
I, 205-08.

[18] PC, Jan. 7, 1793, RG 42, DNA.

[19] John A. Carroll and Mary W. Ashworth, George
Washington: First in Peace, Vol. 7 of Douglas Southall
Freeman, George Washington (New York, 1957), 128.

James Greenleaf moved into the picture. A member of a
prominent Massachusetts family, Greenleaf had formed a
New York City mercantile firm with James Watson in 1788.
That same year, he moved to Amsterdam, and in March of
1793 the Senate confirmed his appointment as United States
Consul in that city. Between January 31, 1789 and August
1, 1792, he negotiated a series of loans for his firm with
the Dutch banking house of Daniel and Gulian Crommelin.
As security for these loans of $1,300,000, Greenleaf
pledged $436,000 of six per cent stock of the United States,
$997,000 of three per cent stock, $375,000 of deferred
stock, and 400 shares, worth $160,000, of stock in the Bank
of the United States. During a visit to the United States
in 1793, Greenleaf purchased land in the Federal City on
the assumption that he would be able to obtain additional
loans in Amsterdam to help finance this new investment.[20]
As Watson refused to participate, they dissolved their
partnership.[21]

In September, 1793, Greenleaf arrived in the future
capital armed with the following letter of introduction
from Washington to the Commissioners:

---

[20]Allen C. Clark, Greenleaf and Law in the Federal
City (Washington, D. C., 1901), pp. 9-18, 80-81, 145.

[21]Ibid., p. 81.

This Gentleman, I understand, had it in
contemplation to make certain proposals to you
for building a number of houses in the Federal
City, provided he can have lots upon such terms
& conditions as may correspond with his interest
in the undertaking while it tends, at the same
time, to promote the great object of the City....
He has been represented to me as a Gentleman of
large property and having the command of much
money in this Country & in Europe; but I can say
nothing on this head from my own knowledge.[22]

On September 23, Greenleaf purchased 3,000 lots,

of 5265 square feet each, for £25, Maryland currency,

or $66.50, per lot. He agreed to pay the money in

seven annual installments, without interest, beginning

on May 1, 1794. The contract required Greenleaf to

build ten houses yearly for ten years. If he sold

any land before January 1, 1796, he was responsible

for the completion of one house on every third lot

sold within four years of the date of sale. In

addition, the Massachusetts speculator was to lend

the Commissioners £1,000, Maryland currency, or

----

[22]August 20, 1793, in "Writings of Washington,"
pp. 87-88. In attempting to untangle the web of
Greenleaf's Federal City speculations, Allen C. Clark
wrote: "To dissipate disappointment an the outset
I confess inability to make a clear and concise
exposition of the entanglement of Greenleaf. I believe
for an exact exhibition, the data does not exist....
Hardly knowing how to advance I enter the wilderness
of barren facts and figures. My readers, if ever I
have any, will, I fear, be discouraged before they
emerge" (Greenleaf and Law, p. 67).

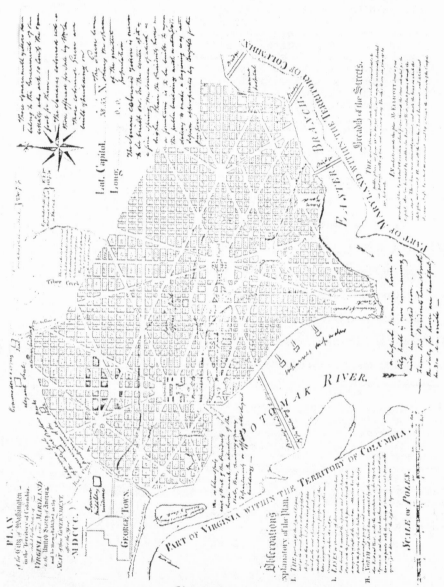

Fig. 10.
Reproduced from the original in the Library of
Congress Geography and Map Division.

approximately $2600, monthly, at six per cent interest,
until all of the public buildings were finished. As
security for these loans, the Commissioners gave
Greenleaf a mortgage on additional lots.[23]

Shortly before he concluded this agreement,
Greenleaf had discussed the potential profits of
the purchase with Morris, who, in turn, conveyed
the information to John Nicholson.[24] On December
24, 1793, Greenleaf and Morris, who also represented
Nicholson, signed a second contract with the Commissioners.[25]
By the terms of this agreement, the speculators purchased
3,000 lots at £35, Maryland currency, or $93.10, per
lot, payable in seven installments, without interest,
beginning on May 1, 1794. The building requirements in this
agreement were the same as in Greenleaf's earlier

---

[23]Clark, Greenleaf and Law, p. 67; Bryan, National
Capital, pp. 215-16; The building regulations, established
by Washington, are printed in Samuel Burch, A Digest
of the Laws of the Corporation of the City of Washington
(Washington, D.C., 1823), pp. 326-30.

[24]RM to Nicholson, Sept. 2, 1793, RMLB, DLC.

[25]PC, Dec. 24-25, 1793, RG 42, DNA.

contract. The Commissioners and the speculators then
decided to combine the two agreements, with the price per
lot averaged at £30, Maryland currency, or $79.80. If the
price per lot is set at $80.00, then the speculators agreed
to pay a total of $480,000 for 6,000 lots in seven yearly
installments of approximately $68,000. Nicholson became
a silent partner by the provision of the agreement that
allowed Morris and Greenleaf "to associate to them one or
more persons in the whole purchase without creating in any
of them" the building obligations imposed on buyers of
lots.[26] The sale, according to the Commissioners, was the
result of "A consideration of the uncertainty of settled
times and an unembarrassed commerce...as well as Mr. Morris's
capital, influence, and activity."[27] In 1794 the three
speculators purchased an additional 1,234 lots from Daniel
Carroll, Notley Young, Uriah Forrest, and Benjamin Stoddert.[28]

Through this sale, the Commissioners hoped to raise
money for the completion of the public buildings in the
District, but the Greenleaf syndicate was only interested in
a quick profit on its investment. When difficulties arose

[26]PC, Dec. 24-25, 1793, RG 42, DNA. A list of the
lots finally assigned to Morris and Nicholson is in
Faehtz, Washington, pp. 35-75.

[27]Commissioners to Washington, Dec. 23, 1793,
RG 42, DNA.

[28]Morris, Account of Property, p. 7.

between the speculators and the Commissioners in 1795,
Morris informed Washington that "Nobody can suppose that
Mr. Nicholson & myself entered into these engagements
with an expectation of holding the property. It was
from the beginning & is now our intention to resell when
it can be done to our satisfaction...."[29] The President,
in fact, had never been enthusiastic about the sales.
He assented to Greenleaf's first contract, although he
thought the price too low, to encourage new purchases
in the District. He objected to the second sale because
he realized that Greenleaf "was speculating deeply, was
aiming to monopolize deeply and was thereby laying the
foundation of immense profit to himself and those with
whom he was concerned."[30]

Under the provisions of the December agreement,
the Commissioners would convey the title to the lots to
the three purchasers proportionately after each installment
was paid. Immediately after the purchase, Greenleaf asked
the Commissioners if the partners could "join in a Bond
for the Payment of the money and performing other parts

[29]Sept. 2, 1795, GWP, DLC.

[30]Washington to Daniel Carroll, Jan. 7, 1795, in
"Writings of Washington," pp. 113-14.

of the contract...."[31] He specifically requested
a deed for 1,000 lots in exchange for which Morris
and Greenleaf "pledged their personal security, united
with that of Mr. Nicholson...." He also wanted a
deed in fee for the remaining 5,000 lots in return for
the speculators' "joint mortgage of the same received as
security for the payment thereof." If the syndicate
sold any of these lots, Greenleaf would give the
Commissioners "funded stocks of America or National Bank
Stock" as security for the purchase money.[32] The President
reluctantly acceded to Greenleaf's first request, and
on April 24, 1794, the Commissioners granted him a deed
in fee for 1,000 lots.[33] By accepting a bond as security
for part of the purchase money, the Commissioners enabled
the trio to claim title to part of the land sooner
than originally provided for.

Washington and the Commissioners granted Greenleaf
the title to these lots in an effort to help him
negotiate a loan in Holland. No Dutch investor could
be expected to subscribe to a negotiation secured
against land to which the owner did not have a clear
title. The loan was critical, as Morris and Nicholson

---

[31]Commissioners to Washington, Dec. 23, 1793,
RG 42, DNA.

[32]PC, Dec. 5, 1794, Greenleaf to Randolph, Jan.
7, 1794, RG 42, DNA; Bryan, National Capital, p. 234;
Edwin M. Williams "Building the Federal City," in John
C. Proctor, ed., Washington: Past and Present, A History
(New York, 1930), I, 55.

[33]Randolph to the Commissioners, Apr. 14, 1794,
Commissioners to Randolph, Mar. 23, 1794, RG 42, DNA.

had invested in the Federal City on the strength of
Greenleaf's promise to secure a foreign loan. Neither
Pennsylvanian had sufficient funds to finance this purchase
without assistance. On November 2, 1793, Greenleaf executed
a power of attorney to Sylvanus Bourne, the United States
Vice-Consul in Amsterdam, to sell the lots or use them as
security for a loan.[34] Bourne contracted with Crommelin
to negotiate a subscription, capitalized at £300,000,
Maryland currency, or $780,000 or 950,000 florins. The
Dutch government approved the proposal on May 6, 1794, by
passing an act that appointed Pieter Godefrey, Butger Jan
Schimmelpenninck, and Crommelin the guardians of the
property. As security for the loan, Greenleaf mortgaged
Federal City lots at the rate of £100 per lot. To increase
the funds at their disposal, the Commissioners accepted
"one third part of the produce of all Bills of Exchange
to be drawn in consequence of the said Loan," payable at the
end of six years, and conveyed to Greenleaf certificates in
fee simple to 1,000 lots, which transferred the legal title
and estate to him, as security for their share of the loan.
They also granted Greenleaf certificates for 1,500 lots,
secured by a bond issued by the three speculators against
their personal estates, and another 500, part in fee simple
and part to be reconveyed to the Commissioners after they
had paid for their one-third of the loan.[35] This subscription

---

[34]RM to Washington, Sept. 21, 1795, GWP, DLC; Clark,
Greenleaf and Law, p. 82.

[35]PC, Apr. 15-24, July 9, Oct. 18, 1794, RG 42, DNA.

was only a partial success. By March, 1795, Dutch
investors had subscribed only $80,000 to the negotiation,
and in July, the guardians reconveyed 1,500 of the 2,000
lots to Greenleaf.[36]

Bourne, although discouraged, turned his attention
to Rotterdam, where he negotiated a loan through Jan
Beeldemaker, the agent for the merchant firm of
Rocquette, Elserier, and Beeldemaker. Bourne offered
the 1,500 lots returned by the Amsterdam guardians as
security for a loan of $400,000, at five and one-half
per cent annual interest. Again, the loan failed.
By July, the subscribers had paid only $48,000,
and Bourne and Beeldemaker altered the original agreement
so that the loan was for only $60,000.[37]

As Morris, Nicholson, and Greenleaf had depended
entirely on the Dutch loan to finance their purchase
of Federal City lots, the syndicate knew well in advance
that they could not meet the second installment due
to the Commissioners in May, 1795. In October, 1794,
the Commissioners "thought proper to comply with Mr.
Greenleaf's request by granting him a Deed for the amount
of money becoming due the 1st of May next on his and
Messrs. Morris and Nicholson's joint notes...."[38] On

[36]Clark, Greenleaf and Law, pp. 82-86.

[37]Morris to Bourne, Oct. 8, 1795, RMLB, DLC;
Clark, Greenleaf and Law, pp. 82-86; Williams, "Federal
City," p. 55; Bryan, National Capital, pp. 234-35.

[38]Commissioners to Randolph, Oct. 18, 1794,
RG 42, DNA.

receipt of these notes, which became due in May, the Bank of
Columbia advanced the Commissioners $60,000. If the
triumvirate failed to meet the May payment, the Commissioners
could sell enough of Greenleaf's property to raise the sum.[39]

Along with the Dutch loans, the speculators tried to raise
funds by selling some of their lots. The largest purchasers
were two Englishmen, Thomas Law and William Mayne Duncanson,
who visited the Federal City in February, 1795. After
this visit, Law confirmed his option of purchase, dated
December 3, 1794, of 445 lots at $293 per lot. Law could
choose the lots he wanted from those to which the three
speculators had the right of possession. Until Morris,
Nicholson, and Greenleaf had acquired clear title to these
squares by paying the Commissioners, they agreed to mortgage
to Law other squares that they already owned. The
mortgage to Law, signed on September 4, 1795, was for
400,000 square feet less than he purchased. Before Law
received the rest of his land, the speculators, facing
bankruptcy, had assigned the land to their creditors.[39]
Duncanson's option, executed on March 10, 1795, required
that he pay $30,222.22 for 544,000 square feet. In
September, he rescinded his option to purchase an
additional 800,000 square feet for $31,200.[41]

News of these sales spread quickly. Washington,
disturbed over the lack of progress in the construction

---

[39]"An Act to establish a Bank in the District of
Columbia," Dec. 28, 1793, JNP, PHMC; PC, Oct. 18, 1794,
Commissioners to Randolph, Jan. 16, 1795, RG 42, DNA.

[40]Law to Nicholson and Morris, Sept. 20, Nov. 4,
1796, JNP, PHMC; Clark, Greenleaf and Law, p. 186.

[41]Clark, Greenleaf and Law, pp. 264-71.

of the public buildings in the city, informed Carroll that
his "sentiments are opposed to any more <u>large</u> sales, if
there be <u>any other</u> resource by which money can be obtained
to carry on your operations....Lately, a Gentleman from
England has paid, or is to pay £50,000 for 500 Lots. Will it
not be asked, why are speculators to pocket so much money?
Are not the Commissioners as competent to make bargains?"[42]

In addition to the failure of the Dutch loans and the
lack of any other significant sales of lots, Morris and
Nicholson had to cope with Greenleaf's financial misconduct.
He failed to honor notes endorsed by his partners, he never
met his share of the installments due for lots, and he used
his partners' money for his personal business. For example,
Morris sent Greenleaf $10,047.40 in notes on April 13, 1795
to discharge the notes "granted to you payable at the Bank
of Columbia on the first of May next." One note was from
Duncanson in favor of Morris for $7,703.70; the other was
a note from Joseph Donaldson to Harrison and Sterett for
$2,343.70, which Sterett endorsed over to Morris. On May
27 the Financier complained that only $7,000 of this sum
had been used for his third of the installment, and that he
expected Greenleaf

> to have compleated my Share of that Paymt from the
> monies which you received of Ca Duncanson in which
> I am one third interested but as it seems you have
> applied this money to your own use the Commissrs
> remain unpaid, which gives me concern....Upon this
> Condition I do agree that in Order to assist you in
> making the Payments, you may draw upon me for any
> Sum not exceeding what remains unpaid of my proportion

---

[42]Jan. 7, 1795, in "Writings of Washington," p. 114.

of the payments.... I shall rely that you will also
provide for my situation to sustain advances for
any length of time.[43]

Morris and Nicholson consistently blamed Greenleaf and

his failure to negotiate the promised Dutch loan as

the cause of their financial difficulties. What sums

had been subscribed, Greenleaf used to cover his

personal expenses.[44] In describing his account with

Greenleaf in 1801, Morris wrote bitterly: "This is an

unsettled Account; and I suppose ever will be so.

"Here commenced that ruin which has killed poor

Nicholson, and brought me to the necessity of giving

an account of my affairs - but I will forbear to say

more, lest I should not know where or when to stop."[45]

By the summer of 1795, the partnership was no

longer tenable. In July, Greenleaf offered to either

buy out Morris and Nicholson or sell them his interest

in the lots."at a price & on Terms which he named."

Morris, at first tempted to sell, decided instead to

purchase Greenleaf's share "because it was more likely

that the Lotts would command money to pay our Debts

than Mr. G's paper." Considerably sobered by the

failure of the Federal City investment, Morris" "only

desire now is to get out of debt, settle account with

every body and quit work...." His experience, however,

---

[43]RMLB, DLC; "Journal C," f. 154, RMP, HSP.

[44]RM to Bourne, Oct. 8, 1795, RMLB, DLC.

[45]Morris, Account of Property, p. 58; RM to
Washington, Sept. 21, 1795, GWP, DLC.

had not completely dampened his enthusiasm. He still
believed that the lots "will be constantly rising in
Value, the more we sell, the more valuable what will
remain, so that after selling one half it is probable
the other half will be worth more than the whole are
now."[46] Accordingly, Morris and Nicholson bought out
Greenleaf at $160 per lot plus six per cent interest
per annum. They agreed to pay him in notes drawn on
and endorsed by each other. Of their total of 7781 lots,
Greenleaf reserved only 25.[47]

After eliminating Greenleaf, the two partners
still owed between $40,000 and $50,000 on the May
payment. The Commissioners had already threatened
to take legal action if the installment was not paid
by May 25.[48] Although the Commissioners temporarily
solved their problem by borrowing $20,000 from the
Bank of Columbia, Washington, a close personal friend
of Morris, grew impatient with the two Pennsylvanians.
He asked Randolph to meet with them to request at least
a partial payment on the overdue installment.
Otherwise, construction on the public buildings would
stop and this "would throw such a cloud over the public

---

[46]Morris to William Constable, July 27, 1795,
RMLB, DLC.

[47]"Memo of an Agreement Between J. Greenleaf &
R. Morris & J. Nicholson relative to the quantity of
lots in the Federal City," May 13, 1796, RMP, NYPL;
Morris, Account of Property, p. 7.

[48]Commissioners to Greenleaf, May 18, 1795,
RG 42, DNA.

& private concerns of the City, & would be susceptible
of such magnified & unfavorable interpretations, as to
give it a vital wound."[49] At the stipulated meeting
Morris and Nicholson promised to pay the arrearages
immediately. They failed to do so by September,
and Washington appealed to Morris out of "private
friendship" as well as "public duty." The President
explained that he had agreed to the sale to the Greenleaf
syndicate because of "the collateral advantages ...
derived from the erection of the buildings and the
advance of money. Withhold these, and the contract
exhibits an unproductive and a disagreeable spectacle."[50]

When Morris denied that he ever knew how
desperately the Commissioners needed funds, they abruptly
reminded him that "the idea of advertising your property
for Sale was not relinquished from any apprehension of
the want of power, but because that measure ought not
to be adopted whilst any Other mode of releif [sic]
remained...." They gave Morris and Nicholson until October
5 to remit $15,000.[51] On that date, Morris promised to send

_____

[49]July 22, 1795, in "Writings of Washington," p. 137.

[50]Sept. 14, Dec. 3, 1795, GWP, DLC.

[51]Commissioners to RM, Sept. 28, 1795, RG 42, DNA;
Washington to RM, Sept. 14, Dec. 3, 1795, GWP, DLC.

the money shortly. In December, Morris and Nicholson met with Commissioner Alexander White, who had replaced Carroll in May, 1795, and promised to pay $10,000 immediately.[52]

Early in 1796, the Commissioners resolved to sell enough of Morris and Nicholson's lots as would cover the sum still due. Washington cautioned them against selling "large parcels to speculators." The President preferred to sell single lots or squares to individuals who would be interested in settling on the land.[53] Attorney General Charles Lee, after considering all of the documents relating to the legality of such a sale, reported that "all the other lots comprised in the contract, remaining in the commissioners, unconveyed either by certificate or deed according to law unto Morris and Greenleaf," may be sold if the purchasers failed to meet their installments or neglected to fulfill the building requirements.[54] By May 2, 1796, Morris and Nicholson had to meet that year's installment and the balance due for 1795 or the Commissioners would advertise their property for sale and file a bill in Chancery to compel them to complete their required number of buildings.[55] To

[52]White to the Commissioners, Dec. 10, 1795, Nicholson to White, Dec. 25, 1795, RG 42, DNA; RM to Commissioners, Oct. 5, 1795, RMLB, DLC.

[53]Washington to the Commissioners, May 22, 1796, in "Writings of Washington," p. 153.

[54]Mar. 20, 1796, RG 42, DNA. See also White to RM and Nicholson, Apr. 26, 1796, to Commissioners, May 2, 1796, RG 42, DNA.

[55]Commissioners to RM, Oct. 15, 1795, to White, Apr. 5, 1796, RG 42, DNA.

prevent this sale, Morris and Nicholson promised to pay $12,000, but the Commissioners had received no money as late as July.[56]

Since Morris and Nicholson had not paid their installments, the Commissioners, by the middle of 1796, needed $100,000 yearly to complete all of the public buildings by 1800. With the help of the two partners, they successfully petitioned Congress for a loan, which was approved on May 8, 1796. In pursuance of this act, Maryland loaned the Commissioners $200,000 of a possible $300,000 in United States 6 per cent stock valued at par. But, by January, 1801, the Commissioners had raised only $130,873.41 from the sale of this stock.[57]

Thus, the Commissioners could tolerate no further delays from Morris and Nicholson. All of the speculators' payments to date did not cover the 1795 installment, no houses had been built in 1796 and 1797, and the two speculators had not fulfilled their promise, given after the passage of the loan act, to sell some of their property to pay the overdue installments. To avoid a sale of lots, the Commissioners offered the partners three alternatives. The Commissioners would accept monthly installments of $12,000 beginning in August,

---

[56]RM and Nicholson to White, May 9, 1796, RMLB, DLC; Commissioners to RM, July 15, 1796, RG 42, DNA.

[57]"Memorial," Jan. 8, 1796, "Committee Report," Mar. 11, 1796, "Commissioners' Report," Jan. 30, 1801, in American State Papers: Documents, Legislative and Executive, of the Congress of the United States: Miscellaneous, I (Washington, D. C., 1834), 133-34, 142-44, 219-31.

or "sell at a Credit of 60 or 90 days, for good negotiable
paper...as much of...[Morris and Nicholson's] City property
as will discharge the debt," or to accept from the
Pennsylvanians judgment bonds at 60 and 90 days. In a tone
that must have irritated the Financier, the Commissioners
reminded him that these propositions, which "shew strong
an inclination to fall on any expedient, rather than carry
things to an extremity," could not be refused "by a
Gentleman of Character, once celebrated for his punctuality
throughout all Europe and America."[58]

Faced with a possible sale of their lots, Morris and
Nicholson searched for new sources of money. They assigned
2,000 of their lots to James Marshall to sell or use as
security for a loan in Europe. Marshall had authority to
continue or close the two Holland loans negotiated by
Bourne. First, Marshall had to determine the amount of the
subscriptions and the purpose to which the money had been
applied. Greenleaf had kept the Pennsylvanians uninformed
about the status of these loans because he did not want them
to know that the loans had largely failed and that he had
misappropriated some of the money subscribed. If Marshall
chose to continue either loan, the partners suggested that
the remainder be subscribed in Antwerp, London, Paris, or
Germany. If the loans could not be filled, then Marshall
was to buy back the subscriptions already pledged. That
way, Morris and Nicholson could reconvey the lots used as

[58]July 15, 1796, RG 42, DNA.

security to themselves or their creditors for sale or use as
security for yet another loan. Marshall's efforts were
futile, and in July, Morris wrote to his son-in-law: "I think
I can perceive a little symptom of despondence in your letters,
but I beg you not to give way to it, keep your Expectations
alive...."[59]

To bring the situation under control, Morris and Nicholson
visited the Federal City. Nicholson left Philadelphia on August
22 or 23, and Morris followed a few weeks later.[60] The
Commissioners informed Washington that to avoid a sale of lots
"Morris and Nicholson have relieved us of $50,000 of our bank
debt and they have reason to expect $20,000."[61] No further
evidence of this transaction has been found.

Once they had prevented this sale, Morris and Nicholson
began the task of selecting, dividing, and selling their lots.[62]
As much as they needed money, they insisted on high prices
for their land. In November, Morris received from 13 to 50
cents per square foot for land he thought worth only 6 cents
when he was in Philadelphia. He refused Henry Lee's offer to

[59]RM and Nicholson to Crommelin and Sons, Jan. 5, 1796, to
Marshall, Oct. 16, 1795, May 24, 1796, RM to Marshall, July 4,
1796, to Franklin, July 18, 1795, to Cranch, July 24, 1795, to
Bourne, Oct. 8, 1795, to Bourdieu, Chollet, and Bourdieu, Oct.
7, 1795, RMLB, DLC; Nicholson to RM, Oct. 12, 1795, JNLB, HSP;
Greenleaf to Crommelin and Sons., Jan., 1796, RMP, NYPL.

[60]RM to Cranch, June 27, 1796, to Commissioners, July 25,
1796, to Nicholson, Aug. 29, 1796, RMLB, DLC; Nicholson to RM,
Aug. 22, 1796, JNLB, HSP.

[61]Oct. 31, 1796, quoted in Bryan, National Capital, I
p. 279, n. 3.

[62]PC, Nov. 12, 16, 19, 23, Dec. 1, 3, 1796, Jan. 19, 1797,
RG 42, DNA.

exchange lots in the Federal City for land in Hardy or
Hampshire Counties, Virginia, but offered to sell him land
at a minimum of 10 cents per square foot.[63]   Although
sales were few, the increase in construction in the city
enabled the speculators to demand and receive high prices
for their property. Regular lots sold for 12 to 20 cents
per square foot, while two choice water lots, purchased
for $160 sold for $4,000 each, and inland lots sold for
$500 to $1,000 each.[64]

This trip to Washington revived Morris' optimism and
enthusiasm. The quality of the land exceeded all of his
expectations. If he held on to the land, he thought it
would be of a "value beyond Calculation." He speculated
that in 1800 the lots would sell for $1,500 to $3,000.[65]
Before Morris left for Philadelphia, where he arrived on
November 17, he executed a power of attorney to William
Cranch to handle all of his Washington interests.[66]

Nicholson remained in Washington to settle the
syndicate's business, while Morris tried, with increasing

[63]RM to Marshall, Nov. 1, 1796, to Lee, Sept. 30,
1796, RMLB, DLC.

[64]Articles of Agreement, Oct. 18, 1796, RM and Levy
Green, Articles of Agreement, Oct. 18, 1796, RM and Daniel
Caffrey, RMP, NYPL; Articles of Agreement, Sept., 1796,
RM and Isaac Reed, JNP, PHMC; RM to Mary Morris, Oct. 19,
1796, RMP, CHHL.

[65]RM to Mary Morris, Sept. 7, 1796, RMP, CHHL; RM to
Marshall, Sept. 17, 1796, to Benjamin Harrison, Jr.,
Sept. 28, 1796, RMLB, DLC.

[66]Nov. 1, 1796, RMP, NYPL; RM to Cranch, Nov. 17,
1796, in Clark, Greenleaf and Law, p. 51.

difficulty, to quiet their Philadelphia creditors, many
of whom faced financial ruin in 1797. American merchants
experienced setbacks in that year because France, which
had reacted angrily to the ratification of the Jay Treaty
in 1796, issued decrees that obstructed the movement of
neutral American vessels in the Caribbean. Between July,
1796 and June, 1797, the French captured more than 300
American ships.[67]

As Morris took stock of his financial situation, the
scope of his investments and the extent of his indebtedness
suddenly overwhelmed him. His credit was not only limited,
it no longer existed. A man known for his hospitality,
charm, sense of humor, and financial wizardry, Morris
uncharacteristically panicked. He grew impatient over
Nicholson's apparent reluctance to return to Philadelphia.
He could not cope with his partner's creditors, who dunned
him for payment on notes he had endorsed for Nicholson.
Morris' letters reveal this change in his attitude. On
his return to Philadelphia, Morris complained to Nicholson
that he lacked the funds needed to satisfy their creditors,
who pressed for payment "in a sour ill tempered manner &
think they grant great favor in consenting to wait a day
or two." By early December he lamented that "The hue and
Cry after money here exceeds all description, and one House

---

[67]Stuart W. Bruchey, Robert Oliver, Merchant of
Baltimore: 1783-1819 (Baltimore, 1956), pp. 176-77, 188-89.
A partial diary of Nicholson's trip to Washington is in
JNP, DLC.

or another seems to be unexpectedly falling into discredit day after day....In short my engagements come too fast for my means...." On December 8, the sheriff arrested Judge James Wilson for nonpayment of debts, and "notice was given" to Morris "to take care...[or] it will be...[his] turn next." After Nicholson failed to return to Philadelphia in December as promised, Morris wrote: "I am quite tired of telling People that you will be here next week and next week, indeed it is almost useless to do so, because they do not believe when they are told so, and those whom I have put off for settlements until your return begin to torment me horribly."[68]

In defense of Nicholson, even Morris admitted that new crises had developed in the Federal City over their land titles, their outstanding debts to the Commissioners and the original proprietors, their failure to comply with the building provisions in their contract, and their inability to pay their workmen, some of whom petitioned the state of Maryland to sell part of Morris and Nicholson's property to pay their wages.[69]

Besides these problems, Law impatiently demanded that the speculators fulfill their contract with him. Morris, Nicholson, and Greenleaf had promised Law certificates of ownership in fee simple for the land he purchased, but the

---

[68]RM to Nicholson, Nov. 20, 24, Dec. 4, 8, 11, 19, 21, 1796, Jan. 4, 1797, RMLB, DLC.

[69]Edward Vidler, Joshua Ward, Thomas Hishes, John Lenox, and William Jackson to the Commissioners, Nov. 4, 1795, RG 42, DNA.

Commissioners could not grant such certificates until the
syndicate had paid for the lots. The Commissioners did
agree to convey such certificates to anyone who purchased
lots from Morris and Greenleaf upon the receipt of payment
for the lots, in cash or negotiable paper, and security
for the required improvements.[70] Greenleaf proposed, while
he was still a partner, to convey 500 lots to Law if the
Commissioners would accept a mortgage on 500 of the trio's
lots. The Commissioners, who needed funds badly and were
disillusioned with Greenleaf, refused because "it is highly
unreasonable that when those Gentlemen are receiving in
ready money more than four times the price given by them to
the public for the same property, that they would at least
let the public participate in the benefits resulting from a
ready payment of the money."[71] During Nicholson's stay in
the District, new problems arose with Law, who still held a
mortgage, dated May 11, 1795, on 4,515,458 square feet as
security for the execution of his contract with the
speculators.[72] As of 1796 this agreement remained
unsatisfied. Morris and Nicholson had not paid for the lots,
and Law, consequently, had not received certificates for them.
On April 10, 1797, the Commissioners agreed to convey the
titles to Law if Morris and Nicholson assigned to them
Law's agreement for the completion of buildings on his

---

[70]Commissioners to Cranch, Mar. 5, 1795, RG 42, DNA.

[71]Commissioners to Randolph, Mar. 20, 1795, RG 42, DNA.

[72]Morris, Account of Property, p. 8.

property. The speculators did so in June.[73]

A second difficulty with Law involved Daniel Carroll of Duddington. Morris and Nicholson owed Carroll $13,000 for lots purchased of him and then conveyed to Law. Carroll refused to convey the titles to Law until the partners had paid for the land.[74] He did agree to accept 100 shares of stock in the North American Land Company, $5,000 in cash, and a 60 day negotiable note for $2,300 as payment, but Nicholson could not raise the $7,300.[75]

Another problem with Carroll stemmed from his contract of September 26, 1793 with Greenleaf. This agreement required that Greenleaf construct twenty houses within three years on all empty lots he purchased or pay a penalty of $266 per lot. When Morris and Nicholson purchased Greenleaf's interest in the Federal City, they also acquired this obligation to Carroll. They agreed to build at least ten houses each and completed thirty before the

[73]RM to Nicholson, Nov. 27, 1796, to Law, Dec. 11, 1796, to the Commissioners, Jan. 30, 1797, RMLB, DLC; RM and Nicholson to the Commissioners, Jan. 12, 1797, Nicholson to Philip Key, Jan. 14, 1797, to RM, Feb. 1, 1797, to Law, Mar. 22, 1797, JNLB, HSP; Commissioners to Nicholson, Jan. 12, 1797, to Washington, Feb. 6, 1797, to RM and Nicholson, Mar. 9, Apr. 10, 1797, Nicholson and RM to the Commissioners, Sept. 30, 1796, Nicholson to the Commissioners, Dec. 24, 1796, Opinion of John McGant, Jan. 12, 1797, Law to Commissioners, Jan. 27, 1797, PC, Feb. 6, Apr. 10, June 13, 1797, RG 42, DNA; Morris, Account of Property, p. 8.

[74]RM to Nicholson, Nov. 20, 1796, to Law, Nov. 22, 1796, RMLB, DLC; Nicholson to RM, Nov. 16, 1796, JNLB, HSP.

[75]RM to Carroll, Dec. 19, 1796, RMLB, DLC; Nicholson to RM, Nov. 16, 1796, JNLB, HSP.

deadline at a cost of $42,000.[76] In May, 1797, Carroll seized
these houses as a result of a suit he brought against Morris
and Nicholson for nonpayment on other lots he had sold to them.
In 1804 Morris and Nicholson's trustees successfully brought
suit against Carroll for failing to maintain the condition of
the houses, and Carroll paid the trustees $39,847.87.[77]

For Morris and Nicholson, the basic problems remained
unsolved in 1797. They could neither pay the installments to
the Commissioners nor complete the 370 houses specified in
their contract. By 1795 they had spent $120,000 on the houses,
but few had been completed. Nicholson then suggested that they
subcontract the annual building of 20 houses. Instead they
hired William Lovering, an architect, at a yearly salary of
$1,800, to finish the houses already in progress. They also
pressured people who had purchased lots from them to complete
the houses on their property.[78] In an effort to raise funds,
they used their lots as security for a loan of $50,000 from
William Sansom, $120,000 from Uriah Forrest, and an undiscovered
sum from Notley Young.[79]

[76]RM to Cranch, Feb. 10, 22, May 22, 1796, RMLB, DLC;
Nicholson to Carroll, Oct. 5, 1796, JNLB, HSP; Clark,
Greenleaf and Law, pp. 124-26.

[77]Clark, Greenleaf and Law, pp. 192-93.

[78]RM and Nicholson to Lovering, Aug. 17, 1795, RMLB, DLC;
Nicholson to Greenleaf, Apr. 13, 1795, to RM, Apr. 13, 1795,
JNLB, HSP; Articles of Agreement, July 6, 1795, RM, Nicholson,
and Lovering, JNP, PHMC.

[79]RM to Young, July 8, 1797, to Forrest, July 12, 1797,
RMLB, DLC; Nicholson to Sansom, July 4, 1796, JNLB, HSP;
Morris, Account of Property, p. 9.

As their financial difficulties increased, more and more creditors brought suit against Morris and Nicholson, who retained Joseph Karrick, Luther Martin, and Philip Key as their attorneys.[80] When the two speculators failed to pay for land in the District they had purchased from the state of Maryland, the State sued them, attached their property, and eventually sold some of the speculators' lots to satisfy this debt. The state of Pennsylvania also attached and sold some of the Washington lots for nonpayment of debts.[81]

With the approach of May, 1797, Nicholson and Morris were again unable to meet the installment on their lots, even though the Commissioners agreed to accept monthly installments of $12,000. The Commissioners gave them until the end of May to arrange for the payment. As the speculators could not reach an acceptable agreement with the Commissioners, the latter advertised part of Morris and Nicholson's property for a sale to be held in early August.[82]

To settle their affairs in the District, Morris, Nicholson, and Greenleaf devised an unusual plan. Back in

---

[80]RM to Karrick, May 10, 1797, RMLB, DLC.

[81]Nicholson to John Vaughan, May 25, 1797, Nicholson and Morris to the Commissioners, May 25, 1797, to William Marbury, May 25, 1797, JNLB, HSP; RM to Charles McNantz, May 4, 1797, RMLB, DLC.

[82]Commissioners to RM and Nicholson, May 4, 1797, RG 42, DNA.

April, 1797, they had approached five of their creditors,
Henry Pratt, Thomas W. Francis, John Miller, Jr., John
Ashley, and Jacob Baker, with the idea of purchasing all
of the speculators' outstanding notes at a price higher
than they would command at a public auction. In return,
the speculators offered their creditors five shillings
in the pound, or one-fourth the nominal value of the notes
in four installments. To raise this money, the trio
intended to sell a portion of their land. As security,
Morris and Nicholson offered shares in the Pennsylvania
Property and Pennsylvania Land Companies, lands in
Kentucky or Virginia, or lots in the Federal City. They
also agreed to secure against their property Greenleaf's
debt of $720,000 to the trustees. At first, Pratt and
his associates demanded additional security, but Morris
and Nicholson reminded them that the more property needed
as security, the less the two Pennsylvanians would be
able to sell to repay the creditors.[83]

An agreement reached in June between the speculators
and their creditors created the so-called Aggregate Fund.
The creditors, as trustees, were to provide security for
all of the partners' debts by selling or mortgaging the
Federal City lots. As a substitute for the property

---

[83]RM and Nicholson to the trustees, Apr. 17, May 15,
16, 1797, RMP, NYPL.

originally offered as security, the trustees accepted a
mortgage on Morris and Nicholson's joint Washington
property up to $300,000. The speculators would add
another $100,000 worth of lots if the creditors remitted
$13,000 to Daniel Carroll and the fourth installment of
$60,000 to the Commissioners. If the trustees paid the
Commissioners, the incumbrance on the Washington lots
would be eliminated, and Morris and Nicholson would
then assign the lots to the trustees as part of the
promised security. Pratt could raise money by selling
the land or mortgaging it as security for a new loan
charged to Morris and Nicholson. The latter agreed to
pay interest on such a loan annually, and the principal
in four installments beginning in 1799. After the
trustees arranged security for Morris and Nicholson's
debts, the speculators hoped that there would be a
surplus for them.[84]

At first, the scheme worked. On August 7, William
H. Dorsey, a Georgetown resident who represented the
trustees, gave the Commissioners a draft for $10,000

---

[84]Articles of Agreement, June 26, 1797, RMP, HSP;
RM and Nicholson to the trustees, June 12, 15, 1797,
Deed Poll, Dec. 28, 1797, Greenleaf, Edward Fox, RM,
Nicholson, and the trustees, RMP, NYPL; Clark, Greenleaf
and Law, pp. 73-74.

payable in 75 days. In return, the Commissioners postponed the sale of Morris and Nicholson's lots until the fall.[85] In addition, the trustees allowed Morris and Nicholson to transfer a mortgage on some of their property to Gustavus Scott, who agreed to pay the Bank of Columbia $6,000 to forestall a sale of lots. Morris and Nicholson had four years to repay Scott.[86]

By November, however, the Aggregate Fund created new problems for the two speculators. The trustees refused to borrow enough money to prevent a future sale of Federal City lots unless the partners provided additional security. This security, the trustees specified, could not consist of shares in any company or a mortgage on Kentucky lands.[87] As a result, a sale of lots advertised on August 10 began on October 18. On the 19th, the Commissioners, upon the receipt of a letter from the trustees, agreed to sell only three lots per day until November 3. By that date, Pratt would either pay the Commissioners or they

---

[85]Nicholson and RM to the Commissioners, Aug. 4, 1797, Commissioners to the trustees, July 26, Aug. 4, 8, 1797, to RM and Nicholson, Aug. 8, 1797, to Dorsey, Aug. 17, 1797, Agreement, Aug. 7, 1797, in PC, Aug. 17, 19, 1797, RG 42, DNA.

[86]RM to James Dunlop, July 8, 1797, to Forrest, July 12, 1797, to Scott, July 30, Aug. 15, 1797, RMLB, DLC; RM and Nicholson to the trustees, July, 1797, RMP, NYPL; Morris, Account of Property, pp. 8-9.

[87]RM to Nicholson, Nov. 21, 1797, RMLB, DLC.

could continue the sale as originally scheduled. As
the Commissioners received no money, the sale resumed in
full on November 6.[88]

In defense of these sales, the Commissioners cited
a Maryland Act of December 28, 1793, which provided
for the sale of lots at public auction if the purchaser
failed to pay for them within 30 days of the specified
date. Morris and Nicholson protested the sales on the
grounds that they had concluded their contract with the
Commissioners a few days before the passage of this
statute. Attorney General Lee, however, reaffirmed his
earlier opinion by maintaining that "By the agreement
of the 24th decr. 1793 the consideration money is to be
paid by instalments and therefore this sale appears to
be within the letter and spirit of the act of 28th december
1793, which more properly comprehends sales made prior
to the passage of the act than sales made subsequent
thereto; and in my opinion comprehends sales of both
descriptions."[89]

In March, 1799, with Morris already in debtors'
prison, the Commissioners proposed several methods
by which the trustees could postpone further

-----

[88]Commissioners to RM and Nicholson, Nov. 15,
1797, to the trustees, Nov. 23, 1797, PC, Oct. 18, 19,
Nov. 2, 1797, RG 42, DNA.

[89]May 1, 1798, RG 42, DNA. See also Lee's earlier
opinion, Mar. 20, 1796, Commissioners to John Adams,
Apr. 20, 1798, PC, Sept. 11, 1798, RG 42, DNA; RM to
the trustees, July 12, 1798, RMP, NYPL.

sales of lots until December, 1800. When they received
no answer from the trustees, the Commissioners decided
to renew the sales in the spring for the balance now
due and to sell lots during the summer to cover the
1800 installment. Once more, the Commissioners offered
to delay the sales upon the receipt of $60,000 in
$12,000 installments beginning on April 1. In December,
they agreed to accept only $40,000, but the trustees
would not even meet this payment. In fact, as late as
May, 1801. the trustees had failed to send any
remittances.[90]

The litigation which resulted from the Federal City
purchase lasted until 1850. At the time of Morris'
bankruptcy proceedings, the Financier was understandably
confused about the state of affairs at the capital. He
had no idea of the nature and extent of Nicholson's
incumbrances. He did know that any surplus from the
Aggregate Fund would have to be used to settle 6 riders
totalling $145,000. He and Nicholson had agreed to
divide any remaining money or property into 300,000
shares. Of Morris' 150,000, he had already transferred
53,650 to his creditors.[91] After his release
from prison, Morris still suggested yet another

---

[90]Commissioners to the trustees, Mar. 20, 22, May 2,
June 3, July 12, Nov. 22, 1799, to Stoddert, Dec. 2,
1799, to Dorsey, Jan. 6, 1800, to Thomas Tingey, an
agent for the trustees, May 11, 19, 1801, Trustees to
the Commissioners, Mar. 26, Apr. 27, May 26, 1799,
RG 42, DNA.

[91]Morris, Account of Property, pp. 9-11.

subscription to a Washington lots scheme.[92]

According to the Commissioners' report to the President
early in 1801, Morris and Nicholson owed a balance of
$195,241.43 to the United States. An appended "list of
notes passed for the purchase money of lots sold at public
sale for default in payment by Morris and Nicholson,
revealed that the Commissioners had sold only $39,263.98
worth of lots at public auction.[93]

The Federal City investment ruined Morris, Nicholson,
and Greenleaf. Again and again the two Pennsylvanians
blamed Greenleaf and his failure to negotiate the Dutch
loan as the reason for their financial collapses.
Undeniably, Greenleaf's misuse of funds created unnecessary
difficulties. Morris and Nicholson originally endorsed
Greenleaf's notes because they anticipated repayment from
the Dutch loan. After Greenleaf's failure in October, 1797,
they were responsible for his notes.[94] In spite of Morris
and Nicholson's enthusiasm for the Federal City lots during
their visit in 1796 and 1797, the truth is that the
investment was never promising. Few people cared about
the development of the city, and the prospect for foreign
investment disappeared after the French invasion of
Holland. Even if the Amsterdam loan had succeeded, the

[92]RM to T. Morris, Jan. 9, 1802, RMP, CHHL.

[93]ASP, Miscellaneous, I, 227-28.

[94]For a defense of Greenleaf, see Clark, Greenleaf and
Law, pp. 173-77; for a critique, see Arbuckle, "Nicholson,"
pp. 374-78.

slow sale of lots would have prevented the speculators
from reimbursing the Dutch. Of course, the loan might
have effected a delay in the trio's bankruptcies. But,
by 1797, Morris and Nicholson had no new sources of money
to tap. For the three speculators, the purchase of the
Washington lots was financial suicide.

Morris knew that his financial world was tumbling
by the middle of 1795, and that he had little to show for
his land investments. The proceeds from the sales of his
New York lands went to pay his French creditors. As he
concluded no other significantly successful sales of large
blocks of real estate, he was unable to pay the Commissioners
or his domestic creditors. In an effort to raise funds, he,
Nicholson, and Greenleaf formed the North American Land
Company on the basis of their holdings in Pennsylvania,
Virginia, North Carolina, South Carolina, Georgia, and
Kentucky.

CHAPTER V

THE NORTH AMERICAN LAND COMPANY

The year 1795 was decisive for Morris and Nicholson.
In addition to the lots in the Federal City, Morris,
Nicholson, and Greenleaf jointly purchased over 6
million acres in New York, Pennsylvania, Virginia,
Kentucky, North Carolina, South Carolina, and Georgia
between 1793 and 1795 at a total cost of $1,233,867.43.[1]
When Greenleaf failed to obtain a Dutch loan to help
finance their Federal City investment, the three speculators
found themselves with millions of acres of land, but no
capital. In particular, they needed money to pay the
Commissioners of the District. Since they were already
unable to satisfy their creditors, additional loans were
out of the question. Instead, they combined most of their
joint holdings and a few of their independent purchases into
the North American Land Company. They hoped to sell

[1]"General Account of Lands bought by Robert Morris
and J. Nicholson on acct of Jas Greenleaf & themselves,"
Aug. 1, 1795, RMP, NYPL.

shares to raise funds and to assign them to creditors
for debts or as security for repayment at a later
date.

Officially, the syndicate formed the Company on
February 20, 1795. The Company's holdings consisted
of the following 6,000,000 acres, valued at 50 cents
per acre, in Pennsylvania, Virginia, North Carolina,
South Carolina, Georgia, and Kentucky:

Pennsylvania,

	Acres	Acres
Northampton county	72,000	
Northumberland	217,046	
Luzerne	4,500	
Mifflin	34,328	
Huntingtnn	29,172	
Westmoreland	40,000	
North and west of Allegany and Ohio rivers	250,000	
		647,046

Virginia,

	Acres	
Monongahela county	19,700	
Washington	25,000	
Harrison	44,155½	
Ohio	30,000	
Randolph	18,825	
Montgomery	484,025 3/4	
Greenbriar	156,355	
Russell	20,000	
Kanhaway	134,560	
		932,621¼

	Acres	Acres
North-Carolina,		
Beauford and Hyde counties	200,000	
Rowan county, on Yadkin river	17,199	
Robinson, Moore, Cumberland, Richmond, and Anson counties	500,000	
		717,299
South-Carolina,		
Orangeburgh District	577,875	
Ninety-six	17,034	
Washington	340,680	
Pinkney	1,883	
Camden	15,130	
Cheraw	4,636	
		957,238
Georgia,		
Washington county	1,453,516	
Franklin	320,370	
Effingham	432,910	
Camden	108,000	
		2,314,796
Kentucky,		
Fayette county	150,943	
Jefferson	29,200	
Lincoln	4,000	
Mason	246,000	
		431,043

$$6,000,043\tfrac{1}{2}$$

The three speculators divided the capital stock
of $3,000,000 into 30,000 shares of 200 acres each.

Thomas Willing, the President of the Bank of the
United States, John Nixon, the President of the
Bank of North America, and John Barclay, the
President of the Bank of Pennsylvania, held title to
the land as the Company's trustees. The first members
of the Board of Managers were Morris, Nicholson,
Joseph Ball, Thomas FitzSimons, and John Vaughan. The
Board had the authority to sell company lands and to
lay out roads and towns. The proceeds of sales would be
deposited in one of the trustees' banks. The Company
guaranteed investors an annual dividend of at least 6
per cent per share. As security for the dividend,
Morris, Nicholson, and Greenleaf each deposited
3,000 shares with the trustees to be sold or,
if necessary, transferred, to pay the dividends. After
15 years, the Managers and shareholders would
liquidate the Company.[2] Willing, Nixon, and Barclay

---

[2]The plan of association of the North American
Land Company is printed in Imlay, _Topographical
Description_, pp. 572-85 and includes the property
schedule quoted above. See also Livermore, _Early
American Land Companies_, pp. 162-68.

refused to serve as trustees because of a possible conflict
of interest with their bank positions and because they
thought that they might be held liable if the Company
failed. Jared Ingersoll, the attorney general of
Pennsylvania, Frederick A. C. Muhlenberg, the Speaker
of the House of Representatives, and Matthew Clarkson,
the mayor of Philadelphia, replaced them.[3]

Once again, Morris optimistically assumed that
the inevitable success of this project would solve
his financial difficulties. His new policy was to
sell, but not to buy any additional, lands. In
January, 1795, he refused at least three purchases
in Virginia and the Federal City.[4]

Of all of the land schemes of the 1790's, the North
American Land Company received the most publicity.
From March through June, 1795, Morris and Nicholson
automatically sent shares in the Company to their
European and domestic agents and creditors, who also
received glowing accounts of the value of the lands and
the unquestionable success of the project. Their
correspondents could either sell or retain these shares.
In this light, Morris informed the Willinks that he

---

[3]RM to Greenleaf, Mar. 26, 1795, to Bourne, Apr. 18,
1795, to Willinks, Apr. 18, 1795, RMLB, DLC; Nicholson to
Greenleaf, Mar. 29, 1795, to Barclay and Nixon, Mar. 23,
1795, to Barclay, Willing, and Nixon, Apr. 14, 1795, to RM,
Mar. 27, 1795, JNLB, HSP.

[4]RM to William Fontain, Jan. 6, 1795, to Thomas and
James Cook, Jan. 16, 1795, to Patrick Fontain, Jan. 17,
1795, RMLB, DLC.

intended to send them 1,000 shares in a new plan
"calculated to promote public Good as well as private
benefit...." Settlers could buy land on credit,
and thus "uncultivated Lands will soon become
settled & improved, and thereby the natural strength
and Wealth of the Country is increased." The
principals, in turn, would benefit from the careful
management of their land. To assure the Willinks
of the quality of the land, Morris reminded them
that since he and Nicholson "made the purchases under
the expectation of keeping the Lands for some years
on our own accounts and then of selling to Persons who
would view for themselves, you will readily suppose
that we took every precaution both as to quality
& Title...." In developing the land, Morris proposed
to follow the example set by Charles Williamson in
the Genesee country. The Company would divide
each tract into farms of 100 to 500 acres. The
first 50 families could purchase the land at
$2.00 per acre, payable in annual installments
with interest. At the end of 4 years, Morris
anticipated "such dividends...as will double or

treble the price of the shares...."[5]

    In addition to this letter campaign, Morris
sent his son-in-law, James Marshall, to Europe
to sell his lands, promote subscriptions to the
North American Land Company, and raise a loan for the
Federal City investment. Morris wrote letters of
introduction for Marshall to all European financiers
with whom he had dealings.[6]

---

[5]RM to Willinks, Mar. 8, 16, 1795, RMLB, DLC.
For similar letters, see RM to Craigie, Jan. 13, Feb. 14,
Mar. 24, 1795, to John Pasley of London, Mar. 18, Apr.
3, May 31, July 27, 1795, to William Constable of
London, Mar. 14, 1795, to Bird, Savage, and Bird, Mar.
20, Apr. 4, 11, June 4, 1795, to Colquhoun, Mar. 18,
Apr. 3, May 28, 1795, to Thomas Russell of Boston,
Mar. 23, 1795, to Henry Cheriot, of New York, Mar. 24,
1795, to James Constable of New York, Mar. 24, 1795,
to Richard Soderstrom, Mar. 24, 1795, to Bourne, Mar.
30, 1795, to James Carey of Baltimore, Apr. 3, 20, 1795,
to Pulteney, Apr. 3, 1795, to Bourdieu, Chollet, and
Bourdieu, Apr. 3, 1795, to William Inman of London,
Apr. 22, 1795, to Franklin, Apr. 22, May 14, 1795,
to James B. Nickolls of Alexandria, Apr. 22, May 4,
1795, to Josiah Watson of Alexandria, Apr. 22, 1795,
RMLB, DLC; Nicholson to Colborne, Barrel, and Servanté
of London, Apr. 2, 1795, to Joseph Barnes of London,
Apr. 2, 1795, to Bird, Savage, and Bird, Apr. 2, 1795,
to Enoch Edwards, Apr. 22, 1795, to Samuel Bayard,
May 13, 1795, to Franklin, May 27, 1795, JNLB, HSP.

[6]RM to Willinks, July 18, 1795, to Cranch, July
24, 1795, to Bourdieu, Chollet, and Bourdieu, Oct. 7,
1795, to Marshall, Oct. 15, 16, 17, 1795, RMLB, DLC.
Morris also wrote letters to Richard P nn, Pulteney,
John Pasley, J. H. Cazenove, Nephew, and Company,
Robert Herries, Bourdieu, Chollet, and Bourdieu,
Thomas Pinckney, Parish and Company, Frege, Gramont
and Company (See the list on page 571 of volume 1 of
RMLB, DLC).

Marshall was not the syndicate's only salesman. Soon, Morris and Nicholson had agents swarming all over Europe. Morris employed his son William, Penn, Franklin, Colquhoun, the Willinks, Pasley, and Bayard, while Nicholson engaged James Tate, Joseph Barnes, and Enoch Edwards. At $2,000 per year, Sylvanus Bourne was the highest paid agent, and Morris and Nicholson sent him to England, France, and Switzerland in an effort to dispose of shares. All of the other agents received yearly salaries of $1,000, a 5 per cent commission on all sales, and one-half the proceeds above the minimum price of the land.[7] In trying to sell shares abroad, Morris and Nicholson thus used all of their contacts, including officers of foreign governments, Americans travelling in Europe, and specially appointed agents.

Unfortunately for the speculators, the Company met a cold shoulder both at home and abroad. As early as July, 1795, the Willinks informed Morris that they could not dispose of the 1,000 shares he had sent to them, and shortly after the Company was formed, Cheriot and Craigie refused to accept any shares. Morris should have expected these disappointments. Merchants with capital found it more profitable to invest in foreign commerce during this period. But Morris had not engaged in trade for so long that his ability

---

[7]Nicholson to Barnes, Apr. 2, 1795, to Edwards, Apr. 22, 24, 29, 1795, Nicholson and Morris to Marshall, Oct. 14, 1795, JNLB, HSP.

to make sound business judgments had been handicapped.
The wars of the French Revolution had opened oceanic
trade to neutral American commerce. France, whose
trade was inhibited by Britain's control of the seas,
opened her ports, particularly in the West Indies, to
American vessels. Britain, on the other hand, tried to
use her power on the seas to seize neutral vessels
carrying goods both to and from French possessions.
On January 8, 1794, Britain modified her policy so that
her ships captured only those vessels that traded
directly between Europe and the French West Indies. To
evade this decree, merchants shipped goods to the United
States, where the products were unloaded and then
re-exported to Europe. The merchant received a drawback
of almost all of the import duties. From 1792 to
1801, re-exports in the United States exceeded exports.
Compared with the profits from these transactions,
land investments were not attractive. Titles were
uncertain and capital invested in land was tied up for
a long period of time. Morris, the former "merchant
prince," never took advantage of the profits to be made
from the re-export trade. In fact, his failure to invest
in shipping during this period reveals his lack of
astuteness in business throughout the 1790's. Morris
could not pay his creditors, who wanted money not

stocks in a new Company, and an end to their participation in any future Morris-Nicholson ventures.[8]

The creditors' suspicions about the Company were in fact well founded. If the assertions in the prospectus are measurements of the reliability of Morris and Nicholson, then the two Pennsylvanians were deliberately lying to the subscribers in order to avoid financial ruin. In the plan of association, they claimed "certainty of title" to the 6 million acres included in the Company. In truth, their titles were clouded because of conditional purchases, mortgages on parts of the property, unpaid land taxes, and conflicting Indian claims. In Pennsylvania, for example, the Company supposedly held title to 647,146 acres. Aside from competition from and conflicting claims with the Holland Land Company, Morris and Nicholson had not fulfilled the provision of the 1792 land act that required a settlement on every 400 acres within 2 years. Morris and Nicholson

---

RM to Cheriot, Apr. 9, 1795, to Craigie, Apr. 14, 1795, to Willinks, July 27, 1795, RMLB, DLC. For a discussion of the profitability of trade during the early national period, see Bruchey, Robert Oliver, pp. 78-89. See also Douglass C. North, "The United States Balance of Payments, 1790-1860," in Trends in the American Economy in the Nineteenth Century (Princeton, 1960), pp. 576-79.

took refuge behind section nine of this act, which
delayed the requirement if enemies of the United States,
in this case the Indians, had prevented settlement.
Squatters, however, had already moved on to these
tracts, which they claimed the two speculators had
forfeited by not completing the settlements required
by law. Whether they were right or wrong, their
accusations and activities discouraged prospective
purchasers of land and subscribers to the Company.

Most of Morris and Nicholson's creditors
recognized that the speculators did not have a
clear title to the lands they were selling and refused
to accept any shares in the Company. In effect, the
two Pennsylvanians were trying to sell shares in a
land company to creditors, even though the land they
were peddling was already mortgaged as security for
their debts. In recognition of this fact, the
prospectus contained a complicated procedure for
settling conflicting claims involving titles to
Company lands.[9]

As chapter four covered Morris' Pennsylvania
holdings, the Virginia lands will be discussed first
here. Almost all of the lands included in the
Company can be accounted for. In May, 1794,

---

[9] Plan of Association, pp. 573-75.

the three speculators purchased 73,026½ acres in
Montgomery County, Virginia, from Benjamin Lodge
and James Carnahan, of Westmoreland County, Pennsylvania.
For this land, they agreed to pay $9,736.84 within
two years.[10] That same month, they acquired 45,999½
acres in Montgomery and Greenbrier Counties from
John and Abraham Singer, who immediately received
$3,076.27.[11] The syndicate purchased all of its
20,000 acres in Russell County from Mordecai Piersol
at a cost of $2,000, due by October, 1794.[12] They also
bought 79,015½ acres from Albert Gallatin and Savary
de Valcoulon in Harrison, Greenbrier, Kanhaway,
Monongahela, and Montgomery Counties for $13,169.25,
payable in two years.[13] Another purchase from Jhhn
Beckley accounted for 20,255 in Greenbrier County.
For this land, they paid $5,138.75.[14] They also
gave Levi Hollingsworth $0.25 per acre for 258,000
in Montgomery, 25,000 in Washington, 16,500
in Harrison, 30,000 in Ohio, 3,000 in Greenbrier,

---

[10]"Journal C," f. 1, 13, 20, 21, RMP, HSP.

[11]"Journal C," f. 20, RMP, HSP.

[12]"Journal C," f. 19, RMP, HSP.

[13]"Journal C," f. 14, RMP, HSP.

[14]"Journal C," f. 10, RMP, HSP.

19,700 in Monongahela, and 18,825 in Randolph Counties.
They had to account for these lands by July, 1797.[15]
From Wilson Carey Nicholas, they acquired 1,000,000
acres in Virginia, of which 320,000 in Greenbrier and
Kanhaway Counties became part of the Company. Nicholas hoped to
received $44,444.44 for the 320,000 acres within
three years.[16] A final purchase from Samuel Pleasants
of Philadelphia accounted for 124,000 acres in Montgomery
County at a cost of $24,800, due in three years.[17]

In Kentucky, Morris, Nicholson, and Greenleaf
purchased 109,943 acres in Fayette County, 29,000
in Jefferson, and 4,000 in Lincoln from Hollingsworth
for $0.25 per acre, payable in three years.[18] Another
purchase from Richard Graham of Dumfries accounted for
246,000 acres in Mason County, for which the triumvirate
owed $61,725.[19]

---

[15]"Journal C," f. 52, RMP, HSP.

[16]"Journal C," f. 80, RMP, HSP.

[17]"Journal C," f. 83, RMP, HSP. For all of the Virginia
lands, see Indenture, Mar. 5, 1795, RM, Nicholson,
Greenleaf and Willing, Nixon, and Barclay, "Alexander
Wilcocks' Remarks respecting Titles," Apr. 2, 1795,
NALCP, HSP; "General Account," Aug. 1, 1795, RMP, NYPL.

[18]"Journal C," f. 52, RMP, HSP.

[19]"Journal C," f. 70, 83, RMP, HSP; Articles of
Agreement, July 14, 1795, JNP, PHMC; "Alexander Wilcocks'
Remarks respecting Titles," Apr. 2, 1795, NALCP, HSP.

All of the Company's North Carolina lands can
be detailed. In June, 1794, the three speculators
bought 200,320 acres of swamp land in Beaufort
and Hyde Counties from John Hall and Gideon Denison
for $40,064.00 All but 320 acres of this land
became part of the North American Land Company.
They also acquired 17,299 acres on the Yadkin River
in Rowan County from Thomas Caron and William Moore
for $6,919,60, payable within one year. By the
end of 1796, Morris was forced to advertise these
lands for sale. Their largest North Carolina
purchase consisted of 500,000,acres, which David
Allison sold them for $66,666.67. To pay for these
lands, located in Robinson, Moore, Cumberland,
Richmond, and Anson Counties, Morris and Nicholson
endorsed $50,000 worth of each other's notes.
In addition, they gave Allison 34 lots in the
Federal City worth $11,333.33 and $5,333.34 worth
of North Carolina certificates.[20]

In South Carolina, the three speculators
acquired much more land than they included in

---

[20]RM to Andrew Caldebeugh, Dec. 30, 1796, RMLB,
DLC; Nicholson to RM, May 6, 15, 21, 1795, to
Allison, May 21, Sept. 26, 1795, JNLB, HSP; "General
Account," Aug. 1, 1795, RMP, NYPL; "Journal C,"
f. 52-53, 174-76, 182, 185, 368, 374, 422, RMP, HSP.

the Company, and no documents have been found that
specify which acres were held by the trustees.
On May 20, they purchased of John Hall and Gideon
Denison, 55,872 acres in the Orangeburgh and Ninety-
Six Districts for $9,312.55.[21] Then, in May,
they acquired 904,018 acres in South Carolina,
counties not specified, from Wade Hampton, an
agent of the Blount family, for $120,535.70. Morris
and Nicholson gave Hampton $55,245.85 worth of notes
in favor of and endorsed by each other. Of this land,
300,000 became part of the Company, while Morris
and Nicholson assigned 604,018 acres to James
Marshall for sale in Europe at 50 cents per acre.
By June, 1796, Morris and Nicholson had mortgaged these
lands to Greenleaf, and later, the lands became
part of the Aggregate Fund.[21] In addition, Morris
bought into Nicholson's ownership of 216,513
acres at a cost of $33,679.80. An undated document

[21]"Journal C," f. 174-75, RMP, HSP; "General
Account," Aug. 1, 1795, RMP, NYPL.

[22]"Journal C," f. 139, RMP, HSP; "General
Account," Aug. 1, 1795, RMP, NYPL; Morris, Account
of Property, p. 17; RM and Nicholson to Marshall,
Oct. 16, 1795, RMLB, DLC; Indenture, June 4, 1799,
RM, Nicholson, and the trustees of the Aggregate
Fund, RM Deeds, HSP.

in the North American Land Company Papers lists
Morris and Nicholson as the owners of 423,831 acres
in Orangeburgh District, 177,200 in Cheraw District,
300,000 in Washington District, and 76,492 in
Camden District.[23]

The largest chunk of territory in the North
American Land Company was in Georgia. How the
speculators acquired the 2,314,796 acres in this
state forms a mini-story in the history of land
speculation. In spite of the fact that historians
of Georgia have, without documentation, involved
Morris, Nicholson, and the North American Land
Company in the Yazoo Frauds, no evidence has been
found of a direct connection.[24] On the other hand,

---

[23]"General Account," Aug. 1, 1795, RMP, NYPL;
"Lands in South Carolina belonging to Robert Morris
and John Nicholson," n.d., NALCP, HSP.

[24]The best accounts of the Yazoo fraud are in
Samuel B. Adams, "The Yazoo Fraud," The Georgia
Historical Quarterly, III (June, 1923), 155-65;
Absalom H. Chappell, Miscellanies of Georgia, Historical,
Biographical, Descriptive, Etc.,(Atlanta, 1874), pp. 66-
137; S. G. McLendon, History of the Public Domain
of Georgia (Atlanta, 1924), pp. 35-75, 130-77;
Charles H. Haskins, "The Yazoo Land Companies,"
Papers of the American Historical Association, V,
(Oct., 1891), 61-103; Louise F. Hays, Hero of
Hornet's Nest: A Biography of Elijah Clark, 1733-1799
(New York, 1946), pp. 280-88; Donald A. MacPhee,
"The Yazoo Controversy; The Beginning of the 'Quid'
Revolt," The Georgia Historical Quarterly, XLIX
(Mar., 1965), 23-43; Jane Elsmere, "The Notorious Yazoo
Land Fraud Case," The Georgia Historical Quarterly, LI
(Dec., 1967), 425-42; William E. Heath, "The Yazoo
Land Fraud," The Georgia Historical Quarterly, XVI
(Dec., 1932), 274-91;

Morris and Nicholson did purchase lands in Montgomery,
Washington, and Franklin Counties, which became part
of the Georgia Pine Barrens speculation.

After the American Revolution, Georgia's only
resource was its back lands. In this, the state
was not alone. In 1789, a new state law gave justices
of the peace the authority to issue warrants for
unappropriated lands, which the claimant surveyed
at his own expense. By this process, speculators
easily acquired large tracts. Between 1789 and 1796,
Georgia officials signed warrants for three times as
much land as existed in the entire state. By
1796, the state had granted warrants for 29,000,000
acres, but the 24 counties contained only 9,000,000.
The technique of this fraud was simple. County
officials could issue warrants, which were later signed
by the Governor. Speculators ran the county governments,
and issued warrants, without surveys, by filling in
fictitious boundaries. These warrants were then sold
to other speculators. Thus, the state issued warrants
for 7,436,995 acres in Montgomery County, which contains
only 407,680.[25]

[25]Chappell, Miscellanies, pp. 43-51; Hays,
Clark, pp. 237-38; E. Merton Coulter, Georgia:
A Short History (3d ed., Chapel Hill, 1960), pp.
191-98; Sakolski, Great American Land Bubble,
pp. 141-46.

Speculators who acquired this land from Georgia landholders were unaware that the region was an undesirable waste covered with pine trees. When Morris discovered the truth, he tried to perpetrate the fraud on other unsuspecting purchasers, to whom he claimed that "Timber is convenient to saw Mills & navigable waters, the Lumber more valuable than any other & always commanding Ready Money at the port of Export."[26] Not all of the land that Morris and Nicholson owned in Georgia became part of the North American Land Company.

In 1794, Morris, Nicholson, and Greenleaf purchased a total of 672,000 acres from George Naylor for $41,603.40 in Washington and Franklin Counties. They also bought tracts from John Hall, Samuel Jack, and Gideon Denison, who were themselves dumping Pine Barrens land on unwitting speculators. From Hall, they acquired 52,100 acres in Washington and Effingham Counties for approximately 13 cents per acre, part due in 1795 and the remainder when all the titles were complete. Jack expected to receive $27,733.34 in 3 years for his 108,000 acres in Camden and 100,000 acres in Franklin which he sold to the syndicate. Together Hall and Denison deeded 782,415 acres to

_____

[26] To Marshall, Nov. 10, 1795, RMLB, DLC.

the speculators in Washington and Effingham Counties
at one-sixth of a dollar per acre, payable in two
years. Late in 1794, Morris and Thomas FitzSimons
transferred their ownership of 459,000 acres in Washington
County to Morris, Nicholson, and Greenleaf for thirty-
three cents per acre. In 1795, the syndicate purchased
72,780 acres in Georgia from Harwood and Pryor for
$12,130. The 50,339 acres in Montgomery County
which Zachariah Cox sold to them for $21,428.58
was not included in the Company's holdings.[27] As all
of these properties, minus the tract from Cox,
total 2,245,295, 68,501 acres of the Company's lands
are unaccounted for.

At some point in 1795, Morris and Nicholson
decided to plunge into the Yazoo speculations. During
that year, the Georgia legislature enacted "An Act
supplementary to an Act, entitled, 'an Act for
appropriating a part of the unlocated territory of this
state, for the payment of the late state troops, and
for other purposes therein mentioned,' declaring

---

[27]"General Account," Aug. 1, 1795, RMP, NYPL.
Although the "General Account" lists 2,729,000 acres in
Georgia, some of these lands were actually in South
Carolina. See also "Journal C,' F. 4, 19, 21, 22, 29,
76, 77, 78 79, 175, 176, 177, 183, RMP, HSP; RM to
Greenleaf, Aug. 3, 9, 1793, Etting Collection, HSP;
RM to _____, Nov. 30, 1793, Gratz Collection, HSP;
Proposal, Jan. 5, 1794, RM, Greenleaf, and Naylor, JNP,
PHMC; George Baker to RM and Greenleaf, Nov. 3, 1794,
Articles of Agreement, June 24, 1794, RM, Nicholson,
Greenleaf, and Cox, Baker to Morris and Nicholson,
May 27, 1794, NALCP, HSP.

the right of this state to the unappropriated territory
thereof, for the protection and support of the frontiers
of this state, and for other purposes."[28] This act
authorized the state to sell 35,000,000 acres of
land to the Georgia, Georgia,Mississippi, Tennessee,
and Upper Mississippi companies for $500,000. Morris
and Nicholson owned 2,500,000 acres in the Georgia
Company and 30 shares in the Tennessee Company, purchased
by James Greenleaf. In 1797 this land became part of
the estate turned over to the trustees of the Aggregate
Fund.[29]

When charges of corruption arose in connection
with these Georgia purchases and sales, Morris and
Nicholson found it impossible to dispose of their
holdings in that state or to sell shares in a company that
was based in part on Georgia lands. In April, 1795, Morris
received copies of letters written by Jonas Fauches of Georgia
and Jean Antoine Joseph Fauchet, the French minister to the
United States. The letters, originally published in Paris in
Feuille de la Republique on January 5, 1795, questioned Morris'

---

[28]Jan. 7, 1795, Microfilm Collection of Early State
Records, DLC. See note 22.

[29]RM and Nicholson to Pratt, Aug. 15, 1797, Feb.
28, 1798, RMLB, DLC.

title to the Georgia lands, as well as the quality
of his holdings in that state. Morris wrote a rebuttal
to Fauchet on April 13 and asked his son William to
aid Dr. Enoch Edwards, who was on his way to Paris
to sell North American Land Company shares, in having
his letter to Fauchet published in the French capital.
Morris published the entire correspondence in Dunlap
and Claypoole's American Daily Advertiser, a Philadelphia
newspaper, on June 15, 1795.[30]

As Morris worked to refute Fauchet's charges,
the Yazoo scandal exploded on to the public scene.
Land speculators had apparently bribed all but one of
the Georgia legislators who had voted for the Yazoo
law. On February 13, 1796, a newly elected state
legislature, rescinded the 1795 act.[31]

In addition to these scandals, Morris and Nicholson
faced other problems. They had underestimated the

-----

[30]RM to William Morris, Apr. 26, 1795, to Bourne,
May 21, 1795, to Willinks, May 31, 1795, RMLB, DLC.

[31]"An Act Declaring null and void a certain usurped
act passed by the last legislature of this state, at
Augusta, on the seventh day of January, one thousand seven
hundred and ninety-five, under the pretended title of 'An
Act supplementary to an act entitled, an act for appropriating
a part of the unlocated territory of this state, for the
payment of the late state troops, and for other purposes
therein mentioned; declaring the right of this state to the
unappropriated territory thereof, for the protection of the
frontiers, and for other purposes:' And for expunging from
the face of the public records the said usurped act, and
for declaring the right of this state to sell all lands
lying within the boundaries therein mentioned" (Microfilm
Collection of Early State Records, DLC).

taxation on the property they owned. In 1796 at
least 100,000 acres of their Georgia holdings were
sold at a sheriff's sale.[32]

At no time did Morris, Nicholson, and Greenleaf
have a clear title to all of the lands they incorporated
into the North American Land Company. They had not
completed payments for most of the land, taxes remained
overdue, and some of the lands had already been mortgaged.
In fact, the trustees of the Company received title to
only 4,479,317 acres. Morris and Nicholson lost
part of the property because of a decision against
them in the Pennsylvania Board of Property. At least
200,000 were subject to a caveat, and several of their
surveyors refused to turn over surveys until they had
been paid.[33]

Of a potential 21,000 shares that Morris, Nicholson,
and Greenleaf put on the market, subscriptions totalled
only 391 in May, 1795.[34] At the end of the Company's
first year, Morris and Nicholson scraped together enough
money to pay the first dividend, which amounted to $3,000.

---

[32]RM to Nicholson, Nov. 3, 1795, to Lewis Sewall,
Nov. 27, Dec. 12, 1795, to Cox, July 9, 1796, to FitzSimons,
Sept. 17, 1796, RMLB, DLC.

[33]Nicholson to Greenleaf, May 2, 1796, JNLB, HSP;
Livermore, Early American Land Companies, p. 168.

[34]"North American Land Company Subscribers," JNP,
PHMC.

At the beginning of 1796, Morris, with a show of
renewed optimism, predicted success for the Company.
He informed Franklin that "The Rise which is taking
Place in the price of Lands generally throughout
the United States will enable the Board of Managers
to make sale this Year of some of the Company's
Lands to a handsome profit, consequently the Dividend
for the year 1796 will be higher...."[35] To Colquhoun
Morris **praised** the advantages of the Jay Treaty for
improved Anglo-American relations and commerce, and
added that "as to the Circumstances of this Country and
its Government there is nothing but what ought to insure
Confidence in the highest degree. I think also that there
are existing Circumstances now in England and other parts
of Europe that will tend to make many Capitalists seek
safety to a part of their property by Investments in American
Lands stocks plans & ca.... I only want to sell as many
Shares as will put me out of debt."[36] Morris hoped that
the prompt payment of the 1795 dividend would establish
the credit of the Company at home and in Europe. He
also assumed that the Federal Land Law of 1796, which

---

[35]Jan. 16, 1796, RMLB, DLC.

[36]Jan. 16, 1796, RMLB, DLC.

fixed the price of lands in the Northwest Territory at $2.00 per acre, would spur sales, and that the signing of Pinckney's Treaty, which opened up the navigation of the Mississippi to United States residents, would increase the value of his Southern tracts.[37]

As usual, Morris expected too much. The Managers of the Company concluded no significant sales of shares in 1796. In addition, Morris and Nicholson's creditors refused to accept shares in the Company as payment or as security for debts. Morris, for example, assigned shares to John B. Church in spite of Church's protests. Then, in May, 1796, the Financier wrote to Church angrily:

> You have threatened me with a Public sale of my North American Land Company Shares, which were entrusted to you by me in the expectation that they would on the terms of that Trust, have produced the discharge of my Debt, and it seems to me that the act of transferring those Shares to your name ought to have convinced you that I never wished or designed you to be insecure. I disclaim any fears or apprehensions from threats, and I will not use any....[38]

As with the Washington lots, Morris and Nicholson blamed Greenleaf for their problems. He had failed to meet his payments for their joint land purchases, and his creditors were dunning Morris and Nicholson for payment on notes that they had endorsed for him. Finally the two Pennsylvanians agreed to buy out their troublesome partner. On May 28 they purchased

[37]To Marshall, Jan. 16, Mar. 4, 25, 1796, to Charles W. Byrd, Mar. 17, 1796, RMLB, DLC.

[38]To Church, May 17, 1796, RMLB, DLC. See also Morris to Church, Oct. 9, 17, 1796, RMLB, DLC.

Greenleaf's 10,000 shares for $1,150,000, payable in from
1 to 4 years in notes drawn by Morris on Nicholson and
by Nicholson on Morris. Greenleaf would transfer his
shares to Morris and Nicholson in proportion to their
yearly payments. If his two former partners failed
to meet any installment, Greenleaf could, after a
30 day waiting period and then a 30 day advertisement
in the newspapers, sell enough of his remaining shares
to cover the overdue installment.[39] A year after the
three speculators concluded this agreement, Greenleaf
began suits against Morris and Nicholson for nonpayment.[40]

At that date, however, Greenleaf was not the only
problem facing Morris and Nicholson. Other difficulties
abounded. They were unable, for example, to meet the
1797 dividend. Morris advertised the dividend payments
in the newspapers on January 10, but he asked Nicholson:
"Where is the money?"[41] Agents, surveyors, and taxes
remained unpaid. Morris thanked David Allison for "the
Information respecting No Carolina Taxes which some

---

[39]Articles of Agreement, May 28, 1796, NALCP, HSP;
RM to Nicholson, Jan. 25, 1796, RMLB, DLC.

[40]RM to Nicholson, Oct. 18, 1797, RMLB, DLC;
[Philadelphia] Aurora, Oct. 3, 1796.

[41]Jan. 6, 1797, RMLB, DLC.

how or other must be provided for, altho' under
present Circumstances I find greater difficulty than
ever in getting money."[42] In addition, Morris and
Nicholson could not find anyone interested in serving
as a Company officer for 1797 and 1798.[43]

At least on the surface, Morris remained calm.
The great hopes he expressed in letters to Marshall
early in 1797 are difficult to understand, except on
the assumption that frankness would have worked to his
disadvantage. Surely Morris could not believe that "The
Lands belonging to this Company are getting into repute and
if the management of the concerns is duely attended to,
the plan will be productive of all the advantages that
ever were expected from it," or that the shares
"are more and more valuable as our agents examine the
quality of the lands."[44] Morris obviously did not
want to discourage Marshall from applying all his
energies to the sale of shares in the Company. By
June, Morris admitted to Colquhoun:

> Mr. Marshall not having had it in his power
> to procure for me any pecuniary aid and

---

[42]June 28, 1797, RMLB, DLC.

[43]To Cottringer, Dec. 22, 1797, RMLB, DLC.

[44]Feb. 10, Apr. 27, May 24, 1797, RMLB, DLC.

there being no Sale for real Estates in this
Country for a considerable time past has put
it out of my Power to face my Engagements as
I ought and wish to do.... The General scarcity
of money caused by merchants over trading themselves
& by other People speculating beyond the
proper Bounds, keeps not only me but almost
every body else involved in scenes of
Distress, that my Property ought to have
secured me from, but in the present situation
of things Property seems to be of little or
no use.[45]

Morris not only avoids admitting that he was one of the

"other People speculating beyond the proper Bounds,"

he only obliquely refers to the fact that most merchants

chose foreign commerce over land investments.

In 1797 Morris informed George Harrison that

"The dividends [for 1798] ... ought to be paid but

there is no money in their Treasury and I have none

or I could advance, If it be possible to raise money

on any part of their property the dividends shall be

paid in January next."[46] During 1798, interested

parties had difficulty in locating the Company

offices or officers.[47] Although Morris and Nicholson's

shares in the Company were sold on their bankruptcies,

litigation concerning the Company continued for more

than 75 years.[48]

Once again, Morris' grand plans were shattered. To

some extent, deservedly so. He knew that many of his

land titles were cloudy and that he had failed to inform

---

[45]June 16, 1797, RMLB, DLC.

[46]Dec. 21, 1797, RMLB, DLC.

[47]Arbuckle, "Nicholson," p. 490.

[48]Livermore, Early American Land Companies, pp. 169-71.

purchasers and subscribers of state laws requiring
settlement on and improvement of the land within a
specified period of time. Neither were Morris and
Nicholson justified in blaming Greenleaf entirely for
the Company's failure. As in the case of the Federal
City speculation, his actions only complicated, but
did not create, the difficulties that beset Morris
and Nicholson.

Again, the Financier and his partners had invested
in large blocks of real estate for which they had
unrealistic expectations. They went on a buying spree
in the mid-1790's while most merchants invested in
trade. Since the speculators had no ready cash, they
intended to pay for the land by selling it at a profit.
They would use the surplus to pay creditors and to
meet their living expenses. They not only overestimated
the demand for American lands, they never considered
the possibility that events on the continent would
interfere with their plans by creating more lucrative
investments for United States merchants in foreign
commerce.

The most that Morris should have expected
from the Company was additional time in which to
raise funds to pay his debts. But his creditors,
already annoyed by his financial manipulations,
refused to jump at this new bait. In December,
1797, no doubt existed in Morris' mind that it was

only a matter of time before he entered debtors' prison.
He described his plight to Charles Young, who was himself
in debtors' prison:

> Notes are our bane....Our situation is become
> deplorable, if we ever had friends, they are
> vanished in these our days of trouble, we have
> no money, nor any immediate prospect of obtaining
> any, Our property is up at Public sale and is or
> will be sacraficed in every direction. Most men
> seem willing to plunder but none to assist us....
> If your creditors will take shares in our
> respective plans, or such Lands as we have, at
> a fair price, we will most chearfully give
> them....[49]

The North American Land Company had failed, but
Morris still owned additional tracts. He purchased well
over 1,000,000 acres on his own in the Southern states,
and he had acquired land with Nicholson and Greenleaf
that did not become part of the North American Land
Company. The Financier tried, also unsuccessfully, to
raise money by selling these lands. He could no longer
avoid the sheriff or his creditors.

---

[49]Dec. 4, 1797, RMLB, DLC.

CHAPTER VI

BANKRUPTCY

As a result of his land purchases with Nicholson and Greenleaf, Morris faced bankruptcy in 1797. In the summer of that year he retreated to "The Hills," where he remained until his arrest in February, 1798. All of his last minute efforts to stall his creditors failed.

Morris' independent purchases of land in the middle and southern states had not netted him the great profits he had expected. But the Financier had had no reason to anticipate failure when he began to acquire these tracts in 1794. From 1791 until 1793, he had raised funds by selling lands in Europe. Although his most significant successes were with Genesee lands, he also concluded agreements concerning two other tracts. He failed to perceive that the outbreak of the French Revolutionary wars in 1792 would create conditions that would lead businessmen to invest in foreign commerce and not in land.

Through his former assistant, Gouverneur Morris, the Financier sold Eden Park, an estate in Delaware, to Louis Philippe, Count de Ségur, for 135,000 livres, which at the current rate of exchange of 12 per cent under par equalled £5625 sterling. As tenant in possession of the land, Robert paid £200 or 4800 livres per year as rent. From 1794 to 1796, Gouverneur, as Robert's agent, met

all of the rent payments for the years 1793 to 1797. Still,
in March, 1796, Ségur complained that he had not received
the titles to the land or the maps promised by the 1791
agreement.[1]

In 1795, Morris sublet Eden Park to Robert Richardson.
Then he decided to sell the estate. Morris had purchased
Eden Park without checking the quality of the land. Now
he found himself burdened with excessive expenses resulting
from constant flood damages. The buyer, Samuel P. Moore
of Wilmington, paid $5,000 in cash and assigned to Morris
30,000 acres, valued at $30,000, in Harrison and Ohio Counties,
Virginia. As for Ségur, Morris offered to return his purchase
money, or to give him the $5,000 and the land received from
Moore, or to allow the Frenchman to retain the estate. Ségur
chose to keep the property. After Richardson assigned the
lease to Moore, who took possession in 1796, Moore became
responsible for all further payments to Ségur.[2]

Along with Eden Park, Morris empowered Gouverneur to sell
Dover Estate, a tract of 2,600 acres in Goochland, Virginia.
Morris had purchased this land from John T. Griffin probably in
1790. Gouverneur intended to use the proceeds from a sale of this
property, or to mortgage the estate, to pay LeCouteulx and Company

[1]G. Morris to RM, Sept. 1, 1791, Mar. 12, 1795, Mar. 1,
Nov. 3, 1796, "Receipt signed by Ségur," Sept. 12, 1792, G.
Morris' "Journal," under the dates of June 1, 1792, Sept. 20,
1794, Jan. 2, 1796, GMP, DLC.

[2]RM to Henry Nash, Feb. 5, 1795, to G. Morris, Jan. 18,
1796, to Moore, July 6, 1796, to Richardson, July 15, 1796,
RMLB, DLC; "Journal C," f. 431, RMP, HSP; Morris, Account
of Property, pp. 15-16.

the debt Robert owed them on account of the French tobacco
contracts. In 1792 Gouverneur concluded a sale to Henry
Cardin Jean Baptiste, Count D'Aguesseau, who was Madame de
Ségur's brother. D'Aguesseau paid £20,000 sterling for the
land, and gave Morris a 9 year lease for an annual rental of
£1,000 sterling.[3] From this £20,000, Morris deducted
Gouverneur's commission of £1,000 and his agent's payments
of £18,800.15.10 sterling to LeCouteulx and Company. Thus,
Morris netted only £2199.4.2 from this sale. At the
current rate of exchange, this sum equalled approximately
$9,675. Gouverneur paid D'Aguesseau the rent from 1794
to 1795, and invested, at D'Aguesseau's request, the 1795
sum in 6 per cent stock of the Bank of the United States.
By the end of 1796, Morris was behind in his payments.[4]

In evaluating this sale in 1793, Gouverneur revealed
his doubts about Robert's ability to manage his finances:
"Thus you are now compleatly clear of all Troubles and
Incumbrances whatever in which I most heartily
congratulate you.... And hereon I now claim the
Performance of your Promise that you will wind up
your Affairs and embark no more in any Undertaking

---

[3]G. Morris to LeCouteulx and Co., Oct. 5, 1791, to
RM, Nov. 21, 1791, Dec. 24, 1792, Jan. 6, Feb. 14, Apr. 5,
1793, to R. Morris, Jr., Feb. 20, 1793, GMP, DLC; G.
Morris, Diary, p. 118; "Journal B," f. 18, RMP, HSP.

[4]G. Morris to RM, May 26, 1793, Mar. 12, Dec. 27, 1795,
Nov. 3, 1796, to R. Morris, Jr., May 27, 1793, G. Morris'
"Journal," under the dates of Aug. 23, 1793, Sept. 20,
1794, Jan. 2, 1796, GMP, DLC: "Journal B," f. 354,
RMP, HSP.

which can employ Time or involve Hazard."[5] Gouverneur's
admonition was ill-founded. In 1796 the Financier deeded
Dover Estate to Gouverneur, who continued to manage
and rent it until at least 1801.[6]

As a result of these sales in Europe, Morris was
full of optimism at the beginning of 1794. In addition
to the lands that became part of the North American Land
Company, Morris purchased, with and sometimes without
Nicholson, tracts in the Southern states. On the whole,
these new acquisitions did not directly contribute to
Morris' financial tumble. Rather, like the Genesee
lands, Morris used these holdings, with increasing
difficulty as his creditors grew more cynical about his
promises to pay them, as security for his debts.

For example, in 1794 Morris purchased on his
joint account with Nicholson and Greenleaf, 1,000,000
acres from Wilson Carey Nicholas in Kanhaway, Greenbrier,
and Wythe Counties, Virginia, for $144,444.44. Of
this land, they assigned 320,000 acres in Kanhaway and
Greenbrier Counties to the trustees of the Company.
John Richard, Jr. paid Nicholas in bonds drawn on
the London firm of Alexander Donald and Robert Burton,

---

[5]Feb. 14, 1793, GMP, DLC.

[6]G. Morris to RM, Dec. 26, 1798, Aug. 23, 1799,
Dec. 11, 1800, to Benjamin Harrison, Jr., Dec. 29,
1798, Feb. 24, July 30, 1799, to Peter Baker, Aug. 23,
1799, to William Wiseham, Apr. 20, 1801, GMP, DLC.

which owed Morris money.[7]

Immediately, Morris authorized George and Robert Philips of Manchester to sell or mortgage the entire 1,000,000 acres. In the meantime, between November, 1794 and March, 1795, William Cramond, of the house of Philips, Cramond, and Company, purchased £45475.18.3 sterling worth of Nicholson's bills of exchange, which Morris had endorsed. Morris told Cramond to draw on the Philips' for this money, which they would pay out of the funds arising from the sale or mortgage of the Virginia lands. Morris also deeded the land, in trust, to Cramond as security for the bills of exchange.[8]

By May, 1795, the Philips' had sold only 200,000 acres to William Constable, at Morris' minimum price of one shilling per acre. They had assigned 480,000 to William Morris to dispose of in ance. The Financier now authorized Franklin to inquire into the status of the remaining 320,000 acres and to sell any unsold land at from one to three shillings per acre. As with the Genesee country, he urged Franklin to negotiate with any company that would develop and sell the land to settlers. Any proceeds from such sales should be

---

[7]Abstract of Title to the Robert Morris Tract of 300,000 Acres of Land, Located in McDowell County, West Virginia (n.p., 1878), pp. 1-6; Morris, Account of Property, p. 16; "Journal C," f. 79, 80, 139, RMP, HSP.

[8]Abstract, p. 6; Morris, Account of Property, p. 16; RM to Richard, Jan. 17, Feb. 14, 1795, to Philipses, Mar. 16, 1795, to Cramond, Mar. 14, Apr. 3, 1795, to Marshall, Oct. 10, 1795, RMLB, DLC.

deposited with the Philipses. Morris' instructions
to Franklin offended the Manchester firm, whose partners
correctly assumed that the Financier was dissatisfied with
their efforts. In October, 1795, when Morris authorized
Marshall to assist with sale of these lands, he humbly
explained to the Philipses that "the more persons
employed in a business of this kind, the more are
the Chances of Success multiplied." Although Morris
deeded the land to Cramond on March 13, 1797, as of
1800, Cramond had not disposed of it.[9]

That same year, 1794, the three speculators, who had
already bought 20,500 from John Beckley, bought
an additional 150,000 from him and Andrew Moore for
$50,000 in Western Virginia in Montgomery and Greenbrier
counties. By May, 1797, Morris and Nicholson admitted
that they had not fulfilled the terms of this contract.[10]

On his own, Morris acquired at least 575,000 acres
in Virginia in 1794. James Brackenridge sold Morris
a tract containing 500,000 acres. Morris agreed to
pay $41,666.67 for the land, which was located
in Russell and Wythe Counties. To fulfill this

---

[9] Abstract, p. 6; Morris, Account of Property, p. 16;
RM to Cramond, Aug. 12, 1796, Mar. 12, 14, May 24, Aug. 30,
1797, to Marshall, Oct. 10, 1795, to Nicholas, Mar. 12,
1797, to Franklin, May 14, 1795, to Philipses, Oct. 10,
1795, RMLB, DLC.

[10] RM to Alexander Welch, Aug. 29, 1796, to John
Stuart, May 24, 1797, RMLB, DLC; Nicholson to RM, Sept.
14, 1795, June 7, 1797, JNLB, HSP; "Journal C," f.
182, 183, RMP, HSP.

obligation, Morris assumed Brackenridge's debt of $7714.62
to Joseph Higbee, and assigned bonds totalling $4745.90
to him. Morris agreed to remit the balance in 6 yearly
installments. Although he managed to meet these payments,
he eventually mortgaged the land to FitzSimons as partial
security for yet another debt.[11]

Morris acquired an additional 75,000 acres in
Wythe County from Robert Pollard of Richmond for
$6,250. His partner in this purchase, Adam Hoops,
relinquished his claims to this tract, which was
one of the few still in Morris' possession in 1800.[12]

In spite of the obvious financial problems that
developed for Morris in 1795, he purchased new tracts
in Virginia in 1796 and 1797. In the first case, he
bought 29,959 acres in Harrison and Ohio Counties from
Matthew Pierce for $10,979.67, due within 2 years.
As Morris failed to send any remittances, Pierce began
proceedings to recover the land.[13]

Then, in 1797, he acquired 44,300 acres from Henry

---

[11]RM to James Wadsworth, Dec. 27, 1794, Jan. 10,
1795, RMLB, DLC; "Journal C," f. 113, 115, 266, 276, 305,
353, RMP, HSP.

[12]Morris, Account of Property, p. 16; "Journal C,"
f. 113, 114, 132, 280, 425, RMP, HSP.

[13]Morris, Account of Property, p. 17; "Journal C,"
f. 277, RMP, DLC.

Lee in Hardy and Shenandoah Counties for $37,037.66.
William Cooper, of Otsego, New York, to whom Lee had
already sold 38,000 acres of this land, agreed to convey
his holdings to Morris. In return, Morris assigned to
Cooper the debt due to him from William Inman, which was
secured against 50,000 acres on the Black River in New
York. By 1800 Morris had mortgaged these Virginia lands
to FitzSimons as security for a debt.[14]

In Kentucky, the Financier fared no better. He
was unable to hold on to his property. In 1788,
for example, he bought 44,000 acres from John T.
Griffin. He sold all but 9,000 acres to pay several
debts. He then assigned the remainder, in trust,
to Rawleigh Colston because of money Morris owed to
the heirs of one Thomas Webb. In February, 1799,
Colston obtained a judgment against Morris and
Carter Braxton for $9,321.83 still due to Webb's
heirs.[15]

During the 1794 buying spurt, Morris expanded his
Kentucky holdings to include 161,937-1/2 acres owned by
William Bell. For these lands, located along Licking,

---

[14]Morris, Account of Property, p. 17; "Journal C,"
f. 236, 246, RMP, HSP; RM to Inman, Mar. 30, 1797, to
Richard, May 5, 1797, RMLB, DLC.

[15]Morris, Account of Property, p. 19; "Journal C,"
f. 416, RMP, HSP; RM to Colston, Oct. 14, 1797, RMLB, DLC.

Clifton, and Rough Creeks, and the Ohio and Sandy Rivers, the Financier assigned to Bell the Franklin Park Estate in New Jersey, valued at $10,000, and a bond for $1333.33. Of the land he purchased from Bell, Morris awarded 10,000 acres to Alexander Mackey. In 1796 he conveyed the remaining 151,937-1/2 acres to Humphrey Marshall, who was empowered to sell it to pay taxes, charges, and $20,000 for debts due to him from the Financier. After these obligations were met, the land was liable to James Marshall for $40,000 he had advanced on his father-in-law's behalf in Europe.[16]

Two years later, Humphrey Marshall assigned to Morris his contract, dated October 24, 1795, with General George Rogers Clark, for the purchase of 74,000 acres near the mouth of the Tennessee River in Kentucky. Morris agreed to pay Clark 50 cents per acre if he freed the land from all Indian and military claims. The Financier later added this land to those tracts assigned to cover his debt to FitzSimons.[17]

The same story applied in North Carolina, where in 1795 John Wilkes Kittera sold Morris

[16]Morris, Account of Property, pp. 18-19; "Journal C," f. 287, 378, 406, RMP, HSP.

[17]RM to Byrd, Nov. 11, 1795, to Marshall, June 3, 1796, to Colston, Oct. 14, 1797, RMLB, DLC.

199, 480 acres in Burke County for $26,597.33. The
Financier's son, Robert, and his bookkeeper, Garrett
Cottringer, were his partners in this transaction.
Morris added this land to James Marshall's growing
list of lands to sell or mortgage in Europe. Always
the optimist, the Financier assured his son-in-law that
"a few years will fill that whole Country with Settlers
and as you know perfectly well the effect which Settlements
have on the Value of Lands it is needless for me to detail
them to you." Although he considered it a low price,
Morris asked only one shilling sterling per acre "In
Consequence of my want of Ready Money." By 1800, the
lands had been sold for taxes.[18]

Yet, in spite of all these holdings, Morris' final
scheme to extricate himself from his financial difficulties
involved only his Pennsylvania lands. He formed the
Pennsylvania Property Company in the spring of 1797 in
order to save his holdings in his home state from sheriff's
sales. Inevitably, Morris burdened Marshall with some
of the shares for sale in Europe, and he began assigning
shares, at will, to various creditors.[19]

In all, Morris conveyed the following 10 pieces of land

---

[18]RM to Marshall, Sept. 24, 1795, RMLB, DLC;
Morris, Account of Property, p. 18.

[19]RM to FitzSimons, Apr. 3, 1797, to Marshall, Apr.
3, 1797, to Joseph Karrick, May 25, 1797, to Stephen
Higginson, June 2, 1797, RMLB, DLC; Plan of Association,
Mar. 18, 1797, BCHS.

to trustees James Biddle and William Bell:

Land	Acres	Value	Value Less Incumbrances
The Hills	300	$150,000	$150,000
Trout Spring	160	158,000	128,000
Morrisville	2,500	250,000	149,333.33
Somerset County	40,000	80,000	50,000
Cunningham's District	90,000	240,000	240,000
Northumberland and Mifflin Counties	80,500	107,313	107,313
Northumberland, Mifflin and Northampton Counties	106,875	142,498	49,498
Westmoreland, Bedford, Green, and Northumberland Counties	60,000	60,000	60,000
Northampton and Luzerne Counties	85,000	170,000	119,000
Northumberland County	2,023	8,092	4,092

Thus, Morris valued this land, free of incumbrances, at $907,236.33. In his Observations on the formation of the Company, Morris began: "It is usual amongst mankin to depreciate property brought into public view, under circumstances like the present; but as that which is contained in this Schedule is mostly been the choice of many years it must be acknowledged to be in almost every instance very valuable, and may reasonably be expected to command sales at prices higher than those at which it is estimated." Because "the present moment is unfavorable for sales, on account of the uncommon pressure for money which is universally felt," the Board of Managers could either

wait to dispose of the land or sell it on credit for more
than the estimated value. Morris emphasized, or rather
overworked, the idea that Pennsylvania's back lands were
limited in quantity, extremely desirable, and destined to
increase in value as long as the population increased.
The Company was composed of 10,000 shares worth $100 each.
Morris promised stockholders an annual dividend of at least
$6.00 per share.[20]

At the same time, Nicholson organized the Pennsylvania
Land Company. The capital consisted of Nicholson's property
in his home state, which he valued at $4,000,672.63.[21]
Neither Company succeeded.. The lands were encumbered, the
chance of profit for prospective subscribers slim, and Morris
and Nicholson's creditors were themselves in need of cash
to pay debts.

Tract by tract, Morris saw his land fall into the hands
of his creditors. The Financier's Pennsylvania lands were
the hardest hit. Suits sprang up in the courts on all sides
as creditors hounded Morris and Nicholson for payment.
Land, and most especially encumbered land, was not an

---

[20]Plan of Association, Mar. 18, 1797, BCHS; "Schedule
of Property," RMP, DLC, RMP, HSP; RM to Jacob F. Levy,
June 30, 1797, RMLB, DLC; Morris, Account of Property,
p. 14; Wilkinson, "Land Policy," pp. 282-88.

[21]Arbuckle, "Nicholson," pp. 289-90, 494.

acceptable substitute for cash. Creditors wanted
money, not mortgages on already encumbered estates.
Most of the suits involving Morris and Nicholson
concerned notes issued by one and endorsed by the
other. Morris saw no difference between these
notes and the "long bobs" and "short bobs" he had
issued during the Revolution. Both, in fact, passed
for currency.[22] In September, 1795, Joseph Drinker
brought suit against Nicholson in the Pennsylvania
Supreme Court for nonpayment of a note he held drawn
by Nicholson in favor of Morris for $669.07, dated May
28, 1795, and payable in 30 days. During the same
session, Drinker also sued Morris as the indorser
of Nicholson's note.[23] By the middle of 1797, Morris
and Nicholson barracaded themselves in their respective
country estates, and refused to leave the grounds for
fear of arrest by the sheriff.[24] Morris soon

---

[22]See, for example, Robert G. Harper to Charles
Carroll, Jan. 10, 1801, Robert Goodhoe Harper Family
Papers, Maryland Historical Society.

[23]"Mr. Wells' Judgments," n.d., JNP, PHMC.

[24]Joseph Reed to James Gibson, July 30, 1796, John C.
Wells to Alexander Wilcox, Mar. 9, 1797, "Account of Sundry
Executions against John Nicholson Esqr.," Feb. 15, 1795,
"List of Casas and Fifas, May 29, 1797, JNP, PHMC; MS Minutes
of the Pennsylvania Supreme Court, Eastern District, Sept.,
1797, Nov., 1797, Nov., 1799, PHMC.

discovered that his 90,000 acres in Allegheny County had been mortgaged to John Cunningham and Dunning McNair for $40,000.[25]

A similar fate awaited his Morrisville estate. In 1794, the Insurance Company of North America agreed to purchase 100 shares of stock in the Bank of Pennsylvania from Robert Morris at $460 per share. The Company advanced the money, but the Financier never delivered the shares. Instead, as security, he mortgaged his Morrisville estate to the Company on January 1, 1795. Before the year had ended, Morris also mortgaged Morrisville to George Clymer, to whom the Financier owed $25,000 because of his purchase of Clymer's house on Chestnut Street. On June 9, 1798, the sheriff sold the Bucks County estate to George Clymer and Thomas FitzSimons for £41,000, Pennsylvania currency.[26]

---

[25] Robert Morris' Property, p. 2. Agreement, McNair and John Field and Son, n.d., Misc. MSS., NYHS.

[26] Indenture, Jan. 1, 1795, RM and the Insurance Company of North America, Indenture, Dec. 3, 1795, RM and George Clymer, BCRD; Deed to Clymer and FitzSimons, Aug. 6, 1798, Bucks County Box, HSP; "Journal C," f. 131, RMP, HSP; Morris, Account of Property, p. 13; Davis, Bucks County, pp. 658-59; Marquis James, Biography of a Business, 1792-1942: Insurance Company of North America (Indianapolis, 1942), pp. 54-72.

In 1794 Morris had borrowed $30,000 from the
Insurance Company of Pennsylvania. To secure this loan,
he mortgaged his estates called "The Hills" and "Trout
Spring" to the Company. Then, in December, 1796, he
mortgaged his Chestnut Street residence to the Willinks
as partial security for his debt to them of $139,000.
On September 15, 1797, the sheriff advertised the
Chestnut Street house and "The Hills" for sale, but
Morris begged for additional time from his creditors.
Finally, in December, 1797, William Sansom, Joseph Ball,
John Reed, and Standish Forde purchased the house at a
sheriff's sale. Early the next year, Reed and Forde also
purchased "The Hills" and "Trout Spring" at a similar sale.
After Morris' debt to Reed and Forde was paid, they
agreed to use the surplus from the sale of these estates
to satisfy Morris' debts to the Willinks and the Insurance
Company.[27]

Morris saw his impending defeat as early as December,
1796, but never accepted it as a just loss. He had
fallen upon hard times and expected understanding and
generosity from his creditors out of respect for his
pre-war reputation as a merchant and out of gratitude
for his services as Financier. As Morris

---

[27]RM to Jonathan Penrose, Dec. 9, 1797, to William
Sansom, Dec. 8, 1797, to Nicholson, Feb. 3, 1798, to
FitzSimons, Jan. 21, 1798, to Edward Tilghman, Jan. 3,
1798, RMLB, DLC; "Journal C," f. 98, 239, 240, 358, RMP,
HSP; Morris, Account of Property, pp. 11-12; Watson,
Annals, III, 262-63.

saw one commercial house after another fail in the

winter of 1796, he wrote to Nicholson, who was in the

Federal City:

> You have no Idea of my present situation. It is
> become precarious in the Extreme, and I hardly
> know which way to turn myself. The Casas out
> against me for your account and my own amount
> to about $19000. I sent notes to the Sheriff
> for $19500, he tryed the market & they would not
> melt, being Reed & Forde endorsed by McClenachan &
> Moore and vice versa and Charles Young endorsed
> Mr Taylor & Forrest & Stoddert without Endorsers
> here. He has sent them back and says that
> either he or I must be taken into Custody
> tomorrow if the money be not produced. I am
> pressing J Ball to come to my relief & Believe
> he will do it, & on him at present I depend. You
> will hear of Jno Barclays Defalcation. His affair
> & B McClenachans plays the Devil, the latter has
> been conveying Property to his Children and his
> Creditors are up in Arms. If I survive tomorrow
> and Keep clear of the Sheriff it will help us, but
> at present the Town says I am tomorrow to be placed
> along side of Poor Wilson. I find that this is
> beléived, & Even Amringe fights Shy waiting for
> the Issue. I am out of money & shall not be able
> to get any untill the fiery Trial of tomorrow is
> over. If I get through that, then comes on Fifa
> in great force, it will require a great deal of
> money to allay her spirit, her Votaries are fierce
> and furious, and for one Sample take a Copy of the
> resolution of the Bank of the U.S. in answer to
> the Letter I wrote them. I shall fight hard to
> weather the storm, but God knows how it will end.
> Some how or other these Judgements must be
> satisfied before the end of this month & the
> amot is very good.[28]

Morris temporarily satisfied Sheriff Baker with a

payment of $5,000 plus "the rest in Train to be

paid tomorrow, next day & so on...."[29]

After Nicholson returned to Philadelphia, Morris'

---

[28]Dec. 11, 1796, RMLB, DLC; See also RM TO Nicholson,
Dec. 4, 1796, RMLB, DLC.

[29]   to Nicholson, Dec. 13, 1796, RMLB, DLC.

spirits revived. He firmly held to the legitmacy of
his position. He was sorry that he could not pay
his creditors, but he had managed his affairs as
ably as he could and they would just have to be
patient. He informed Cranch "that the disappointments
& Wants to which you have been exposed have not
arisen from neglect or any other Causes than the
impossibility of raising money."30 He pleaded with
James Dunlop, a creditor who had endorsed Morris
and Nicholson's notes to the Bank of Columbia, for
more time:

> I must confess that appearances are so strongly
> against us as to justify your apprehensions. The
> situations of Money Matters in this City is at
> least as bad as in any other part of the United
> States and I beleive [sic] that universal Distress
> is prevalent, Personal Confidence is destroyed and
> the few that have possession of Money are afraid
> to part with it on any real Estate because altho
> their money be ultimately safe, yet that kind
> of Security cannot assure punctual Reimbursement.
> Under this situation of things our Expectation
> of raising Money by sales of Property or upon Loan
> has hitherto been defeated. We are run very hard
> and are in great Want, but Hope, the great Sweetner
> of Life stands by us if nothing else does, and under
> the influence of this divine Goddess we continue our
> Zealous Endeavors to acquire the needful & we have not
> a View of obtaining about $8000 to $10,000 towards
> the notes on which your name and Mr. Carletons is....
> With respect to the Commissioners we consider their
> Advertizement as put forth for their own Justification
> and only to be carried into Effect in case we fail
> to make monthly Payments to them.... You may depend
> on our Exertion and attention. Everything we can
> accomplish shall for our own sakes be accomplished
> & our Diligence shall be doubled for your sake.31

30May 14, 1797, RMLB, DLC.

31June 10, 1797, RMLB, DLC.

Which of Morris' creditors actually sent him
to debtors' prison is not known. On September 16,
1797, Amos Alexander and William Whare asked for
a writ against Morris for an unpaid debt of $20, 19.44,
and William Clifton did the same for Morris' debt to
him of $5,015.75. On December 30, 1797, Blair
McClenachan had the sheriff issue a writ for $16,017.71.
John Ely and John Bell signed orders committing Morris
to debtors' prison early in 1798.[32] From the Financier's
correspondence, Charles Eddy appears to have been
the man. On February 14, 1798, Morris informed
Nicholson that he was sending "for Jno Baker that I
may surrender myself to him rather than to Charles
Eddy."[33] On the next day, the former merchant prince,
while in the sheriff's custody, wrote pitifully to his
partner: "As I believe you want money as much, if
not more than I do at this moment I return the
forty dollars received in your note of this day, with
thanks for the kind intention."[34] Arrested on the 16th,
he described his confinement as "attended with disagreable

---

[32]Writs by Alexander and Whare and Clifton, RMP,
DLC: Benson J. Lossing, "The Arrest of Robert Morris,"
The American Historical Record, II (1873), 229; Henry
Simpson, The Lives of Eminent Philadelphians, Now
Deceased (Philadelphia, 1859), p. 713.

[33]RMLB, DLC.

[34]RMLB, DLC.

and uncomfortable circumstances, for having no
particular place allotted for me, I feel myself
an intruder in every place into which I go."[35] In
1798, William B. Wood, an actor who was also in the
Prune Street prison, described Morris' behavior:

> His person was neat, and his dress, although
> a little old-fashioned adjusted with much
> care....
>
>   Mr. Morris appeared cheerful, returned
> my salutation in the politest manner, but
> in silence, continuing his walk, and dropping
> from his hand, at a given spot, a pebble on
> each round, until a certain number which he
> had in his hand was exhausted. For some
> mornings the same silence prevailed, until
> at length, observing my languid deportment,
> he suddenly stopped, inquired whether I was
> ill, and added, with something like severity:
> "Sir, this is but an ill place for one so
> sickly, and apparently so young." He seemed
> to wait for some kind of explanation, which
> I found myself either unable or unwilling to
> give and then passed on. From this time he
> spoke to me almost daily, and always with
> great kindness. On one occasion he unbent
> much more than usual, and offered some remarks
> which embraced much good counsel. In more
> than one instance he favored me with frienly
> notice.[36]

On November 27, 1798, in a dramatic show of friendship,
Washington, who was in Philadelphia for meetings

---

[35]RMLB, DLC.

[36]Wood, Personal Recollections of the Stage,
Embracing Notices of Actors, Authors, and Auditors
During a Period of Forty Years (Philadelphia, 1855),
pp. 38-39

[37]John C. Fitzpatrick, ed., The Diaries of George
Washington, 1748-1799 (4 vols; Boston, 1925), IV, 289.

concerning the organization of the additional army
to be raised for the Quasi-War, dined in prison with
Morris.[37] Then, in 1800, Nicholson joined Morris in
debtors' prison, where, until his death on December 5,
1800, he edited a newspaper aptly entitled, The
Supporter or Daily Repast.

Historians and contemporaries of Morris' have
long debated the question of the morality of Morris'
imprisonment. One either contends that a man, who
once served his nation as Morris had, should be
forgiven for later sins, or one holds that all men,
regardless of past services, exist equally under the
law. Morris' failure and imprisonment, along with the
general commercial recession of the late 1790's,
brought about agitation for a national bankruptcy
act.

The issue of bankruptcy legislation was not new, but
with the commercial prosperity of the 1790's demands for
such legislation subsided. Only with the business failures
of 1796 and 1797 did Congress respond to the increasing
support for a national bankruptcy law. On April 4, 1800,
Congress enacted "An Act to establish an uniform system
of bankruptcy throughout the United States." Essentially
a Federalist Bill, it favored the moneyed classes.

The provisions applied only to a "merchant, or other person, actually using the trade of merchandise, by buying and selling in gross or by retail or dealing in exchange, or as a banker, broker, factor, underwriter, or insurer." On the request of one creditor for a debt of $1,000, two for $1,500, or three for $2,000, the Federal Court would appoint a commission of bankruptcy. If two-thirds of the debtor's creditors, in number and value, agreed, the bankrupt would be discharged.[38]

On July 28, 1801, Judge Richard Peters of the District Court of the United States for Pennsylvania, issued a commission of bankruptcy against Morris, and appointed John Hallowell, Joseph Hopkinson, and Thomas Cumpston as the commissioners. Approximately 61 creditors proved their debts against Morris, which amounted to $2,948,711.11, mainly in unpaid Morris-Nicholson notes.[39]

In accordance with the commissioners' instructions, Morris prepared "a full disclosure and discovery of his

---

[38]2 Stat. 19-36; Annals of Congress, IX, 50, 51, 68, 110, 115, 116, 125, 126, 388-89, 508, 519, 533-34; George P. Bauer, "The Movement Against Imprisonment for Debt in the United States" (unpublished Ph.D. dissertation, Harvard University, 1935), pp. 79-80; 114-23; Charles Warren, Bankruptcy in United States History (Cambridge, 1935), pp. 6, 12, 19.

[39]Morris' bankruptcy proceedings and papers are in RG 21, Records of the United States District Court for the Eastern District of Pennsylvania, Robert Morris Bankruptcy Case Records, DNA.

estate and effects." His reports were published at
an unknown date in a pamphlet entitled In the Account
of Property. In this pamphlet, he explained, as best he
could, all of his land purchases, and provided the
commissioners with an inventory of articles found in
his rooms at the prison. He also listed and described
all of the accounts which remained open on his books.[40]

The first part of his pamphlet was inevitably
incomplete, although remarkably accurate with regard
to those purchases that Morris did discuss. The items
in the inventory, which Edward Fox and Garrett
Cottringer valued at $403, is interesting. First,
it shows the true state of poverty to which the Financier
and his family had been reduced. All of their furniture
had been sold, and Mrs. Morris lived on items she had
borrowed from FitzSimons and Marshall. Most significant,
however, is Morris' list of the records and accounts
then in his possession. If he did destroy the records
of his transactions in the 1780's and 1790's, he waited
until after his release from prison, because they
were all available in 1800-1801.

In th list of open accounts, Morris assures
the Commissioners that there is money still due to him.
Frequently, as with Matthew Clarkson, John Willcocks,

---

[40](Philadelphia, n.d.).

William Crouch, the account remained unsettled. Others, such as Samuel Delap and James Nielson, died insolvent. On most of these unsettled accounts, Morris generously gives himself benefit of the doubt and assumes that a final settlement would reveal a small sum in his favor. In describing his relations with Nicholson, Morris unjustifiably viewed himself as the reluctant participant:

> ...a heavy balance will be found due to me on the accounts depending between this my fellow sufferer and myself, probably upwards of $600,000 specie, when all entries are made that the transaction require.
>
> With the purest Intentions, he unfortunately laid a train that ended as it hath done, I here say he laid the train, because there are living witnesses, that I opposed as soon as I knew it, altho' from Infatuation, Madness, or Weakness, I gave way afterwards.

As the bulk of Morris' debts stemmed from those infamous Morris-Nicholson notes, the Financier clearly addressed himself to this problem:

> It is well known that Mr. Nicholson and myself owe a very large debt by Notes drawn and endorsed by each. The issuing of these notes, is the blameable part of our conduct, which we have both felt and acknowledged. But as no use can arise to the holders of such Paper from any Reflections, I can now make, I will forbear any attempt to justify that Business; altho' circumstances might be adduced that would at least soften the disposition to censure.
>
> I do not pretend to name the amount of notes out as I have not a correct account of what was issued, nor what has been paid or otherwise satisfied. Mr. Nicholson was to have kept a Register thereof, but when I entered with him into an examination it was found very

> inaccurate, therefore the Amount of these
> Notes that are or may be proved before the
> Commissioners, must be taken as the nominal
> Amount that remain unsatisfied. As to the
> value received for them,--I must be silent.

Judge Peters released Morris from prison on August 31,
even though the proceedings remained unsettled until
December 4. Once free, Morris' confidence surfaced, and
although he was "a free Citizen...without one cent" he asked
fellow merchants about the possibility of reestablishing his
business. When they responded unenthusiastically, Morris
vainly assumed that their lack of confidence was the result
of the blow dealt to American commerce by the establishment
of peace between Britain and France.[41] Actually, his reputation
was not completely shattered. On March 12, 1801, Thomas
Jefferson informed his Secretary of State, James Madison: "What
a misfortune to the public that R. Morris has fallen from his
height of character. If he could get from confinement, and
the public give him confidence, he would be a most valuable
officer in that station [Secretary of the Navy] and in our
council. But these are two impossibilities in the way."[42]
Morris lived in a house on Twelfth Street, between Market and
Chestnut Streets, until his death in 1806 on the pension
secured for him by Gouverneur Morris from the Holland Land
Company.

The disposition of his land and the satisfaction
of his creditors remained an issue until at least the

[41]RM to T. Morris, July 29, Aug. 27, Dec. 5, 1801,
RMP, CHHL.

[42]Quoted in Oberholtzer, Morris, p. 353.

1890's. On December 8, 1801, at the request of Morris'
creditors, the Commissioners of Bankruptcy assigned
his estate and effects to John R. Smith, John Craig,
and William Field, as trustees. All three men refused
the trust. In 1825, Henry Morris, Robert's son, applied
to have the commission vacated and superseded, because
Morris' estate "had been wasted and misapplied without
benefit to the creditors or the bankrupt." Judge
Joseph Hopkinson of the District Court granted this
petition in 1830, and in 1836 he rejected the request
of William Sansom, a creditor, to reinstate the commission.
On August 1, 1839, Morris' surviving creditors met in
Philadelphia to protest the court's decision by which
"the property of a confessed bankrupt has been taken
from his creditors by a court of justice, and given to
his family, upon the allegation that his creditors were
not making a diligent use of it." This Committee of
creditors appointed a submommittee to inquire into "the
extent the value and situation of the property of Robert
Morris, to consult, counsel as to the most effectual
means of making that property available to the creditors,
and to institute such proceedings in the courts of justice,
or such applications to the legislature, as may be
advised."[43] This effort appears to have failed.

---

[43]At a very numerous Meeting of the Creditors of
"Robert Morris, A Bankrupt," and John Nicholson, held
pursuant to public notice, and adjournment at Evan's
Hotel, George Street, the following Report and
Resolutions were submitted, spproved and adopted,
Aug. 1, 1839, HSP.

Still, Morris' title to certain tracts continued
to haunt the courts until the end of the nineteenth
century. In 1891, J. W. Maynard, of the United States
Circuit Court, delivered his opinion on the largest
realty suit ever begun in Pennsylvania up to that
date. The suit pitted the Robert Morris Land and Coal
Company against the Reading Railroad Company. Stewart
Newell, of New York, was president of the Land and Coal
Company, which had been formed specifically for this
suit. At issue was 8,949 acres in Northumberland County
that Morris had purchased in 1793 in the names of Thomas
Grant, James Davidson, Deborah Grant, and others. In
1794 Morris sold this land to Nicholson. In 1802, after
Nicholson had died intestate, his heirs authorized William
P. Farrand to sell the acres for them. The land passed
from Farrand to Henry K. Strong to H. Hoff to Stewart
Newell, who acquired the tract in 1849. At that date,
the Reading Coal and Iron Company and the Reading Rail
Road Company, which jointly operated the land, refused
Newell the right of entry on to the tract, then worth
$30,000,000. In 1891 Newell reached a settlement
with V. H. Wheeler, who represented the companies.
The two men agreed to combine their property and
divide it into 10,000 shares, which might be used to
form one or more coal companies. A similar suit
involved 10,000 acres in Northumberland, Schuylkill,
and Columbia Counties. There, in 1872, Wheeler
and Newell conveyed the rights to the 10,000 acres,

in trust to Francis Jordan, who also had a claim to the tracts involved.[44]

During the same period, Morris' heirs in Ohio initiated a suit in New York to recover land in western New York, then valued at $50,000,000. The Financier had mortgaged this property to the Holland Land Company, whose affairs were settled in 1845 by the Farmer's Loan and Trust Company of New York. According to Morris' heirs, irregularities in the proceedings of the Dutch concern gave them title to some of the lands disposed of by the Loan and Trust Company. No further record of this suit has been found.[45] A later article in the New York Herald states that Congress enacted a law in the late 1880's to reimburse the heirs of Morris $1,500,000, but no such statute appears on the books.[46]

Thus, the merchant prince ended his career in poverty. Scholars who study his career prefer to concentrate on his successful years as a merchant and his administration of the office of Superintendent of Finance. Yet, his later years are equally revealing of the man. The eternal optimist, the infallible

---

[44]These suits are described in two different pamphlets, which are both entitled Opinions in Reference to the Title to twenty-five Tracts of Coal Lands situated in the Counties of Northumberland, Columbia and Schuylkill, Pennsylvania, with Abstract of Title (Philadelphia, n.d.).

[45]The New-York Times, Oct. 15, 1890.

[46]June 2, 1891.

Financier, Morris plunged head on into speculations in
all phases of the nation's economic life because of his
belief in the United States' inevitable growth, and thus,
his expectations of immediate profits. He rarely
questioned the wisdom or scope of his investments. When
he invested in land in the 1790's, he abruptly ended his
mercantile career. The land market, however developed
slowly, and Morris had no funds to draw on for his personal
expenses. Already in trouble because of the French tobacco
contracts, Morris counted on his speculations in land to
relieve his situation. If he had stopped with the Genesee
country, he might have succeeded. But his involvement
with Nicholson and Greenleaf was the equivalent of a lease
on an apartment in Philadelphia's debtors' prison.[47]

On the basis of his activities in the 1790's,
historians must reconsider certain assumptions about
Robert Morris, the Financier. Was he growing senile
throughout the decade or was he the victim of his own
enthusiasm regarding the growth of the new nation? To
what extent was his bankruptcy the result of poor business
judgment on his part and what roles were played by luck
and bad timing? If Morris was largely responsible for his

[47]For defenses of Morris, see John Kennedy, The Genesee
Country (Batavia, 1895), p. 65; Katharine Beals, "The Land
Speculations of a Great Patriot," Bulletin of the Business
Historical Society, III (Apr., 1929), 1-9; A. M. Sakolski,
"Robert Morris, Patriot and Bankrupt," Nation's Business,
XVIII (Apr., 1930), 36-38, 202-06; Morris Weisman, "The
Bankruptcy of Robert Morris," Commercial Law Journal, XLV
(July, 1940), 163-66.

own decline, does this conclusion call for a reassessment
of his earlier career to determine if he really had
superior financial talents or if the odds were simply more
in his favor during his younger years?

Morris' choice of investments during the 1790's
raises questions about his awareness as a businessman.
After the failure of the French tobacco contracts, he
turned his back on all future trade activities. He must
have known of the profits other businessmen were reaping
from expanding foreign trade, but he failed to take
advantage of any such opportunities throughout the decade.
Instead, he invested all of his capital in the land market,
which tied up assets for years. Morris' greatest error in
judgment in the 1790's was his failure to diversify his
investments by putting some of his available funds into
the re-export trade. Unlike other businessmen, he never
anticipated the fact that the outbreak of war between
France and Great Britain would result in increased
opportunities for American neutral shipping. In short,
he was blind to all investments except for land, and in
this respect, he appears as one of the less perceptive
entrepreneurs of the period.

Morris' failure is also, in large part, a condemnation
of the land policies of the state and federal governments.
Indeed, all levels of government sought to use the public
lands to raise funds. The fact that many of the leading
state politicians were also the nation's largest

speculators only increased the opportunities for
corruption in securing title to large tracts of valuable
land at the expense of soldiers and individual settlers.

In the end, however, Morris must bear the
responsibility for his financial tumble. Surely he knew
the risks of issuing notes for which he had no funds to
pay. Speculators began speculating in Morris-Nicholson
notes, which in 1797 sold for a maximum of ten cents on
the dollar.[48] He was also a careless purchaser, who
bought land on the recommendation of men he hardly knew.
He never checked if the title to the land was encumbered
or if the surveys sent to him were accurate. In the case
of his Georgia holdings, the salesmen were themselves
speculators looking to unload worthless or nonexistent
lands. In that state, Morris found himself the unwitting
victim of a fraudulent land deal.

In the simplest terms, Morris had overextended himself.
The land market did not yield a profit until the early
1800's, and Morris' creditors, also in financial
difficulties, could no longer wait for payment. Friends,
such as Washington and Gouverneur Morris, remained loyal
to Morris in spite of their vocally expressed opposition
to his speculative activities.

Morris was indeed pure speculator. The few plans he
supported in the way of internal improvements served only

---

[48]Jonas P. Phillips to Nicholson, Feb. 23, 1797, JNP,
PHMC.

to increase the value of his property to future purchasers. With the exceptions of his private estates, he never looked to attract artisans or to develop the natural resources of the property. Under no circumstances did he choose to offer small lots to individual settlers, because they could not pay ready cash and he could not afford to extend credit to them. Development required capital to build roads and towns. Capital was what Morris lacked. He counted on quick sales of large tracts to maintain his solvency.

Factors beyond his control, but not beyond his perception, contributed to his downfall. After the success of the Genesee sales in Europe, he assumed that Europeans would always be eager purchasers of American lands. He never considered the negative effects of the wars of the French Revolution on the European money market and on immigration until he experienced them. In spite of reports from William Morris, Gouverneur Morris, and William Temple Franklin, which described declining European interest in American property, Morris still sent James Marshall abroad laden with lands for sale. Despite Marshall's discouraging letters, the Financier forwarded lists of yet additional tracts to sell or mortgage as well as shares to sell in the North American Land Company and the Pennsylvania Property Company.

Notwithstanding his decline into bankruptcy, Morris' place in history is rightfully high. His contributions as Financier and his proposals for the nation's economic growth have earned him increasing praise from recent scholars. He was always a nationalist of great vision, whose programs anticipated the needs of an ever-expanding people and economy. Hamilton's program of the 1790's was in large measure a restatement of the proposals Morris presented to the Continental Congress as Financier. Even his land activities reflect this spirit. He invested in land because he believed in the growth of the United States, by immigration and natural increase, and he expected that growth to be swift and uninterrupted. If he had died rich and successful, historians and contemporaries would have hailed his speculations as a major factor in opening up the nation's back lands to settlement. His failure offers temptation to the same critics to condemn his methods.

The Financier miscalculated his financial means as well as the demand for lands. He assumed that land would rise in value quickly because of the natural increase in population, a high level of immigration, the desire of European investors to sink large sums into American lands, and because Hamilton's financial program insured the financial stability and reliability of the United States. As most land speculators learned, land rarely assured its owners a quick profit on their investments.

Morris was not unique in his failure; other businessmen

found the land market a poor investment. But he was alone in the scope and extent of his holdings, and with the possible exception of Nicholson, in the amount of his indebtedness. Never again in United States history would one man attempt to corner such a large chunk of the land market.

Perhaps most disillusioning to Morris was the realization that he had overestimated the strength of his reputation and the limits of his own credit. The Robert Morris of the 1790's paid for the enthusiasm and optimism he had developed as Financier the heavy price of bankruptcy and three and a half years in debtors' prison.

Bibliography

Manuscript Collections

Bucks County Historical Society, Doylestown, Pennsylvania.
  Land Records.

Columbia University Libraries, Special Collections,
  New York City.
  Gouverneur Morris Papers.

Crawford County Historical Society, Meadville, Pennsylvania.
  Pennsylvania Population Company Minute Books

Gemeentearchief, Amsterdam, The Netherlands.
  The Holland Land Company Papers, including the
  Theophile Cazenove Letter Books.

Hall of Records, New York City.
  New York Chancery Court Minutes and Papers.

The Historical Society of Pennsylvania, Philadelphia.
  Robert Morris Papers, including "Journal B, 1791-
  1801" and "Journal C," 1794-1801."
  John Nicholson Letter Books.
  Asylum Company Papers
  Bucks County Box
  Logan Papers.
  John J. Maitland Family Papers.
  North American Land Company Papers.
  Etting Papers.
  Grantz Collection.
  Robert Morris Deeds Collection.
  Woodhouse Collection.
  Willing Letter Books.

Henry E. Huntington Library and Art Gallery, San Marino,
  California.
  Robert Morris Papers.

Library of Congress, Washington, D. C.
  The Papers of Robert Morris, including his private
  Letter Books, Dec. 22, 1794 - Mar. 7, 1798.
  The Papers of George Washington
  The Papers of Gouverneur Morris, including Letter Books.
  The Papers of Alexander Hamilton.
  The Papers of Thomas Jefferson.
  The Papers of John Nicholson.

The Papers of Andrew Ellicott.
The Taggart Collection.
District of Columbia Papers.
Minutes of the Asylum Company.
Miscellaneous Manuscripts.
Microfilm Collection of Early State Records.

Maryland Historical Society, Baltimore.
Robert Goodloe Harper Family Papers.

National Archives, Washington, D. C.
RG 59, Domestic Letters of the Department of State,
1784-1906.
RG 60, Letters from and Opinions of Attorneys
General, 1791-1811.
RG 42, Records of the District of Columbia Commissioners
and of the Offices Concerned with Public Buildings,
1791-1867,
RG 21, Records of the United States District Court
for the Eastern District of Pennsylvania, Robert
Morris Bankruptcy Case Records.

The New-York Historical Society, New York City.
Henry O'Rielly Papers.
Miscellaneous Manuscripts.

The New York Public Library, New York City.
Robert Morris Papers.
William Constable Papers.

New York, Secretary of State, Miscellaneous Records,
Division of Corporations and State Records, Albany.
Deeds.

The New York State Library, Albany.
Holland Land Company Papers.
Phelps and Gorham Papers.

Ontario County Historical Society, Canandaigua, New York.
Robert Morris Letters.
Documents relating to the Genesee country.
William Temple Franklin's Journal, 1790-1791.

Pennsylvania Historical and Museum Commission, Harrisburg.
John Nicholson Papers.
MS Minutes of the Supreme Court of Pennsylvania.

Queens College of the City University of New York.
New York Chancery Court Papers Before 1800, Historical
Documents Collection.

Recorder of Deeds, County of Bucks, Doylestown, Pennsylvania.
Land Records.

Rochester Public Library and Monroe County Library,
Rochester, New York.
Osgood Papers.

United States Naval Academy, Annapolis, Maryland.
   Talleyrand Letter.

Western Reserve Historical Society, Cleveland, Ohio.
   John Nicholson's Account Current Book with
   Robert Morris.

Primary Sources

Documents

American State Papers: Documents, Legislative and
   Executive, of the Congress of the United States.
   38 vols. Washington, D. C., 1832-61.

Burch, Samuel. A Digest of the Laws of the Corporation
   of the City of Washington. Washington, D. C., 1823.

The Debates and Proceedings of the Congress of the United
   States.... 42 vols. Washington, D. C., 1834-49.

Hogan, Edmund. The Pennsylvania State Trials: Containing
   the Impeachment, Trial, and Acquittal of Francis
   Hopkinson, and John Nicholson, Esquires. Philadelphia,
   1794.

Journals of the Continental Congress, 1774-1789. 34 vols.
   Washington, D. C., 1906.

Mitchell, James T., and Flanders, Henry, ed. The Statutes
   at Large of Pennsylvania from 1682 to 1801.
   Philadelphia, 1896-1908.

The Public Statutes at Large of the United States of
   America. 17 vols. Boston, 1850-73.

U.S. Reports.

Books and Pamphlets

Abstract of Title to the Robert Morris Tract of 320,000
   Acres of Land, Located in McDowell County, West
   Virginia. n.p., 1878.

Balch, Thomas W., ed. Willing Letters and Papers.
   Philadelphia, 1922.

Bingham, Robert W., ed. Holland Land Company's Papers:
   Reports of Joseph Ellicott as Chief of Survey
   (1797-1800) and as Agent (1800-1812) of The Holland
   Company's Purchase in Western New York. 2 vols.
   Buffalo, 1937, 1941.

Burnett, Edmund C., ed. Letters of Members of the
   Continental Congress. 8 vols. Washington, D. C.,
   1921-36.

Clark, Allen C. Greenleaf and Law in the Federal City. Washington, D. C., 1901.

Cooper, Thomas, Some Information Respecting America. Dublin, 1794.

Cruikshank, E. A., ed. The Correspondence of Lieut. Governor John Graves Simcoe, with Allied Documents relating to His Administration of Upper Canada. 3 vols. Toronto, 1923-31.

Faehtz, Ernest F. M. and Pratt, Frederick W., Washington in Embryo Or, the National Capital from 1791-1800. Washington, D. C., 1874.

Fairchild, Helen L., ed. Journals of John Lincklaen: Travels in the Years 1791 and 1792 in Pennsylvania, New York and Vermont. New York, 1897.

Fisher, Miers. Brief of the Titles of Robert Morris, Esquire, to a Tract of Country in the County of Ontario, in the State of New-York, One of the United States of America. Philadelphia, 1791.

Fitzpatrick, John C., ed. The Diaries of George Washington: 1748-1799. 4 vols. Boston, 1925.

Fitzpatrick, John C., ed. The Writings of George Washington. 39 vols. Washington, D. C., 1931-44.

[Franklin, William Temple.] Observations on the Present Situation of Landed Property in America. [London], 1792.

Henkels, Stan V. The Confidential Correspondence of Robert Morris the Great Financier of the Revolution, Being Letters from the Leading Statesmen, Military and Naval Heroes and Patriots of that Time. Philadelphia, 1917.

Huth, Hans, and Pugh, Wilma J., eds. & trans. Talleyrand in America as a Financial Promoter, 1794-1796. Washington, D. C., 1942.

Imlay, Gilbert. A Topographical Description of the Western Territory of North America. 3d ed. London, 1797.

Jeremy, David J., ed. Henry Wansey and His American Journal, 1794. Philadelphia, 1970.

Kite, Elizabeth S., ed. L'Enfant and Washington, 1791-1792. Baltimore, 1929.

La Rochefoucauld-Liancourt. Travels through the United States of North America, the Country of the Iroquois, and Upper Canada, in the Years 1795, 1796, and 1797; with an Authentic Account of Lower Canada. Translated by H. Neuman. 2 vols. London, 1799.

Maclay, William, The Journal of William Maclay: United States Senator from Pennsylvania, 1789-1791. New York, 1927.

Mathews, Catharine, ed. Andrew Ellicott: His Life and Letters. New York, 1908.

Morris, Anne C., ed. The Diary and Letters of Gouverneur Morris: Minister of the United States to France; Member of the Constitutional Convention, etc. 2 vols. New York, 1888.

Morris, Gouverneur, A Diary of the French Revolution. Edited by Beatrix C. Davenport. 2 vols. Boston, 1939.

Morris, Robert, Account of Robert Morris' Property. Philadelphia, n.d.

Morrison, Alfred J., ed. The District in the XVIIIth Century. History, Site-Strategy, Real Estate Market, Landscape, & c., as Described by the Earliest Travellers: Henry Wansey, Francis Baily, Isaac Weld, Duke of La Rochefoucauld-Liancourt, John Davis of Salisbury. n. p., 1909.

Munro, Robert [Charles Williamson]. A Description of the Genesee Country. New York, 1804.

O'Callaghan, E. B., ed. The Documentary History of the State of New-York. 4 vols. Albany, 1849-50.

Opinions in Reference to the Title to Twenty-Five Tracts of Coal Lands situated in the Counties of Northumberland, Columbia and Schuylkill, Pennsylvania, with Abstract of Title. Philadelphia, n.d. There are two different pamphlets by this same title.

Phillips, P. Lee, The Beginnings of Washington, as Described in Books Maps and Views. Washington, D. C., 1917.

Plan of Association of the Asylum Company. As Established April 22d 1794. And Improved April 25, 1795. Philadelphia, 1795.

Rutt, John T., ed. Life and Correspondence of Joseph Priestley 2 vols. London, 1831-32.

Sibbald, George, Notes and Observations on the Pine Lands of Georgia. Augusta, 1801.

Stadnitski, Pieter, Voorafgaand Bericht wegens eene
Negotiatie op Landen in America. Amsterdam, 1792.

Syrett, Harold C., ed. The Papers of Alexander Hamilton.
19 vols. to date. New York, 1961- .

Wharton, Francis, ed. The Revolutionary Diplomatic
Correspondence of the United States. 8 vols.
Washington, D. C., 1889.

Williamson, Charles, Description of the Settlement of
the Genesee Country, in the State of New-York.
In a Series of Letters from a Gentleman to His
Friend. New York, 1799.

Wood, William B. Personal Recollections of the Stage,
Embracing Notices of Actors, Authors, and Auditors
During a Period of Forty Years. Philadelphia, 1855.

Articles

"Extracts from Jos. Ellicott's Letter Books and Early
Correspondence," Publications of the Buffalo
Historical Society, XXVI (1922), 49-166.

"Letters by Augustus Porter." Publications of the
Buffalo Historical Society, VII (1904), 323-30.

"Memorandum of Agreement between Robert Morris and John
Dickinson, for the lot on Chestnut Street, in
Manuscript Department, Historical Society of
Pennsylvania." Pennsylvania Magazine of History
and Biography, XXXIV (Apr., 1910), 237-38.

Morris, Thomas. "Narrative of Events in the History
and Settlement of Western New York ... Communicated
by Henry O'Rielly," The Historical Magazine,
2nd ser., V (June, 1869), 368-88.

Osborne, John B. "The First President's Interest in
Washington as Told by Himself, Records of the
Columbia Historical Society, IV (1901), 173-98.

Porter, Augustus, "Narrative of Early Years in the Life
of Judge Augustus Porter," Publications of the
Buffalo Historical Society, VII (1904), 277-322.

Richardson, A. J. H., and Cowan, Helen I., eds. "William
Berczy's Williamsburg Documents." Publications
of the Rochester Historical Society, XX (1942).

Vail, R. W. G. "A Rare Robert Morris Caricature."
Pennsylvania Magazine of History and Biography,
LX (Apr., 1936), 184-86.

"Warrantees of Land in the Several Counties of the State
of Pennsylvania, 1730-1898." Pennsylvania Archives,
2nd ser., XXIV, XXV, XXVI (1897).

"The Writings of George Washington Relating to the National
Capital," Records of the Columbia Historical Society,
XVII (1914), 2-232.

Secondary Sources

Books

Abernathy, Thomas P. Western Lands and the American
Revolution. New York, 1959.

Barber, John W. Historical Collections of the State of
New York. New York, 1851.

Bausman, Joseph H. History of Beaver County, Pennsylvania
and its Centennial Celebration. 2 vols. New York,
1904.

Bedini, Silvio A. The Life of Benjamin Banneker. New York,
1972.

Beers, Frederick W. Gazetteer and Biographical Record of
Genesee County, N. Y., 1788-1890. Syracuse, 1890.

Bidwell, Percy W., and Falconer, John I. History of
Agriculture in the Northern United States, 1620-1860.
Washington, D. C., 1925.

Black, Henry Campbell. Black's Law Dictionary: Definitions
of the Terms and Phrases of American and English
Jurisprudence, Ancient and Modern. 4th ed. St. Paul, 1951.

Bruchey, Stuart W. Robert Oliver, Merchant of Baltimore:
1783-1819. Baltimore, 1956.

Bryan, Wilhelmus B. A History of the National Capital, from
Its Foundation through the Period of the Adoption of the
Organic Act. 2 vols. New York, 1914-16.

Carroll, John A., and Ashworth, Mary W. George Washington:
First in Peace. Vol. 7 of Douglas Southall Freeman,
George Washington. New York, 1957.

Chappell, Absalom H. Miscellanies of Georgia, Historical,
Biographical, Descriptive, Etc. Atlanta, 1874.

Chazanof, William. Joseph Ellicott and the Holland Land
Company: The Opening of Western New York. Syracuse, 1970.

Childs, Frances S. French Refugee Life in the United States,
1790-1800: An American Chapter of the French Revolution.
Baltimore, 1940.

Clark, T. Wood. Emigrés in the Wilderness. New York, 1941.

Conover, George S. The Genesee Tract: Cessions between New York and Massachusetts. The Phelps and Gorham Purchase. Captain Charles Williamson and the Pulteney Estate. Geneva, 1889.

Conover, George S., ed., and Aldrich, Lewis Cass, comp. History of Ontario County, New York: With Illustrations and Family Sketches of Some of the Prominent Men and Families. Syracuse, 1893.

Coulter, E. Merton. Georgia: A Short History. 3rd ed. Chapel Hill, 1960.

Cowan, Helen I. Charles Williamson: Genesee Promoter, Friend of Anglo-American Rapprochement. Rochester, 1941.

Davis, Joseph S. Essays in the Earlier History of American Corporations. 2 vol. Cambridge, 1917.

Davis, W. W. H. The History of Bucks County, Pennsylvania, From the Discovery of the Delaware to the Present Time. Doylestown, 1876.

Donaldson, Thomas, The Public Domain: Its History with Statistics. Washington, D. C., 1884.

East, Robert A. Business Enterprise in the American Revolution. New York, 1938.

Episodes of History in the Stories of the United States and the Insurance Company of North America as Bound up Together in National Achievement, 1792-1917. Chicago, 1916.

Evans, Paul D. The Holland Land Company. Buffalo, 1924.

Ferguson, E. James. The Power of the Purse: A History of American Public Finance, 1776-1790. Chapel Hill, 1961.

The Genesee County Pioneer Association. A History of its Organization, List of Officers and Members, and the Annual Address delivered June 11, 1878, by Hon. Norman Seymour. Batavia, 1879.

Gordon, Thomas F. Gazetteer of the State of New York.... Philadelphia, 1836.

Green, Constance M. Washington: Village and Capital, 1800-1878. 2 vols. Princeton, 1962-63.

Hadley, Frank. Joseph Ellicott. n. p., 1936.

Hansen, Marcus L. The Atlantic Migration: 1607-1860. New York, 1961.

Hays, Louise F. Hero of Hornet's Nest: A Biography of Elijah Clark, 1733-1799. New York, 1946.

Hibbard, Benjamin H. A History of the Public Land Policies. New York, 1924.

Higgins, Ruth L. Expansion in New York with Especial Reference to the Eighteenth Century. Columbus, 1931.

A History of the Treaty of Big Tree and an Account of the Celebration of the One Hundredth Anniversary of the Treaty, Held at Geneseo, N. Y., September the Fifteenth Eighteen Hundred, Ninety-Seven. Published by the Livingston County Historical Society. Dansville, 1897.

A History of the Insurance Company of North America. Philadelphia, 1885.

Holt, Anne. A Life of Joseph Priestley. London, 1931.

Hotchkin, James H. A History of the Purchase and Settlement of Western New York, and of the Rise, Progress, and Present State of the Presbyterian Church in that Section. New York, 1848.

Hungerford, Edward. The Genesee Country. New York, 1946.

Huston, Charles. An Essay on the History and Nature of Original Titles to Land in the Province and State of Pennsylvania. Philadelphia, 1849.

Hames, Marquis, Biography of a Business, 1792-1942: Insurance Company of North America. Indianapolis, 1942.

Kennedy, John. The Genesee Country. Batavia, 1895.

Kennedy, John. Robert Morris and the Holland Purchase. Batavia, 1894.

Konkle, Burton A. Thomas Willing and the First American Financial System. Philadelphia, 1937.

Lacour-Gayet, G. Talleyrand, 1754-1838. Paris, n.d.

Livermore, Shaw. Early American Land Companies: Their Influence on Corporate Development. New York, 1939.

McLendon, S. G. History of the Public Domain of Georgia. Atlanta, 1924.

McNall, Neil A. An Agricultural History of the Genesee Valley: 1790-1860. Philadelphia, 1952.

Magrath, C. Peter. Yazoo: Law and Politics in the New Republic, The Case of Fletcher v Peck. New York, 1966.

Malone, Dumas, The Public Life of Thomas Cooper: 1783-1839. Columbia, 1961.

Martin, Margaret E. Merchants and Trade of the Connecticut River Valley, 1750-1820. Northampton, 1939.

Mather, Joseph H., and Brockett, L. P. Geography of the State of New York. Hartford, 1847.

Mau, Clayton, The Development of Central and Western New York: From the Arrival of the White Man to the Eve of the Civil War as Portrayed Chronologically in Contemporary Accounts. Rochester, 1944.

Murray, Elsie. French Exiles of 1793 in Northern Pennsylvania. New York, 1935.

Murray, Louise W. A History of Old Tioga Point and Early Athens Pennsylvania. thens, 1908.

Murray, Louise W. The Story of Some French Refugees and their "Azilum," 1793-1800. Athens, 1903.

Nettels, Curtis P. The Emergence of a National Economy: 1775-1815. New York, 1962.

Oberholtzer, Ellis P. Robert Morris: Patriot and Financier. New York, 1903.

O'Rielly, Henry. Sketches of Rochester; with Incidental Notices of Western New-York. Rochester, 1838.

Porter, John A. The City of Washington: Its Origins and Administration. Baltimore, 1885.

Price, Jacob M. France and the Chesapeake: A History of the French Tobacco Monopoly, 1674-1791, and of Its Relationship to the British and American Tobacco Trades. 2 vols. Ann Arbor, 1973.

Report of the Secretary of Internal Affairs. Harrisburg, 1892.

Robbins, Roy, M. Our Landed Heritage: The Public Domain,
    1776-1936. Princeton, 1942.

Rosengarten, J. G. French Colonists and Exiles in the
    United States. Philadelphia, 1907.

Sakolski, A. M. The Great American Land Bubble: The
    Amazing Story of Land-Grabbing, Speculations, and
    Booms from Colonial Days to the Present Time.
    New York, 1932.

Smith, Edgar F. Priestley in America, 1794-1804.
    Philadelphia, 1920.

Smith, Walter B., and Cole, Arthur H. Fluctuations in
    American Business, 1790-1860. Cambridge, 1935.

Spafford, Horatio G. A Gazetteer of the State of
    the State of New-York. Albany, 1824.

Spofford, Ainsworth R. The Founding of Washington City,
    with Some Considerations on the Origins of Cities
    and Location of National Capitals. Baltimore, 1881.

Stevens, William B. A History of Georgia. 2 vols.
    Philadelphia, 1847-59.

Stone, William L. The Life and Times of Sa-Go-Ye-Wat-Ha,
    or Red Jacket. Albany, 1866.

Sumner, William G. The Financier and the Finances of
    the American Revolution. 2 vols. New York, 1891.

Sumner, William G. Robert Morris. New York, 1892.

Tiffany, Nina Moore, and Francis. Harm Jan Huidekoper.
    Cambridge, 1904.

Todd, Charles B. The Story of Washington: The National
    Capital. New York, 1889.

Treat, Payson J. The National Land System, 1785-1820.
    New York, 1910.

Turner, Chipman P. The Pioneer Period of Western New
    York. Buffalo, 1888.

Turner, Orsamus. History of the Pioneer Settlement of
    Phelps and Gorham's Purchase, and Morris' Reserve....
    Rochester, 1851.

Turner, Orsamus. _Pioneer History of the Holland Purchase of Western New York...._ Buffalo, 1849.

Vanderhoof, Elisha W. _Historical Sketches of Western New York._ Buffalo, 1907.

Varnum, Joseph B. _The Seat of Government of the United States. A Review of the Discussions, in Congress and Elsewhere, on the Site and Plans of the Federal City; with a Sketch of Its Present Position and Prospects._ New York, 1848.

Ver Steeg, Clarence L. _Robert Morris: Revolutionary Financier, with an Analysis of His Earlier Career._ Philadelphia, 1954.

Warren, Charles. _Bankruptcy in United States History._ Cambridge, 1935.

White, George. _Statistics of the State of Georgia._ Savannah, 1849.

Willis, Clarency. _The Pulteney Land Title: Genesee Tract._ New York, 1921.

Young, Eleanor. _Forgotten Patriot: Robert Morris._ New York, 1950.

Young, James S. _The Washington Community, 1800-1828._ New York, 1966.

Articles

Adams, Samuel B. "The Yazoo Fraud." _The Georgia Historical Quarterly_, III (June, 1923), 155-65.

"Address of Nathaniel Burt, February 12, 1875, on the Washington Mansion in Philadelphia. _Pennsylvania Historical Society, Miscellaneous Papers_, I (1875), 1-35.

Alexander, Sally K. "A Sketch of the Life of Major Andrew Ellicott." _Records of the Columbia Historical Society_, II (1899), 158-203.

Bartlett, G. Hunter. "Andrew and Joseph Ellicott." _Publications of the Buffalo Historical Society_, XXVI (1922), 1-48.

Beals, Katharine. "The Land Speculations of a Great Patriot." _Bulletin of the Business Historical Society_, III (Apr., 1929), 1-9.

Bedini, Silvio A. "Benjamin Banneker and the Survey of the District of Columbia, 1791." Records of the Columbia Historical Society, LXIX-LXX (1969-70), 7-30.

Bowling, Kenneth. "Dinner at Jefferson's" A Note on Jacob E. Cooke's 'The Compromise of 1790,'" William and Mary Quarterly, 3d ser., XXVIII (Oct., 1971), 629-48.

Brotherhead, William. "Robert Morris." The Lives of Eminent Philadelphians, Now Deceased. Edited by Henry Simpson. Philadelphia, 1859.

Brown, Glenn. "The Making of a Plan for Washington City." Records of the Columbia Historical Society, VI (1903), 1-10.

Clark, Allen C. "Origin of the Federal City." Records of the Columbia Historical Society, XXXV-XXXVI (1935), 1-97.

Cooke, Jacob E. "The Compromise of 1790." William and Mary Quarterly, 3d ser., XXVII (Oct., 1970), 523-45.

Cowan, Helen I. "Williamsburg: Lost Village on the Genesee." Rochester History, III (July, 1942), 5-24.

Craft, David. "A Day at Asylum." Proceedings and Collections of the Wyoming Historical and Geological Society, VIII (1904), 46-86.

Craft, David. "The French at Asylum." Proceedings and Collections of the Wyoming Historical and Geological Society, V (1900), 75-110.

Dana, Robert S. "Morrisville and Its Vicinity." Collections of the Bucks County Historical Society, III (1909), 244-57.

Elsmere, Jane. "The Notorious Yazoo Land Fraud Case." The Georgia Historical Quarterly, LI (Dec., 1967), 425-42.

Ely, Warren S. "Andrew Ellicott, The Great Surveyor." Collections of the Bucks County Historical Society, V (1926), 745-51.

Evans, Paul D. "The Frontier Pushed Westward." Conquering the Wilderness. Vol. 5 of History of the State of New York. Edited by Alexander C. Flick. 10 vols. New York, 1934.

Evans, Paul D. "The Pulteney Purchase." Quarterly Journal of the New York State Historical Association, III (Apr., 1922), 83-104.

Hart, Armine N. "Robert Morris." Pennsylvania Magazine of History and Biography, I (1877), 333-43.

Hart, Armine N. "Robert Morris." Annals of Philadelphia, and Pennsylvania, Edited by John F. Watson, III (1887), 260-261.

Hart, Charles Henry. "Mary White-Mrs. Robert Morris." Pennsylvania Magazine of History and Biography, II (1878), 157-84.

Haskins, Charles H. "The Yazoo Land Companies." Papers of the American Historical Association, V (Oct., 1891), 61-103.

Heath, William E. "The Yazoo Land Fraud." The Georgia Historical Quarterly, XVI (Dec., 1932), 274-91.

Heiges, George L. "Robert Morris in Manheim." Papers Read before the Lancaster County Historical Society, XXXIV (June, 1930), 121-34.

Henderson, Elizabeth K. "The Northwestern Lands of Pennsylvania, 1790-1812." Pennsylvania Magazine of History and Biography, LX (Apr., 1936), 131-60.

Humphrey, George H. "Nathaniel Gorham." Publications of the Rochester Historical Society, VI (1927), 297-99.

Lossing, Benson J. "The Arrest of Robert Morris." The American Historical Record, II (1873), 229.

Lossing, Benson J. "Robert Morris in Jail." The American Historical Record, II (1873), 305-07.

McClintock, Walter J. "Title Difficulties of the Holland Land Company in Northwestern Pennsylvania." The Western Pennsylvania Historical Magazine, XXI (June, 1938), 119-38.

MacPhee, Donald A. "The Yazoo Controversy: The Beginning of the 'Quid' Revolt." The Georgia Historical Quarterly, XLIX (Mar., 1965), 23-43.

Milliken, Charles F. "The Phelps and Gorham Purchase." History of the Genesee Country. Edited by Doty R. Lockwood. 4 vols. Chicago, 1925.

Milliken, Charles F. "Thomas Morris." Publications of the Rochester Historical Society, VII (1928), 41-53.

Moore, Charles, "The Making of a Plan for the City of Washington," Records of the Columbia Historical Society, VI (1903), 11-23.

Murray, Elsie. "Early Land Companies and Titles of Northumberland County." Proceedings of the Northumberland County Historical Society, XX (1954), 16-33).

Murray, Elsie. "French Experiments in Pioneering in Northern Pennsylvania." Pennsylvania Magazine of History and Biography, LXVIII (Apr., 1944), 175-88.

North, Douglass C. "The United States Balance of Payments, 1790-1860." Trends in the American Economy in the Nineteenth Century. Princeton, 1960.

Nourse, Michael. "Robert Morris, the Financier." The Bankers' Magazine, IX (Feb., 1860), 577-91.

Nussbaum, Frederick L. "American Tobacco and French Politics, 1783-1789." Political Science Quarterly, XL (Dec., 1925), 497-516.

Oberholtzer, Ellis P. "A Great Philadelphia: Robert Morris." Pennsylvania Magazine of History and Biography, XXVIII (July, 1904), 273-94.

Oberholtzer, Ellis P. "Robert Morris, Founder of Morrisville." Collections of the Bucks County Historical Society, III (1909), 345-55.

Osborne, Richard H. S. "Historic 'Summerseat.'" Collections of the Bucks County Historical Society, III (1909), 237-42.

Osgood, Howard L. "History of the Title of the Phelps and Gorham Purchase." Publications of the Rochester Historical Society, I (1892), 19-51.

Park, Mary C. "Joseph Priestley and the Problem of Pantisocracy." Proceedings of the Delaware County Institute of Science, XI (1947), 1-60.

Parker, Arthur C. "Charles Williamson: Builder of the Genesee Country." Publications of the Rochester Historical Society, VI (1927), 1-34.

Phillips, P. Lee. "The Negro Benjamin Banneker; Astronomer and Mathematician, Plea for Universal Peace." Records of the Columbia Historical Society, XX (1917), 114-20.

"Robert Morris Envisioned Bucks County Development: Document in State Land Office Gives Early Statesman's Views." Bulletin of the Department of Internal Affairs of the Commonwealth of Pennsylvania, XX (July, 1952), 7-9.

Robinson, Charles M. "The Life of Judge Augustus Porter:
A Pioneer in Western New York." Publications
of the Buffalo Historical Society, VII (1904),
229-75.

Ryan, William C. "Founding of Morrisville." Collections
of the Bucks County Historical Society, III (1909),
361-67.

Sakolski, A. M. "Robert Morris, Patiot and Bankrupt."
Nation's Business, XVIII (Apr., 1930), 36-38, 202-06.

Silsby, Robert W. "The Holland Land Company in Western
New York." Adventures in Western New York History,
VIII (1961), 1-16.

Silsby, Robert W. "Mortgage Credit in the Phelps-Gorham
Purchase." New York History, XLI (Jan., 1960),
3-34.

Turner, D. K. "Robert Morris the Financier of the
Revolution." Collections of the Bucks County
Historical Society, II (1909), 157-72.

Waln, Robert. "Robert Morris." Biography of the Signers
to the Declaration of Independence, V (1824),
189-315.

Wandell, Samuel H. "Oliver Phelps." New York History,
XXIII (July, 1942), 275-82.

Weisman, Morris. "The Bankruptcy of Robert Morris."
Commercial Law Journal, XLV (July, 1940),
163-66.

Wilkinson, Norman B. "The 'Philadelphia Fever' in
Northern Pennsylvania." Pennsylvania History,
XX (Jan., 1953), 41-56.

Wilkinson, Norman B. "Robert Morris and the Treaty of
Big Tree." Mississippi Valley Historical Review,
XL (Sept., 1953), 257-78.

Williams, Edwin M. "Building the Federal City."
Washington: Past and Present, A History. Edited
by John C. Proctor. 2 vols. New York, 1930.

Yerkes, Harman. "Morrisville the Capital." Collections
of the Bucks County Historical Society, III (1909),
355-60.

Unpublished Sources

Arbuckle, Robert D. "John Nicholson, 1757-1800: A Case Study of an Early American Land Speculator, Financier and Entrepreneur." Unpublished Ph.D. dissertation, The Pennsylvania State University, 1972.

Baldridge, Jr., Edwin R. "Talleyrand in the United States, 1794 to 1796." Unpublished Ph.D. dissertation, Lehigh University, 1963.

Bauer, George P. "The Movement Against Imprisonment for Debt in the United States." Unpublished Ph.D. dissertation, Harvard University, 1935.

Bowling, Kenneth R. "Politics in the First Congress, 1789-1791." Unpublished Ph.D. dissertation, The University of Wisconsin, 1968.

Davis, William A. "William Constable: New York Merchant and Land Speculator, 1772-1803." Unpublished Ph.D. dissertation, Harvard University, 1955.

Garff, Royal L. "Social and Economic Conditions in the Genesee Country, 1787-1812." Unpublished Ph.D. dissertation, Northwestern University, 1939.

Hale, R. Nelson. "Pennsylvania Population Company." Unpublished Ph.D. dissertation, 1950.

Keith, Alice B. "Three North Carolina Blount Brothers in Business and Politics, 1783-1812." Unpublished Ph.D. dissertation, University of North Carolina, 1940.

Kline, Mary-Jo, "Gouverneur Morris and the New Nation, 1775-1778." Unpublished Ph.D. dissertation, Columbia University, 1970.

Robb, Arthur. "The Founding of Washington." United States, Department of Justice, Columbia University Law Library. (Typewritten.)

Ruddy, Joseph C. "The Policy of Land Distribution in Pennsylvania Since 1779." Unpublished M.A. thesis, Pennsylvania State College, 1933.

Silsby, Robert W. "Credit and Creditors in the Phelps-Gorham Purchase." Unpublished Ph.D. dissertation, Cornell University, 1958.

Tailby, Donald G. "Chapters from the Business Career of William Constable: A Merchant of Post-Revolutionary New York." Unpublished Ph.D. dissertation, Rutgers, The State University, 1961.

Tripp, Wendell. "Robert Troup: A Quest for Order and Security, 1757-1832." Unpublished Ph.D. dissertation, Columbia University, 1973.

Wilkinson, Norman B. "Land Policy and Speculation in Pennsylvania: 1779-1800." Unpublished Ph.D. dissertation, University of Pennsylvania, 1958.

Zoller, Lucille L. "The French Settlement at Asylum, Pennsylvania." Unpublished M.A. thesis, University of Pittsburgh, 1936.

Newspapers

[Philadelphia] Aurora.

Dunlap and Claypoole's [Philadelphia] American Daily Advertiser.

New York Herald.

The New-York Times.

Dissertations in American Economic History
An Arno Press Collection

1978 Publications

Alston, Richard Moss. **Commercial Irrigation Enterprise, the Fear of Water Monopoly, and the Genesis of Market Distortion in the Nineteenth Century American West.** (Doctoral Thesis, Cornell University, 1970). 1978

Buss, Dietrich G. **Henry Villard.** (Revised Doctoral Dissertation, Claremont Graduate School, 1976). 1978

Chernow, Barbara Ann. **Robert Morris: Land Speculator, 1790-1801.** (Doctoral Dissertation, Columbia University, 1974). 1978

Cranmer, H. Jerome. **The New Jersey Canals.** (Doctoral Dissertation, Columbia University, 1955). 1978

Dick, Trevor J. O. **An Economic Theory of Technological Change.** (Revised Doctoral Dissertation, University of Washington, 1970). 1978

Eis, Carl. **The 1919-1930 Merger Movement in American Industry.** (Doctoral Dissertation, The City University of New York, 1968). 1978

Esbitt, Milton. **International Capital Flows and Domestic Economic Fluctuation.** (Doctoral Thesis, Michigan State University, 1970). 1978

Godfrey, John Munro. **Monetary Expansion in the Confederacy.** Doctoral Dissertation, University of Georgia, 1976). 1978

Golembe, Carter H. **State Banks and the Economic Development of the West, 1830-44.** (Doctoral Dissertation, Columbia University, 1952). 1978

Govan, Thomas Payne. **Banking and the Credit System in Georgia, 1810-1860.** (Doctoral Thesis, Vanderbilt University, 1937). 1978

Gray, Jean Mathieson. **The Term Structure of Interest Rates in the United States: 1884-1914.** (Doctoral Dissertation, University of California, Berkeley, 1969). 1978

Heavner, Robert Owen. **Economic Aspects of Indentured Servitude in Colonial Pennsylvania, 1771-1773.** (Doctoral Dissertation, Stanford University, 1976). 1978

Herbst, Lawrence A. **Interregional Commodity Trade from the North to the South and American Economic Development in the Antebellum Period.** (Doctoral Dissertation, University of Pennsylvania, 1974). 1978

Klepper, Robert. **The Economic Bases for Agrarian Protest Movements in the United States, 1870-1900.** (Doctoral Dissertation, University of Chicago, 1973). 1978

Kline, Mary-Jo. **Gouverneur Morris and the New Nation, 1775-1788.** (Doctoral Dissertation, Columbia University, 1970). 1978

Koller, Roland H., II. **Predatory Pricing in a Market Economy.** (Doctoral Dissertation, University of Wisconsin, 1969). 1978

Lavin, Marilyn Anne. **William Bostwick.** (Doctoral Dissertation, Columbia University, 1977). 1978

Lee, Ronald Demos. **Econometric Studies of Topics in Demographic History.** (Doctoral Thesis, Harvard University, 1970). 1978

Leet, Don R., **Population Pressure and Human Fertility Response.** (Doctoral Dissertation, University of Pennsylvania, 1972). 1978

Libecap, Gary D. **The Evolution of Private Mineral Rights.** (Doctoral Dissertation, University of Pennsylvania, 1976). 1978

MacDowell, Michael Alan. **Public Understanding of Economic Policies.** (Doctoral Dissertation, Ball State University, 1974). 1978

Miller, Randall M. **The Cotton Mill Movement in Antebellum Alabama.** (Doctoral Dissertation, Ohio State University, 1971). 1978

Morrison, Grant. **Isaac Bronson and the Search for System in American Capitalism, 1789-1838.** (Doctoral Dissertation, The City University of New York, 1973). 1978

Munyon, Paul Glenn. **A Reassessment of New England Agriculture in the Last Thirty Years of the Nineteenth Century.** (Revised Doctoral Dissertation, Harvard University, 1975). 1978

Perry, Joseph McGarity. **The Impact of Immigration on Three American Industries, 1865-1914.** (Doctoral Dissertation, Northwestern University, 1966). 1978

Ready, Milton L. **The Castle Builders.** (Revised Doctoral Dissertation, University of Georgia, 1970). 1978

Soper, John Charles. **The Long Swing in Historical Perspective.** (Doctoral Dissertation, University of Massachusets, 1970). 1978

Spencer, Austin H. **An Examination of Relative Downward Industrial Price Flexibility, 1870-1921.** (Doctoral Thesis, Indiana University, 1972). 1978

Sushka, Marie Elizabeth. **An Economic Model of the Money Market in the United States, 1823-1859.** (Doctoral Dissertation, University of Georgia, 1974). 1978

Synnott, Thomas Whitney, III. **Investment Policies, Growth and Profitability in the New England Cotton Textile Industry, 1830-1914.** (Doctoral Dissertation, Yale University, 1968). 1978

Vatter, Harold G. **Some Aspects of the Problem of Small Enterprise As Seen in Four Selected Industries.** (Doctoral Dissertation, University of California, Berkeley, 1950). 1978

Wilkenfeld, Bruce Martin. **The Social and Economic Structure of the City of New York, 1695-1796.** (Doctoral Dissertation, Columbia University, 1973). 1978

Womack, Roy Douglas. **An Analysis of the Credit Controls of the Second Bank of the United States.** (Doctoral Dissertation, University of Alabama, 1971). 1978

Xander, James Allen. **Vault Cash and the Role of Commercial Banks in Regional Economic Development—United States, 1870-1913.** (Doctoral Dissertation, University of Georgia, 1974). 1978

1977 Publications

Ankli, Robert Eugene. **Gross Farm Revenue in Pre-Civil War Illinois.** (Doctoral Dissertation, University of Illinois, 1969). 1977

Asher, Ephraim. **Relative Productivity, Factor-Intensity and Technology in the Manufacturing Sectors of the U.S. and the U.K. During the Nineteenth Century.** (Doctoral Dissertation, University of Rochester, 1969). 1977

Campbell, Carl. **Economic Growth, Capital Gains, and Income Distribution: 1897-1956.** (Doctoral Dissertation, University of California at Berkeley, 1964). 1977

Cederberg, Herbert R. **An Economic Analysis of English Settlement in North America, 1583-1635.** (Doctoral Dissertation, University of California at Berkeley, 1968). 1977

Dente, Leonard A. **Veblen's Theory of Social Change.** (Doctoral Dissertation, New York University, 1974). 1977

Dickey, George Edward. **Money, Prices and Growth;** The American Experience, 1869-1896. (Doctoral Dissertation, Northwestern University, 1968). 1977

Douty, Christopher Morris. **The Economics of Localized Disasters:** The 1906 San Francisco Catastrophe. (Doctoral Dissertation, Stanford University, 1969). 1977

Harper, Ann K. **The Location of the United States Steel Industry, 1879-1919.** (Doctoral Dissertation, Johns Hopkins University, 1976). 1977

Holt, Charles Frank. **The Role of State Government in the Nineteenth-Century American Economy, 1820-1902:** A Quantitative Study. (Doctoral Dissertation, Purdue University, 1970). 1977

Katz, Harold. **The Decline of Competition in the Automobile Industry, 1920-1940.** (Doctoral Dissertation, Columbia University, 1970). 1977

Lee, Susan Previant. **The Westward Movement of the Cotton Economy, 1840-1860:** Perceived Interests and Economic Realities. (Doctoral Dissertation, Columbia University, 1975). 1977

Legler, John Baxter. **Regional Distribution of Federal Receipts and Expenditures in the Nineteenth Century:** A Quantitative Study. (Doctoral Dissertation, Purdue University, 1967). 1977

Lightner, David L. **Labor on the Illinois Central Railroad, 1852-1900:** The Evolution of an Industrial Environment. (Doctoral Dissertation, Cornell University, 1969). 1977

MacMurray, Robert R. **Technological Change in the American Cotton Spinning Industry, 1790 to 1836.** (Doctoral Dissertation, University of Pennsylvania, 1970). 1977

Netschert, Bruce Carlton. **The Mineral Foreign Trade of the United States in the Twentieth Century:** A Study in Mineral Economics. (Doctoral Dissertation, Cornell University, 1949). 1977

Otenasek, Mildred. **Alexander Hamilton's Financial Policies.** (Doctoral Dissertation, Johns Hopkins University, 1939). 1977

Parks, Robert James. **European Origins of the Economic Ideas of Alexander Hamilton.** (M. A. Thesis, Michigan State University, 1963). 1977

Parsons, Burke Adrian. **British Trade Cycles and American Bank Credit:** Some Aspects of Economic Fluctuations in the United States, 1815-1840. (Doctoral Dissertation, University of Texas, 1958). 1977

Primack, Martin L. **Farm Formed Capital in American Agriculture, 1850-1910.** (Doctoral Dissertation, University of North Carolina, 1963). 1977

Pritchett, Bruce Michael. **A Study of Capital Mobilization, The Life Insurance Industry of the Nineteenth Century.** (Doctoral Dissertation, Purdue University, 1970). Revised Edition. 1977

Prosper, Peter A., Jr. **Concentration and the Rate of Change of Wages in the United States, 1950-1962.** (Doctoral Dissertation, Cornell University 1970). 1977

Schachter, Joseph. **Capital Value and Relative Wage Effects of Immigration into the United States, 1870-1930.** (Doctoral Dissertation, City University of New York, 1969). 1977

Schaefer, Donald Fred. **A Quantitative Description and Analysis of the Growth of the Pennsylvania Anthracite Coal Industry, 1820 to 1865.** (Doctoral Dissertation, University of North Carolina, 1967). 1977

Schmitz, Mark. **Economic Analysis of Antebellum Sugar Plantations in Louisiana.** (Doctoral Dissertation, University of North Carolina, 1974). 1977

Sharpless, John Burk, II. **City Growth in the United States, England and Wales, 1820-1861:** The Effects of Location, Size and Economic Structure on Inter-urban Variations in Demographic Growth. (Doctoral Dissertation, University of Michigan, 1975). 1977

Shields, Roger Elwood. **Economic Growth with Price Deflation, 1873-1896.** (Doctoral Dissertation, University of Virginia, 1969). 1977

Stettler, Henry Louis, III. **Growth and Fluctuations in the Ante-Bellum Textile Industry.** (Doctoral Dissertation, Purdue University, 1970). 1977

Sturm, James Lester. **Investing in the United States, 1798-1893:** Upper Wealth-Holders in a Market Economy. (Doctoral Dissertation, University of Wisconsin, 1969). 1977

Tenenbaum, Marcel. **(A Demographic Analysis of Interstate Labor Growth Rate Differentials;** United States, 1890-1900 to 1940-50. (Doctoral Dissertation, Columbia University, 1969). 1977

Thomas, Robert Paul. **An Analysis of the Pattern of Growth of the Automobile Industry:** 1895-1929. (Doctoral Dissertation, Northwestern University, 1965). 1977

Vickery, William Edward. **The Economics of the Negro Migration 1900-1960.** (Doctoral Dissertation, University of Chicago, 1969). 1977

Waters, Joseph Paul. **Technological Acceleration and the Great Depression.** (Doctoral Dissertation, Cornell University, 1971). 1977

Whartenby, Franklee Gilbert. **Land and Labor Productivity in United States Cotton Production, 1800-1840.** (Doctoral Dissertation, University of North Carolina, 1963). 1977

1975 Publications

Adams, Donald R., Jr. **Wage Rates in Philadelphia, 1790-1830.** (Doctoral Dissertation, University of Pennsylvania, 1967). 1975

Aldrich, Terry Mark. **Rates of Return on Investment in Technical Education in the Ante-Bellum American Economy.** (Doctoral Dissertation, The University of Texas at Austin, 1969). 1975

Anderson, Terry Lee. **The Economic Growth of Seventeenth Century New England:** A Measurement of Regional Income. (Doctoral Dissertation, University of Washington, 1972). 1975

Bean, Richard Nelson. **The British Trans-Atlantic Slave Trade, 1650-1775.** (Doctoral Dissertation, University of Washington, 1971). 1975

Brock, Leslie V. **The Currency of the American Colonies, 1700-1764:** A Study in Colonial Finance and Imperial Relations. (Doctoral Dissertation University of Michigan, 1941). 1975

Ellsworth, Lucius F. **Craft to National Industry in the Nineteenth Century:** A Case Study of the Transformation of the New York State Tanning Industry. (Doctoral Dissertation, University of Delaware, 1971). 1975

Fleisig, Heywood W. **Long Term Capital Flows and the Great Depression:** The Role of the United States, 1927-1933. (Doctoral Dissertation, Yale University, 1969). 1975

Foust, James D. **The Yeoman Farmer and Westward Expansion of U.S. Cotton Production.** (Doctoral Dissertation, University of North Carolina at Chapel Hill, 1968). 1975

Golden, James Reed. **Investment Behavior By United States Railroads, 1870-1914.** (Doctoral Thesis, Harvard University, 1971). 1975

Hill, Peter Jensen. **The Economic Impact of Immigration into the United States.** (Doctoral Dissertation, The University of Chicago, 1970). 1975

Klingaman, David C. **Colonial Virginia's Coastwise and Grain Trade.** (Doctoral Dissertation, University of Virginia, 1967). 1975

Lang, Edith Mae. **The Effects of Net Interregional Migration on Agricultural Income Growth:** The United States, 1850-1860. (Doctoral Thesis, The University of Rochester, 1971). 1975

Lindley, Lester G. **The Constitution Faces Technology:** The Relationship of the National Government to the Telegraph, 1866-1884. (Doctoral Thesis, Rice University, 1971). 1975

Lorant, John H[erman]. **The Role of Capital-Improving Innovations in American Manufacturing During the 1920's.** (Doctoral Thesis, Columbia University, 1966). 1975

Mishkin, David Joel. **The American Colonial Wine Industry:** An Economic Interpretation, Volumes I and II. (Doctoral Thesis, University of Illinois, 1966). 1975

Winkler, Donald R. **The Production of Human Capital:** A Study of Minority Achievement. (Doctoral Dissertation, University of California at Berkeley, 1972). 1977

Oates, Mary J. **The Role of the Cotton Textile Industry in the Economic Development of the American Southeast:** 1900-1940. (Doctoral Dissertation, Yale University, 1969). 1975

Passell, Peter. **Essays in the Economics of Nineteenth Century American Land Policy.** (Doctoral Dissertation, Yale University, 1970). 1975

Pope, Clayne L. **The Impact of the Ante-Bellum Tariff on Income Distribution.** (Doctoral Dissertation, The University of Chicago, 1972). 1975

Poulson, Barry Warren. **Value Added in Manufacturing, Mining, and Agriculture in the American Economy From 1809 To 1839.** (Doctoral Dissertation, The Ohio State University, 1965). 1975

Rockoff, Hugh. **The Free Banking Era: A Re-Examination.** (Doctoral Dissertation, The University of Chicago, 1972). 1975

Schumacher, Max George. **The Northern Farmer and His Markets During the Late Colonial Period.** (Doctoral Dissertation, University of California at Berkeley, 1948). 1975

Seagrave, Charles Edwin. **The Southern Negro Agricultural Worker:** 1850-1870. (Doctoral Dissertation, Stanford University, 1971). 1975

Solmon, Lewis C. **Capital Formation by Expenditures on Formal Education, 1880 and 1890.** (Doctoral Dissertation, The University of Chicago, 1968). 1975

Swan, Dale Evans. **The Structure and Profitability of the Antebellum Rice Industry:** 1859. (Doctoral Dissertation, University of North Carolina at Chapel Hill, 1972). 1975

Sylla, Richard Eugene. **The American Capital Market, 1846-1914:** A Study of the Effects of Public Policy on Economic Development. (Doctoral Thesis, Harvard University, 1968). 1975

Uselding, Paul John. **Studies in the Technological Development of the American Economy During the First Half of the Nineteenth Century.** (Doctoral Dissertation, Northwestern University, 1970). 1975

Walsh, William D[avid]. **The Diffusion of Technological Change in the Pennsylvania Pig Iron Industry, 1850-1870.** (Doctoral Dissertation, Yale University, 1967). 1975

Weiss, Thomas Joseph. **The Service Sector in the United States, 1839 Through 1899.** (Doctoral Thesis, University of North Carolina at Chapel Hill, 1967). 1975

Zevin, Robert Brooke. **The Growth of Manufacturing in Early Nineteenth Century New England.** 1975

DATE DUE